Decoding Smart Money Concepts

Deepanshu Suman

2025 — First Edition

See What Institutions See — Trade What They Trade

Copyright

Title: Decoding Smart Money Concepts
Author: Deepanshu Suman

First Edition
ISBN: 978-93-344-4475-9

Disclaimer: This book is for educational and informational purposes only. It provides insights into market structure, institutional trading behavior, and Smart Money Concepts (SMC) and ICT methodologies. It does not constitute financial, investment, legal, or professional advice. Trading and investing involve risk, including the potential loss of capital. Readers are advised to perform their own due diligence or consult with a qualified professional before making financial decisions.

All brand names, product names, and company names mentioned are the property of their respective owners. References are provided solely for illustrative and educational purposes and do not imply any endorsement, affiliation, or sponsorship. The author disclaims any ownership of third-party trademarks or content referenced herein.

Dedication

To the traders who refused to quit,

who stared at red charts and still showed up the next day.

To the ones who lost money, sleep, and confidence —
but never their curiosity.

May this book remind you that the market was never your enemy —
only your greatest mirror.

Trade with patience. Learn with humility.
Think like the institutions, not the crowd.

Acknowledgments

This book represents not just an analysis of the markets but a journey of deep intellectual effort and perseverance. It's a mirror of the market itself: often humbling, occasionally unpredictable, yet ultimately profoundly rewarding.

My deepest thanks go to the global trading community. The countless mentors, analysts, and fellow traders who share knowledge with such openness and passion are the true backbone of understanding in this space. Your continuous charting, open discussions, and collective insights have been instrumental in shaping and simplifying the complex Smart Money Concepts (SMC) and ICT methodologies presented here.

I owe a special debt of gratitude to the original pioneers and educators of institutional trading concepts. Their work successfully bridged the gap between basic retail trading perceptions and the true institutional reality of how price moves. They inspired a generation of traders to look past simple indicators and understand the actual psychology and intent driving market price action.

To my readers: thank you for committing your time, curiosity, and patience. You are the reason this manuscript became a book. My hope is that it allows you to trade with newfound confidence, see structure where there was only chaos, and build unshakable conviction in the face of uncertainty.

To my friends and peers who supported this project, back when it was nothing more than sleepless nights and disorganized notes—your encouragement was the momentum that pushed this effort through to mastery.

And finally, to the market itself—the ultimate teacher. This book is a tribute to the challenging learning curve: to every loss, every difficult stop-out, and every moment of doubt that forced a deeper, more profound understanding. It is dedicated to all traders who choose to stay the course.

— *Deepanshu Suman*

Preface

There comes a moment in every trader's journey when the charts stop looking like random noise and start whispering intent. What once seemed like chaos begins to make sense — not through indicators or luck, but through understanding how the market truly moves. This book was born from that moment.

Author's Journey & Trading Story

Like many retail traders, my journey began with curiosity and overconfidence. I was captivated by the idea of "financial freedom" and believed that with enough effort, a few moving averages and YouTube strategies could get me there. It didn't take long for the market to humble me.

The early days were marked by blown accounts, emotional trades, and countless hours searching for the "perfect system." Every loss felt personal; every win felt like proof I had finally figured it out — until the next loss came. Over time, I realized that trading wasn't about predicting price; it was about understanding **behavior** — not of the charts, but of the people and institutions behind them.

The turning point came when I discovered **Smart Money Concepts (SMC)** and **ICT methodology**. For the first time, the market started to feel logical. Liquidity wasn't just random volatility — it was **fuel**. Order blocks weren't mysterious rectangles — they were **institutional footprints**. I began to see how price hunts liquidity, mitigates imbalances, and moves in stages that reflect intent rather than emotion.

Trading transformed from gambling to structured reasoning. And with structure came confidence — not in predicting, but in reading.

Why Retail Traders Struggle

Retail traders don't fail because they lack intelligence. They fail because they are conditioned to see the market through the wrong lens. They chase certainty in a probabilistic game. They seek patterns where institutions see liquidity. They look for confirmation where professionals seek inefficiency.

Most educational material reinforces this trap — emphasizing indicators over intent, entry signals over context, and precision over understanding. Retail traders are taught **what** to trade, not **why** price behaves the way it does. And without that depth of reasoning, every strategy eventually breaks under pressure.

Trading isn't about predicting what will happen next — it's about understanding **why** it's happening now. That shift in perspective separates the crowd from the consistently profitable.

How SMC + ICT Can Change Trading Outcomes

Smart Money Concepts (SMC) and Inner Circle Trader (ICT) methodologies changed the way I viewed every chart. They revealed that markets are engineered — not manipulated in conspiracy, but structured through design. Liquidity isn't random; it's intentional. Price doesn't move **to** a level — it moves **through** liquidity to reach imbalance. Every stop hunt, every breaker, every mitigation is part of a larger institutional playbook.

By learning to think like the institutions — identifying order flow, imbalances, and liquidity pools — traders can begin to align their trades with the underlying engine of the market. The difference isn't subtle; it's transformational. What once felt like uncertainty becomes structured opportunity.

SMC and ICT offer something far beyond "entry setups" — they offer a framework for **thinking**. They replace randomness with reasoning, chaos with causality, and emotion with precision. And while no system guarantees success, the edge comes from seeing what others overlook — the invisible hand behind the chart.

This book distills that understanding — from market structure and liquidity theory to mindset and execution. It's not a shortcut, but a map. A guide to help you trade with the clarity of institutions, the patience of professionals, and the discipline of probability.

— *Deepanshu Suman*

Introduction

Markets are not random. They are structured, purposeful, and deeply psychological. Every candlestick, every liquidity grab, and every fake breakout tells a story — the story of money moving from weak hands to strong hands. And behind that movement lies *intention* — the quiet, calculated intention of institutions, market makers, and algorithmic systems that dominate today's trading landscape.

For decades, retail traders have been told that markets are unpredictable, that success is a matter of luck or indicators. But beneath the surface noise lies a hidden structure — a logic that governs liquidity, order flow, and market behavior. Understanding that logic is what separates amateurs from professionals.

This book is about uncovering that logic — decoding the blueprint of institutional activity through **Smart Money Concepts (SMC)** and **ICT (Inner Circle Trader)** methodologies. It's about seeing what institutions see, trading what they trade, and finally learning to align yourself with the flow of the real market.

What Are Smart Money Concepts?

Smart Money Concepts (SMC) are a framework for analyzing markets through the lens of institutional behavior. Rather than relying on lagging indicators or arbitrary chart patterns, SMC focuses on how *liquidity, order blocks, imbalances, and market structure shifts* drive price.

At its core, SMC teaches traders to understand:

- **Where liquidity lies** — the zones where large players target retail stop losses.
- **How market structure evolves** — the transition between accumulation, manipulation, and distribution.
- **Why price moves** — not because of news or emotions, but because institutions are engineering liquidity to fill their orders efficiently.

ICT (Inner Circle Trader) refined these ideas into a practical methodology — mapping how the "smart money" manipulates price to accumulate positions before major moves. ICT's teachings on fair value gaps (FVGs), market structure breaks (MSBs), and daily profiles have given traders the ability to see behind the curtain.

In essence, SMC + ICT help you understand that markets aren't random; they're *engineered.* Once you recognize those patterns, you stop being liquidity — and start following the liquidity.

Importance of Thinking Like Institutions

Most retail traders lose not because they lack effort, but because they think like *retail traders.* They chase candles, trade emotionally, and react to price instead of anticipating it. Institutions, on the other hand, create the very moves retail traders react to.

To succeed, you must stop following the crowd and start thinking like the architects of the market. That means:

- Viewing the market as a *liquidity ecosystem*, not a gambling machine.
- Understanding *time and price delivery* — how sessions, kill zones, and liquidity sweeps are orchestrated.
- Learning to be *patient*, waiting for confirmation through structure and displacement.

When you start thinking institutionally, you no longer trade every move — you wait for the high-probability setups they are engineering. You learn to spot manipulation before it happens and position yourself *with* the smart money, not against it.

This mindset shift is the foundation of consistent profitability. Once you think like a liquidity engineer instead of a liquidity provider, everything changes.

How This Book Is Structured

This book is designed to take you from *conceptual understanding* to *strategic mastery.* Each section builds progressively — from decoding institutional behavior to applying advanced ICT-based models in live trading.

Here's what to expect:

1. **Foundations of Smart Money** — Learn the core principles: market structure, liquidity, order blocks, and the psychology of price delivery.
2. **Institutional Frameworks in Action** — Explore ICT concepts like fair value gaps, optimal trade entry (OTE), and session-based liquidity.

3. **Strategy & Application** — Combine theory with practice: build setups, manage risk, and apply a professional execution model.

4. **The Probabilistic Mindset** — Shift from prediction to probability. Master emotional neutrality and the mental models used by elite traders.

5. **Advanced Models & Case Studies** — Study real-world examples of how SMC and ICT concepts align to produce asymmetric trades.

6. **Appendices & Tools** — Access glossaries, resources, and frameworks for journaling, backtesting, and continuing your learning journey.

Each chapter is structured to blend clarity, depth, and practical insight — so you can internalize not just *what* to trade, but *how to think*.

In Closing

This book isn't a get-rich-quick manual. It's a roadmap for transformation — from reactive retail trader to confident, calculated liquidity engineer. By the end, you'll no longer be chasing price. You'll understand how and why price moves — and most importantly, how to align yourself with the forces that truly drive the market.

Welcome to the other side of trading.
Welcome to the Smart Money world.

How to Read This Book

Trading is both art and science. This book is written to help you understand not only the logic behind institutional trading but also the psychology that drives it. To get the most out of this material, it's important to know how to approach it — how to read, reflect, and apply.

This is not a book you read once and put away. It's a framework to revisit — one that deepens in meaning each time you study the charts and the logic behind them. Every section builds upon the last, blending market theory, psychological insight, and practical execution.

Recommended Reading Flow

Smart Money Concepts and ICT models require both conceptual clarity and practical repetition. The order in which you absorb these ideas matters.

Step 1: Build the Foundations

Start with the early chapters on **market structure**, **liquidity**, and **institutional behavior**. These are the pillars on which all Smart Money understanding rests. Before you can interpret fair value gaps or breaker blocks, you must first understand *why* price moves the way it does and *who* moves it.

Step 2: Study Institutional Frameworks

Once the fundamentals are clear, move into the sections on **ICT principles** — including market sessions, order flow, displacement, and optimal trade entry (OTE). These chapters decode how large players accumulate, manipulate, and distribute positions. Read slowly, take notes, and visualize how these patterns repeat daily across timeframes.

Step 3: Apply and Journal

After the conceptual foundation is laid, practice. Go through live charts, backtest examples, and mark key structural points. Keep a **trading journal** where you log your thoughts, hypotheses, and emotional reactions. True transformation comes not from reading — but from observing and recording your evolution as a trader.

Step 4: Embrace Probabilistic Thinking

The later chapters will focus on mindset — shifting from prediction to probability, from reaction to anticipation. This is where you'll develop emotional neutrality and understand that consistency is not about winning every trade — it's about executing a repeatable edge with discipline.

Notes on Charts, Diagrams, and Examples

Throughout this book, you'll find charts, schematic diagrams, and price examples. These visuals are not meant for aesthetic appeal; they're strategic learning tools designed to anchor complex ideas.

- **Charts are conceptual, not predictive.** They illustrate principles — liquidity sweeps, market structure breaks, order blocks — not forecasts of future price.
- **Examples are simplified for clarity.** Real market conditions will often be more chaotic, with multiple overlaps and fake-outs. Learn to interpret the principle, not memorize the pattern.
- **Recreate them yourself.** Use your preferred charting platform to redraw examples. This tactile learning process sharpens pattern recognition and builds deep visual memory.
- **Timeframes matter.** ICT and SMC concepts are fractal. What happens on a 1-minute chart mirrors what happens on a 1-hour or 1-day chart. Learn to zoom in and out without losing structural context.

In Summary

Read this book with patience and intention. Take notes. Mark your realizations. Question your assumptions. Most importantly — don't rush.

The markets will always be there. But mastery comes to those who move slowly, think deeply, and learn continuously. Treat this book not as a course to finish, but as a manual for evolution — a lens through which you begin to see what the institutions already know.

Welcome to the study of Smart Money.
Trade with intention. Learn with curiosity.

Contents

Part I

Foundations

Chapter 1

Introduction to Smart Money & ICT

Markets are more than charts and indicators — they are living ecosystems, moving in response to the intentions of the strongest players. Every swing, every spike, every stop hunt has a purpose. Behind these movements is what traders call the "Smart Money" — institutions, banks, and professional traders orchestrating liquidity and exploiting market inefficiencies.

Before you can trade like them, you must understand who they are, how they operate, and how retail traders often misstep. This chapter sets the foundation for everything that follows, helping you see the market through the lens of the institutions rather than the crowd.

1.1 Definition of Smart Money

Smart Money represents the capital controlled by professional market participants — institutions, banks, hedge funds, proprietary trading firms, and high-net-worth investors. Unlike retail traders, who often trade reactively or emotionally, Smart Money operates with intention, information advantage, and strategic foresight. Understanding Smart Money is not just about spotting where price moves; it is about recognizing who is moving it and why.

The Core Concept

At its essence, Smart Money is **capital guided by superior insight and strategy**. These market participants have the resources, data, and patience to shape price action in ways that retail traders rarely perceive. They do not chase trends or react impulsively; instead, they create conditions in the market that allow them to accumulate or distribute positions efficiently, often at the expense of uninformed participants.

Key Characteristics:

- **Size and Influence:** Smart Money has the ability to move markets due to the sheer volume of capital controlled.
- **Strategic Intent:** Every action is planned with a specific outcome in mind, often targeting long-term profitability over short-term gains.
- **Data and Analysis:** Institutions have access to order flow, volume profiles, historical data, and proprietary research tools.
- **Patience and Discipline:** They operate over multiple timeframes, waiting for high-probability opportunities rather than forcing trades.
- **Liquidity Awareness:** Smart Money identifies where retail liquidity pools exist and exploits these zones to enter or exit positions with minimal slippage.

How Smart Money Operates

Smart Money does not merely follow price; it *creates price movements.* Understanding their operations requires insight into key mechanisms:

1. **Accumulation and Distribution:** Institutions accumulate positions quietly during low-volatility periods and distribute them after liquidity has been created. This process often precedes large trends that retail traders perceive as "sudden."
2. **Manipulation of Retail Behavior:** Smart Money intentionally triggers stop-losses and false breakouts to fill orders efficiently. These moves are not random; they are engineered to exploit predictable retail psychology.
3. **Market Structure Engineering:** By understanding how price forms swings, breakouts, and retracements, institutions manipulate short-term volatility to optimize entry and exit points while maintaining control over market direction.
4. **Liquidity Targeting:** Retail traders often cluster stops and limit orders at obvious price levels. Smart Money drives price toward these liquidity zones to execute large orders with minimal slippage.

Common Tools and Footprints of Smart Money

Smart Money leaves identifiable "footprints" in the market. Recognizing these structures is crucial for aligning trades with institutional activity:

- **Order Blocks (OBs):** Zones where institutions have previously placed significant buy or sell orders, often acting as support or resistance.
- **Liquidity Pools:** Areas where retail orders cluster, frequently targeted for stop hunts.

- **Fair Value Gaps (FVGs):** Imbalances created when price moves too quickly, leaving behind areas of unfilled liquidity.
- **Stop Hunts and Breakers:** Deliberate moves to trigger retail stops, creating liquidity for institutional trades.

Why Smart Money Matters to Traders

For a retail trader, understanding Smart Money is transformative:

- **Shift from Reactive to Strategic Trading:** Instead of chasing price, traders learn to anticipate moves based on where Smart Money is likely acting.
- **Higher-Probability Setups:** By aligning trades with institutional footprints, traders increase the likelihood of profitable outcomes.
- **Reduced Emotional Trading:** Recognizing that stop hunts and manipulations are intentional reduces frustration and impulsive trading.
- **Framework for Probabilistic Thinking:** Traders stop seeking certainty and start thinking in terms of probabilities, risk management, and expected value.

The Mindset Behind Smart Money

Understanding Smart Money is not just a technical skill — it is a mindset:

- Think in multiple timeframes. Institutions operate fractally — what happens on a 1-minute chart mirrors higher timeframes.
- Observe patiently. Not every market move is actionable; high-probability setups are rare and must be respected.
- Learn to read intent. Recognize accumulation, manipulation, and distribution patterns rather than blindly following indicators.
- Embrace uncertainty. Smart Money thrives in uncertainty by exploiting retail predictability, and traders must adopt probabilistic thinking to align with it.

Summary

Smart Money is the invisible force driving market structure. By studying its behavior, footprints, and strategies, retail traders can transition from being reactive participants to proactive, strategically-aligned traders.

In the chapters that follow, we will explore how to identify these footprints, leverage ICT methodology to read the market, and build a framework for trading with the probability edge that institutions inherently possess.

1.2 Difference: Retail vs Institutional Traders

Understanding the market requires knowing who moves it. Broadly, traders can be divided into two groups: **retail traders** and **institutional traders.** The distinction is not merely one of capital size; it is a difference in perspective, methodology, and purpose. Recognizing these differences is critical for aligning your trading strategy with high-probability setups.

Retail Traders

Retail traders are individual market participants who trade their own capital, often with limited access to institutional-level data and resources. Key characteristics include:

- **Reactive Trading:** Retail traders typically respond to price movements, news, or technical indicators rather than anticipating them.
- **Short-Term Focus:** Many retail traders focus on immediate gains, chasing trends or quick profits without considering broader market structure.
- **Emotional Bias:** Fear, greed, FOMO (Fear of Missing Out), and revenge trading often drive retail decisions.
- **Limited Resources:** Retail traders lack access to sophisticated order flow data, large-scale liquidity insights, and professional-grade analytics.
- **Crowd Mentality:** Retail participants often herd, amplifying volatility at predictable levels (e.g., clustered stop-losses or breakout zones).

Institutional Traders

Institutional traders include banks, hedge funds, proprietary trading desks, and other entities controlling significant capital. Their approach is fundamentally different:

- **Proactive Trading:** Institutions act with foresight, creating price movements and targeting liquidity to execute large orders efficiently.
- **Long-Term Perspective:** Positions may be held for multiple sessions, days, or even months, aligning with strategic objectives rather than short-term fluctuations.
- **Data-Driven Decisions:** Institutions have access to market depth, order flow analytics, economic data, and proprietary algorithms that inform every trade.

- **Liquidity Engineering:** They manipulate market liquidity through stop hunts, fake breakouts, and engineered volatility to create optimal entry and exit conditions.
- **Risk Management:** Advanced hedging, position sizing, and correlation strategies reduce exposure and increase expected value.

Key Behavioral Differences

The contrast between retail and institutional traders is best understood through behavior and mindset:

1. **Reaction vs. Anticipation:** Retail traders react to price; institutions anticipate it.
2. **Emotion vs. Discipline:** Retail trading decisions are often emotional; institutional trades follow disciplined plans.
3. **Fragmented vs. Cohesive:** Retail actions are dispersed and inconsistent; institutional orders are coordinated and strategically executed.
4. **Noise vs. Signal:** Retail activity often creates noise that institutions exploit to enter or exit positions efficiently.

Practical Implications for Traders

Recognizing these differences allows retail traders to improve their approach:

- **Stop Being Liquidity:** Most retail traders inadvertently provide liquidity for institutional orders. Understanding Smart Money behavior helps avoid being on the wrong side of these moves.
- **Think Like an Institution:** Focus on market structure, liquidity zones, and probabilistic setups rather than chasing candles or news.
- **Patience is a Strength:** Align with high-probability setups instead of trading every market movement.
- **Risk-First Approach:** Manage exposure carefully, using proper position sizing and risk-to-reward analysis, emulating institutional risk practices.

Summary

The difference between retail and institutional traders is not only capital or experience but also perspective, discipline, and strategic approach. Retail traders often act as liquidity providers for the institutions, while institutional traders move markets with purpose and foresight.

For traders aiming to master Smart Money Concepts (SMC) and ICT methodologies, the goal is to bridge this gap: adopt institutional thinking, recognize market manipulation, and execute trades with discipline, patience, and a probabilistic mindset.

Understanding this distinction lays the foundation for all subsequent chapters, from market structure to order blocks and liquidity analysis.

1.3 Introduction to ICT Methodology

The Inner Circle Trader (ICT) methodology is a framework designed to help traders understand the market from the perspective of institutional participants. While Smart Money Concepts (SMC) provide the foundational knowledge of liquidity, market manipulation, and order flow, ICT translates these principles into actionable trading strategies. This section introduces the core philosophy, tools, and mindset of ICT.

The Philosophy Behind ICT

ICT emphasizes that trading is not about guessing where price will go; it is about **reading market intent and acting with probability**. The methodology teaches traders to:

- Observe market structure and identify institutional footprints.
- Anticipate moves before they happen by understanding liquidity and manipulation.
- Execute trades with precision, patience, and calculated risk.

In essence, ICT transforms the abstract principles of Smart Money into practical steps that can be applied across markets, assets, and timeframes.

Core Concepts of ICT

Several key concepts form the backbone of ICT methodology:

1. **Optimal Trade Entry (OTE):** A Fibonacci-based approach to identify high-probability entry zones after a trend or retracement, aligning with institutional accumulation or distribution.
2. **Market Structure:** Understanding swings, break of structure (BoS), and change of character (CHoCH) allows traders to anticipate trend continuation or reversal.
3. **Liquidity Pools and Stops:** Identifying areas where retail traders cluster stop-losses or limit orders provides insight into where Smart Money is likely to target liquidity.

4. **Fair Value Gaps (FVGs):** Imbalances left on the chart during rapid price movements indicate areas that institutions may revisit to fill unexecuted orders.

5. **Session Bias and Time of Day:** Markets have different behaviors during London, New York, and Asian sessions. ICT teaches how to align trades with session-specific liquidity dynamics.

6. **Order Blocks (OBs):** Zones of previous institutional activity where significant buying or selling occurred, serving as support/resistance and potential trade areas.

The ICT Trading Mindset

ICT emphasizes a disciplined, probability-based approach:

- **Patience Over Action:** Not every market movement is an opportunity. The highest-probability trades often require waiting for the perfect confluence of market conditions.
- **Alignment With Smart Money:** Trades should always align with the market's strongest players. Going against institutional flows increases risk and reduces expected value.
- **Fractal Thinking:** Patterns repeat across multiple timeframes. Understanding higher-timeframe structure provides context for lower timeframe entries.
- **Probabilistic Decision Making:** Every trade is treated as an opportunity with expected probability and risk-to-reward, not a certainty.

Practical Application of ICT

ICT methodology is applied through a structured process:

1. **Analyze Higher Timeframes:** Identify overall market bias, trend direction, and key structural levels.
2. **Locate Liquidity Zones:** Determine where retail stop-losses, limit orders, and previous highs/lows cluster.
3. **Identify Order Blocks and FVGs:** Map institutional footprints to understand where price may reverse or continue.
4. **Determine Optimal Entry Points (OTE):** Use Fibonacci retracement and confluence with OBs and FVGs to plan entries.
5. **Execute With Discipline:** Apply proper risk management, set stops, and monitor price action without emotional interference.
6. **Review and Journal:** Post-trade analysis and journaling reinforce learning and build statistical confidence.

Summary

ICT methodology bridges the gap between theory and execution. While Smart Money Concepts teach *what* drives the market, ICT teaches *how* to interpret those movements and act with high probability. By combining market structure, order flow, liquidity analysis, and disciplined execution, traders can align themselves with institutional activity and significantly increase the odds of consistent profitability.

Mastering ICT requires practice, observation, and reflection. The subsequent chapters will explore each component — order blocks, liquidity, fair value gaps, and trade execution strategies — in detail, providing actionable tools to trade like the institutions.

1.4 Core Principles of SMC: Liquidity, Order Blocks, Market Manipulation

Smart Money Concepts (SMC) are built on the idea that the market is predominantly influenced by institutional players rather than retail traders. Understanding these core principles — **Liquidity**, **Order Blocks**, and **Market Manipulation** — is essential for interpreting price action, anticipating market behavior, and executing high-probability trades.

Liquidity

Definition: Liquidity refers to areas in the market where a significant number of buy or sell orders are clustered. These areas provide institutions with the ability to enter or exit positions efficiently without moving the market excessively.

Key Insights:

- Retail traders often place stop-losses and limit orders at obvious price levels, creating predictable liquidity pools.
- Smart Money targets these pools to execute large trades, often triggering retail stop-losses in the process.
- Understanding liquidity zones allows traders to anticipate potential market reversals or accelerations.

Practical Example: If a major swing low has accumulated many stop-loss orders from retail traders, Smart Money may push the price slightly below that level to trigger these stops, thereby creating liquidity for institutional buying.

Order Blocks (OBs)

Definition: Order Blocks are areas on the chart where institutions have previously placed significant buy or sell orders. These zones often act as support or resistance in future price movements.

Types of Order Blocks:

- **Bullish Order Block:** A zone where institutions have accumulated long positions before pushing price higher.
- **Bearish Order Block:** A zone where institutions have accumulated short positions before pushing price lower.

Identification Criteria:

- Sharp directional moves following consolidation or retracement.
- Presence of liquidity pools that were likely targeted before the move.
- Subsequent retests of the same zone acting as support or resistance.

Practical Application: Traders use order blocks to identify high probability entry and exit points, especially when combined with other confluences such as fair value gaps, liquidity pools, or optimal trade entry zones.

Market Manipulation

Definition: Market manipulation refers to intentional price actions by Smart Money to create liquidity and mislead retail traders. These moves are not random; they are engineered to facilitate accumulation or distribution of large positions.

Common Techniques:

- **Stop Hunts:** Driving price to trigger retail stop-losses and create liquidity for institutional orders.
- **Fake Breakouts:** Simulating a trend continuation or reversal to mislead retail traders before reversing the market.
- **False Structure Shifts:** Creating the appearance of a break of structure to induce panic or euphoria, allowing institutions to accumulate or distribute positions.

Key Takeaways:

- Retail traders often act as the source of liquidity for these moves.
- Recognizing manipulation patterns helps traders avoid traps and align with institutional flows.
- Combining market manipulation insights with liquidity zones and order blocks increases the probability of successful trades.

Integration of Principles

The true power of SMC lies in integrating these three principles:

- Identify **liquidity zones** where retail orders are likely concentrated.
- Map **order blocks** to see where institutions have previously executed positions.
- Recognize **market manipulation** patterns to distinguish intentional moves from random volatility.

When used together, these principles allow traders to anticipate market behavior, plan high-probability trades, and trade in harmony with institutional activity rather than against it.

Summary

> "Price is never random; it is engineered by the strongest participants. Understanding liquidity, order blocks, and market manipulation is the key to reading the market like an institution."

By mastering these core principles, traders gain the ability to:

- Identify where institutions are likely to act next.
- Avoid retail traps and false signals.
- Build a structured, probability-based trading approach aligned with Smart Money.

This foundation sets the stage for advanced topics such as fair value gaps, breaker blocks, and optimal trade entries, which will be explored in the subsequent chapters.

1.5 Common Retail Mistakes and Why They Fail

Trading is deceptively simple: buy low, sell high. Yet, most retail traders consistently fail to achieve sustainable profitability. Understanding **why retail traders fail** is crucial for bridging the gap between amateur and professional trading. This section explores the most common mistakes and their underlying causes.

Chasing Trends and Reacting to Price

Mistake: Retail traders often jump into a trade after a strong price move, fearing they will miss out on profits.

Why It Fails:

- Retail traders react to price rather than understanding market structure.
- Buying after a strong upward move increases the risk of entering at the tail end of an institutional accumulation.
- Trend-chasing ignores liquidity zones where Smart Money is likely accumulating or distributing.

Solution: Wait for high-probability setups that align with institutional order blocks, fair value gaps, or liquidity pools. Patience is more profitable than impulsivity.

Ignoring Market Structure

Mistake: Many retail traders focus solely on indicators or candlestick patterns without understanding the context of higher timeframe market structure.

Why It Fails:

- Lack of market structure awareness leads to trading against the trend or institutional flow.
- Retail traders often interpret random noise as actionable signals.

Solution: Analyze multi-timeframe structure, identifying swing highs/lows, break of structure (BoS), and changes of character (CHoCH) to align trades with market direction.

Overtrading and Emotional Trading

Mistake: Trading too frequently, based on emotion or a perceived "need to be in the market," leads to overtrading.

Why It Fails:

- Each trade incurs cost (spread, slippage), which erodes profitability.
- Emotional decision-making (fear, greed, revenge trading) leads to inconsistent execution.

Solution: Develop a trade plan with predefined setups, risk-to-reward parameters, and daily limits. Only take trades that meet strict criteria.

Improper Risk Management

Mistake: Retail traders often risk too much on a single trade or ignore position sizing rules.

Why It Fails:

- High-risk positions amplify losses and emotional stress.
- Ignoring stop placement and risk-reward ratio leads to negative expectancy over time.

Solution: Use proper position sizing based on account size, calculate risk-to-reward ratios before entry, and adjust exposure according to confidence in the setup.

Relying Solely on Indicators or Signals

Mistake: Many retail traders depend on moving averages, RSI, MACD, or buy/sell signals from others without understanding market context.

Why It Fails:

- Indicators are lagging tools that often generate false signals.
- Without understanding liquidity, order blocks, or institutional intent, signals are low-probability.

Solution: Treat indicators as supportive tools, not decision-makers. Focus on market structure, liquidity zones, and institutional footprints.

Ignoring Psychology and Discipline

Mistake: Underestimating the mental and emotional challenges of trading.

Why It Fails:

- Fear of missing out (FOMO) and revenge trading cause inconsistent entries and exits.
- Impatience leads to premature exits or overtrading.

Solution: Develop self-discipline, maintain a trading journal, and practice mindfulness. Treat trading as a probabilistic game, not a series of certainties.

Summary of Key Lessons

- **Patience is critical:** Wait for setups that align with Smart Money, rather than chasing price.
- **Understand the market structure:** Multi-timeframe awareness reduces risk and increases probability.

- **Control risk:** Position sizing, stop placement, and risk-to-reward ratios protect capital.
- **Align with institutional flow:** Trade where liquidity and order blocks suggest Smart Money is active.
- **Maintain discipline:** Avoid emotional trading and overtrading.

By avoiding these common mistakes and adopting a Smart Money-aligned mindset, retail traders can transition from reactive participants to strategic, probabilistic traders who consistently improve their edge in the market.

1.6 Institutional Algorithmic Behavior Basics

Modern financial markets are dominated by automated systems. It is estimated that 80–90% of daily trading volume is generated by institutional algorithms operated by banks, hedge funds, market-making firms, and high-frequency trading engines. To understand Smart Money Concepts (SMC) and ICT methodology, it is essential to understand how these institutional algorithms behave, because price is ultimately a reflection of their programmed intent.

Algorithms Do Not Predict, They Execute

Institutional traders do not "predict" market direction. Instead, they deploy algorithmic engines designed to:

- Fill large orders at optimal prices,
- Seek liquidity to minimize slippage,
- Accumulate or distribute without revealing intent,
- Hedge exposure across correlated markets.

These algorithms operate without emotion. Their systematic rules create recurring price behaviors that SMC traders can recognize.

Liquidity as the Primary Objective

The first principle of institutional algorithms is that **liquidity is required to fill large orders**. Liquidity clusters typically exist at:

- Equal highs and equal lows,
- Previous swing highs and lows,
- Fair Value Gaps (FVGs),
- Order Blocks (OBs),

- Session highs and lows,
- Psychological round numbers.

Algorithms deliberately push price toward these areas to capture stops and trigger pending orders. What retail traders perceive as "support" and "resistance" are often simply *liquidity reservoirs* used by institutions.

The Three-Stage Algorithmic Cycle

Institutional price movement typically follows a structured three-stage sequence:

1. Liquidity Capture

The algorithm first seeks liquidity by:

- Running above old highs,
- Sweeping below old lows,
- Creating sharp wicks,
- Spiking into imbalance zones.

2. Displacement

After liquidity is collected, the algorithm initiates a directional move characterized by:

- Strong impulsive candles,
- Breaks of structure (BOS),
- Fair Value Gaps left behind,
- Clear momentum signatures.

3. Rebalancing and Mitigation

Following displacement, price often returns to:

- Order Blocks,
- Fair Value Gaps,
- Mitigation Blocks,
- Imbalance zones.

This retracement allows institutions to refine entries or mitigate earlier positions.

Algorithms Target Inefficiencies

Markets become inefficient during rapid moves, leaving behind:

- Fair Value Gaps (FVGs),
- Price imbalances,
- Thin liquidity zones.

Institutional algorithms tend to revisit these areas to rebalance price and finalize order execution. This behavior is foundational to SMC methodology.

Time-Based Algorithmic Behavior

Institutional activity is concentrated during high-liquidity periods, often referred to as ICT killzones:

- London Open (LO),
- New York Open (NYO),
- London Close,
- New York Lunch Fade.

During these windows, algorithms initiate liquidity hunts, displacement moves, and trend continuation or reversal setups.

Concealment of Institutional Intent

Institutional engines must execute large orders without revealing direction. Common concealment mechanisms include:

- Hovering price around key levels,
- False breakouts and fake structure shifts,
- Stop runs prior to reversal,
- Slow accumulation or distribution phases.

These behaviors are engineered to mask intent while ensuring optimal execution.

Why Understanding Algorithmic Behavior Matters

Mastering algorithmic behavior enables retail traders to:

- Avoid trading in liquidity zones targeted for sweeps,
- Ignore emotional reactions to manipulative moves,
- Interpret price through the lens of institutional logic,
- Anticipate the sequence of liquidity $\rightarrow$ displacement $\rightarrow$ mitigation,
- Trade in alignment with the algorithmic flow rather than against it.

Summary

Institutional algorithms:

- Hunt and utilize liquidity,
- Move price through predictable sequences,
- Create BOS, CHoCH, FVGs, and other SMC structures,
- Follow time-of-day cycles,
- Conceal large order execution,
- Maintain market efficiency.

Understanding these behaviors is the foundation upon which all Smart Money Concepts are built.

Chapter 2

Market Structure

Markets are often perceived by retail traders as chaotic, unpredictable, or random — a series of candles fluctuating on a screen. Yet, beneath this apparent chaos lies a structured rhythm dictated by the movements of Smart Money. Understanding **market structure** is akin to learning the grammar of a language: once you understand the rules, reading and anticipating price action becomes intuitive.

The purpose of this chapter is to equip you with the ability to see beyond the noise. By analyzing trends, swings, and shifts in market character, you will begin to recognize where liquidity lies, how institutions maneuver, and where the market is likely to go next. This knowledge forms the foundation for identifying high-probability setups and aligning your trades with the market's strongest participants.

We will explore key concepts such as trends, break of structure (BoS), changes of character (CHoCH), and the significance of swing highs and lows. Additionally, we will contrast how institutional traders interpret these movements versus how retail traders commonly perceive them. By the end of this chapter, you will understand not just *where price moves*, but *why* it moves — the first step toward trading with a strategic, probability-based approach.

2.1 Trend Analysis: Uptrend, Downtrend, Sideways

Understanding trends is the first step in mastering market structure. While many retail traders react to price movements without context, institutions operate by identifying and exploiting trends, aligning their trades with high-probability directional moves. Trend analysis is not just about determining whether price is moving up or down; it is about understanding the underlying forces shaping the market and identifying where liquidity resides.

What is a Trend?

A trend is a general direction in which the market moves over a specific period. It is the collective outcome of supply and demand forces, driven predominantly by Smart Money. Trends provide context, allowing traders to differentiate between impulsive moves and corrective retracements, and to anticipate future price action.

Types of Trends:

1. **Uptrend:** Characterized by higher highs (HH) and higher lows (HL). Price demonstrates consistent upward momentum as institutions accumulate positions, and retail traders often follow after the move is underway.

2. **Downtrend:** Characterized by lower lows (LL) and lower highs (LH). Institutions are distributing or shorting positions, while retail traders often buy prematurely at perceived "support" levels.

3. **Sideways (Range-Bound):** Price moves within horizontal support and resistance levels. Institutions are often accumulating or distributing during these phases, waiting for liquidity and a trigger for the next directional move.

Institutional vs Retail Perspective

Retail Traders: Retail participants often focus on candle patterns, oscillators, or breakout signals, reacting to price rather than understanding structure. They may misinterpret retracements as reversals or chase trends too late, entering after liquidity has been consumed by institutions.

Institutional Traders: Institutions view trends as opportunities to accumulate or distribute positions with precision. They analyze market structure, liquidity clusters, and session behavior to determine the optimal entry, target, and exit points. For example, a retracement to a previous swing low in an uptrend may be used to add to long positions, rather than signaling a reversal.

Identifying Trends Across Timeframes

Trends exist on multiple timeframes simultaneously. Recognizing the dominant trend on higher timeframes is critical before making intraday or swing trades.

- **Higher Timeframes (Daily, Weekly):** Show the overall market bias and institutional intent.

- **Lower Timeframes (Hourly, 15-min):** Reveal short-term liquidity hunts, stop runs, and entry opportunities for high-probability setups.

Aligning trades with higher timeframe trends increases the probability of success and minimizes conflict with institutional flows.

Characteristics of Trends

1. **Impulse vs Corrective Moves:** - **Impulse moves** occur in the direction of the trend, often strong and rapid, reflecting institutional activity. - **Corrective moves** are counter-trend retracements, often shallow and containing liquidity traps for retail traders.

2. **Trend Exhaustion:** Signs of weakening momentum, such as failure to make higher highs in an uptrend, may indicate accumulation or distribution zones for the next move.

3. **Volume and Liquidity Clues:** Volume spikes often accompany institutional accumulation or distribution. Identifying these points helps anticipate the next leg of a trend.

4. **Psychology of Trend Participants:** Retail traders fear missing out during strong trends and often enter late, while institutions control liquidity and execute strategically.

Sideways Markets and Accumulation/Distribution

Sideways markets are often misinterpreted by retail traders as indecisive. However, these phases are critical for institutions:

- **Accumulation:** Institutions quietly build long positions at support levels before a bullish breakout.

- **Distribution:** Institutions sell or short near resistance levels before a bearish breakout.

- **Liquidity Creation:** Sideways consolidation accumulates retail stops and limit orders, which institutions later use to fuel directional moves.

Recognizing whether a sideways market represents accumulation or distribution is key to anticipating breakouts or trend reversals.

Practical Applications for Traders

- Trade in the direction of the dominant trend to align with institutional flows.

- Use retracements to enter trades at liquidity zones rather than chasing price.

- Identify when a trend is losing momentum to prepare for potential reversals or market manipulation.

- Apply multi-timeframe analysis to combine context (higher timeframes) with precision entry (lower timeframes).

- Avoid trading during sideways markets unless institutional footprints indicate accumulation or distribution.

Summary

Trend analysis is the foundation of market structure. Recognizing uptrends, downtrends, and sideways phases allows traders to:

- Align with institutional intent.
- Anticipate liquidity hunts and stop runs.
- Enter high-probability trades at optimal points rather than reacting to noise.

By mastering trends, traders shift from being passive participants to proactive, probability-driven strategists capable of reading the market like Smart Money.

2.2 Break of Structure (BoS)

The concept of **Break of Structure (BoS)** is central to understanding market dynamics and Smart Money behavior. A BoS represents a significant shift in market direction, indicating that the previous trend or range has been invalidated. Recognizing BoS is crucial for anticipating institutional moves and avoiding common retail pitfalls.

Definition of BoS

A **Break of Structure** occurs when price decisively breaks a previous swing high or swing low, signaling that the market may be transitioning to a new trend or that institutions are manipulating liquidity to create favorable conditions for their positions.

- **Uptrend BoS:** Price breaks a previous swing high, confirming bullish continuation.
- **Downtrend BoS:** Price breaks a previous swing low, confirming bearish continuation.
- **Range BoS:** A breakout from sideways consolidation that establishes directional intent.

Institutional Perspective

Institutions do not trade randomly. BoS represents moments where they deliberately push price beyond key levels to:

- Trigger retail stop-losses clustered around obvious swing highs/lows.
- Create liquidity pools for institutional entry or exit.

- Test market sentiment to gauge participation and strength.

From an institutional point of view, a BoS is not merely a breakout; it is a strategic move designed to facilitate accumulation or distribution while minimizing slippage and execution risk.

Retail vs Institutional Interpretation

Retail Traders: Retail participants often interpret BoS as a simple "breakout" signal and rush to enter the market, frequently resulting in late entries or getting trapped in fake breakouts.

Institutional Traders: Institutions anticipate where retail traders will place stops and entries. They often manipulate price to trigger these levels before continuing in their intended direction. Recognizing a BoS in context allows traders to avoid traps and align with Smart Money flow.

Identifying BoS in Practice

1. **Swing High/Low Analysis:** Identify the last significant swing high and swing low. A break beyond these points signals potential structural change.

2. **Momentum Confirmation:** Look for strong directional candlesticks or volume spikes supporting the break.

3. **Retest and Validation:** Often, price may retest the broken level. This retest can serve as a high-probability entry aligned with institutional intent.

4. **Multi-Timeframe Alignment:** Confirm that the break is in alignment with higher timeframe trends to avoid false signals.

BoS and Liquidity

Breaks of structure are often strategically used to hunt liquidity. Retail traders' stops are commonly placed just beyond swing highs/lows. Institutions push price to these points to:

- Fill their own orders without causing excessive market impact.

- Remove weak hands from the market, ensuring stronger follow-through.

- Signal the next directional leg after absorbing retail liquidity.

Practical Applications for Traders

- Use BoS as a context tool rather than a standalone signal. Combine with liquidity zones, order blocks, and fair value gaps for higher probability trades.
- Avoid entering immediately after a break; wait for retests or confluence with other structural elements.
- Analyze the BoS within higher timeframe structure to determine whether it is a continuation, reversal, or manipulation.

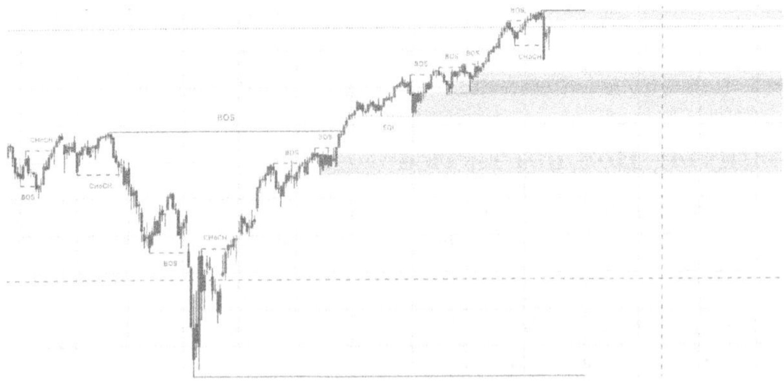

Figure 2.1: Schematic of a Bullish Market Structure Shift. Note the Change of Character (CHoCH) breaking the previous Lower High, followed by the Break of Structure (BoS) confirming the new trend.

Summary

The Break of Structure is more than just a technical breakout; it is a reflection of institutional intent and liquidity engineering. By understanding and correctly interpreting BoS, traders can:

- Identify where institutional activity is likely occurring.
- Avoid being caught in retail traps or false breakouts.
- Align trades with the strongest market participants for higher-probability outcomes.

Recognizing BoS sets the stage for understanding more subtle shifts in market behavior, such as **Change of Character (CHoCH)**, which will be discussed in the next section.

2.3 Change of Character (CHoCH)

While the Break of Structure (BoS) identifies a significant shift in market direction, the **Change of Character (CHoCH)** provides an earlier, more subtle signal that a trend may be weakening or reversing. Understanding CHoCH is crucial for anticipating institutional activity and positioning trades with high probability.

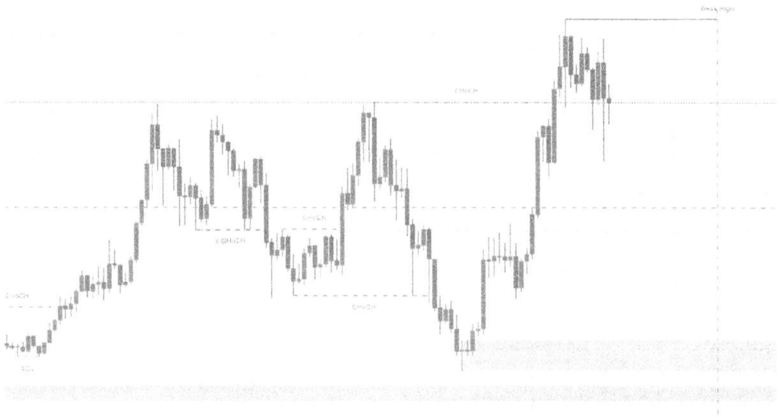

Figure 2.2: The first sign of reversal: A Change of Character (CHoCH) occurs when price breaks the most recent swing point in the opposite direction, signaling a potential shift in trend.

Definition of Change of Character

A Change of Character occurs when the market shows signs of hesitation or reversal within an existing trend. Unlike a BoS, which confirms structural change after price decisively breaks a key swing high or low, CHoCH signals the potential for that break before it happens.

- **Uptrend CHoCH:** The market fails to make a higher high or creates a lower low relative to the previous swing, suggesting bullish momentum is waning.
- **Downtrend CHoCH:** The market fails to make a lower low or creates a higher high relative to the previous swing, suggesting bearish momentum is fading.

Institutional Perspective

Institutions use CHoCH to manipulate retail participants and to manage liquidity efficiently:

- **Early Signaling:** A subtle CHoCH can indicate that Smart Money is beginning to distribute (in an uptrend) or accumulate (in a downtrend) positions.
- **Liquidity Hunting:** By creating early signs of reversal, institutions can trigger retail stops and orders in preparation for the next major move.
- **Trend Reversal or Continuation:** CHoCH helps institutions identify whether to maintain their positions, exit partially, or reverse the market entirely.

CHoCH vs BoS

	Change of Character (CHoCH)	**Break of Structure (BoS)**
Timing	Early, subtle indication of potential trend reversal	Confirmed structural shift after swing high-/low is broken
Signal Strength	Weak to moderate; requires context	Strong; visible break with momentum
Retail Perception	Often ignored or misinterpreted	Frequently triggers late entries or stop-losses
Institutional Use	To manipulate liquidity and gauge retail behavior	To execute accumulation/distribution efficiently

Identifying CHoCH in Practice

1. **Observe Swing Behavior:** Watch for a failure to create a new higher high in an uptrend or a new lower low in a downtrend.
2. **Momentum Analysis:** Weakening candlestick strength, volume divergence, or slower directional moves may indicate CHoCH.
3. **Liquidity Context:** Identify nearby liquidity pools or previous swing highs/lows that institutions may target following CHoCH.
4. **Retest Confirmation:** Often, CHoCH is followed by a retest of key levels before a BoS occurs. This retest provides a high-probability entry aligned with institutional intent.

Practical Applications for Traders

- Use CHoCH to anticipate trend exhaustion before it is confirmed by BoS.
- Combine CHoCH with order blocks, fair value gaps, and liquidity zones for high-probability setups.

- Avoid entering immediately on the first sign of CHoCH; wait for confirmation through retests or additional structural cues.
- Recognize that CHoCH provides a **probabilistic early warning**, not a guaranteed reversal.

Psychology of CHoCH

Retail traders often misinterpret CHoCH signals as minor pullbacks within the trend, leading to premature entries or missed opportunities. Institutions, on the other hand, use these subtle shifts to:

- Gauge retail sentiment and positioning.
- Accumulate or distribute positions ahead of a major trend continuation or reversal.
- Execute liquidity hunts without causing excessive market impact.

Summary

> "Change of Character is the whisper before the roar; it signals that the market may be ready to turn, giving those who recognize it a strategic advantage."

By mastering CHoCH:

- Traders can anticipate trend reversals earlier than most retail participants.
- Trade entries can be timed more precisely, aligning with institutional intent.
- Probabilistic thinking is reinforced — no signal is guaranteed, but understanding CHoCH improves the odds of success.

In the next sections, we will explore how swing highs and lows act as liquidity zones and how institutional bias differs from retail perception, further solidifying the framework for reading market structure like Smart Money.

2.4 Swing Highs/Lows as Liquidity Zones

Swing highs and lows are not just points on a chart; they represent critical zones of liquidity that institutional traders actively monitor and manipulate. Understanding how these levels function as liquidity zones is fundamental to trading like Smart Money.

Definition of Swing Highs and Lows

- **Swing High:** A price peak preceded and followed by lower highs, representing a temporary resistance area.
- **Swing Low:** A price trough preceded and followed by higher lows, representing a temporary support area.

These points are psychologically significant because retail traders commonly place stop-loss orders just beyond them. Institutions exploit these clusters to access liquidity for larger trades without causing significant market disruption.

Swing Points as Liquidity Zones

Why Swing Highs/Lows Matter:

- Retail traders often set stop-losses above swing highs in short positions or below swing lows in long positions.
- Limit orders accumulate near these levels as traders anticipate reversals.
- Institutions target these zones to trigger stop-losses and absorb liquidity, enabling them to execute large positions efficiently.

Liquidity Pool Concept: Liquidity zones are areas where multiple retail orders cluster. Swing highs/lows act as natural boundaries where these pools form, creating opportunities for Smart Money to hunt liquidity.

Institutional Tactics Around Swing Liquidity

Institutions manipulate swing highs/lows strategically:

- **Stop Hunts:** Push price slightly beyond a swing high/low to trigger retail stop-losses, creating liquidity for institutional orders.
- **Fake Breakouts:** Break a swing point briefly to lure retail traders before reversing in the intended direction.
- **Order Absorption:** Use liquidity at swing levels to accumulate or distribute positions quietly, maintaining market stability.

Identification in Practice

To identify swing highs/lows and treat them as liquidity zones:

1. Mark the most recent significant swings on multiple timeframes.
2. Observe where previous attempts to break these swings failed; these points often form strong liquidity clusters.

3. Look for volume spikes or price rejection at these levels to confirm institutional activity.
4. Use these zones in combination with order blocks, fair value gaps, and market structure for high-probability entries.

Practical Trading Applications

- **Entry Timing:** Wait for price to approach a swing high/low zone that aligns with institutional order blocks.
- **Stop Placement:** Position stops just outside liquidity zones to avoid being trapped by stop hunts.
- **Trend Alignment:** Combine swing liquidity analysis with dominant trend direction to reduce risk and increase probability.
- **Confirmation Signals:** Retests of swing levels, rejection wicks, and candlestick patterns can provide confluence for entry.

Summary

Swing highs and lows are more than mere chart points; they are active **liquidity zones** shaped by the collective positioning of retail traders. Recognizing and respecting these zones allows traders to:

- Anticipate where institutional activity is likely to occur.
- Avoid retail traps and false breakouts.
- Align trade entries with Smart Money for higher-probability outcomes.

In the next section, we will explore **Institutional Bias vs Retail Perception**, highlighting how professional traders interpret these liquidity zones differently from retail participants, further refining your ability to read market structure accurately.

2.5 Institutional Bias vs Retail Perception

Understanding the market from the perspective of institutional traders is essential for consistently profitable trading. Retail traders often interpret price action superficially, reacting to what they see on the screen, while institutions operate with a probabilistic, liquidity-driven mindset. This section explores the key differences between institutional bias and retail perception, and how adopting the former can improve trading outcomes.

Defining Institutional Bias

Institutional bias refers to the strategic framework institutions use to evaluate market direction and liquidity. Rather than reacting to each candle or indicator, institutions consider:

- Where liquidity pools are likely to exist (e.g., swing highs/lows, stop clusters).
- The dominant trend across multiple timeframes.
- Market manipulation techniques to accumulate or distribute positions.
- Optimal entry and exit points for high-volume trades without moving the market excessively.

Institutional bias is probabilistic rather than deterministic: it identifies areas with higher likelihood of movement in a preferred direction based on market structure and participant behavior.

Retail Perception of the Market

Retail traders, in contrast, often focus on:

- Short-term price fluctuations without context.
- Technical indicators as primary signals (RSI, MACD, moving averages).
- News events or headlines as catalysts for immediate action.
- Emotional responses like fear, greed, or FOMO rather than structured analysis.

This perspective often results in:

- Entering trades late or against institutional flow.
- Being caught in stop hunts, fake breakouts, and liquidity traps.
- Overtrading or reacting impulsively to minor market fluctuations.

Key Differences Between Institutional and Retail Perspectives

	Institutional Bias	Retail Perception
Focus	Market structure, liquidity, order flow	Price movements, indicators, news
Decision Process	Probabilistic, long-term, strategic	Reactive, short-term, emotional
Trend Approach	Align with dominant trend and liquidity pools	Chasing trends or attempting reversals
Risk Management	Position sizing, stops at strategic levels, hedging	Improper risk, random stop placement
Execution	Gradual, efficient, minimal market impact	Impulsive, late entries, emotional exits

Examples of Institutional Bias in Action

1. **Liquidity Hunting:** Institutions push price above a swing high to trigger retail stops before continuing the dominant trend.
2. **Trend Continuation:** A series of retracements within an uptrend may appear as indecision to retail traders, but institutions are accumulating positions for the next impulsive leg.
3. **Market Reversal Signals:** Subtle changes like CHoCH provide early indications of trend weakening, which retail traders often miss.

Aligning Your Trading with Institutional Bias

To trade like Smart Money:

- Focus on higher timeframe trends to determine overall bias.
- Identify liquidity zones (swing highs/lows, order blocks, fair value gaps).
- Wait for confirmations such as BoS or retests before entering trades.
- Avoid reacting impulsively to short-term fluctuations or indicator noise.
- Maintain a probabilistic mindset: every trade has a likelihood, not a certainty.

Psychological Implications

Adopting an institutional perspective requires retraining your mindset:

- Patience over impulsivity: wait for high-probability setups rather than reacting to every move.
- Discipline over emotion: avoid revenge trading, FOMO, or premature exits.
- Strategic thinking: view the market as a game of probability and liquidity, not as random chaos.

Summary

Retail traders often see the market as a series of disconnected events, while institutions view it as a structured system driven by liquidity, accumulation, and distribution. By understanding and adopting an **institutional bias**, traders can:

- Identify high-probability trade setups.
- Avoid common retail mistakes like chasing price or entering during stop hunts.
- Make strategic decisions aligned with Smart Money activity.
- Improve risk management and long-term profitability.

With a clear grasp of market structure, trends, BoS, CHoCH, swing liquidity, and institutional bias, you are now equipped to read charts like the banks. This foundation sets the stage for the next phase: applying Smart Money Concepts to entry and exit strategies with precision.

2.6 Internal Structure vs External Structure

One of the most important distinctions in market structure analysis is the difference between **External Structure** and **Internal Structure**. Institutional trading algorithms rely heavily on these two structural layers to engineer liquidity, manipulate short-term flows, and execute large-scale directional moves. Understanding how they interact is essential for accurate trend identification, bias formation, and timing precision within Smart Money Concepts (SMC) and ICT methodology.

External Structure (Macro Structure)

External structure refers to the large, dominant swing points that form on higher timeframes such as:

- Monthly (MN),
- Weekly (W1),
- Daily (D1),
- 4-Hour (H4).

It defines:

- the overall market direction,
- major swing highs and lows,

- macro liquidity targets,
- the institutional directional bias.

External structure can be thought of as the *macro map* of the marketplace. It reveals where liquidity resides and which direction institutional algorithms are likely positioned.

Examples include:

- a weekly Break of Structure (BOS),
- a daily Change of Character (CHoCH),
- large external swing highs targeted for liquidity,
- long-term premium and discount zones.

External structure provides the **true trend direction** and overarching context. Most retail traders lose because they allow internal structure noise to override the external trend.

Internal Structure (Micro Structure)

Internal structure is formed on lower timeframes such as:

- H1,
- M15,
- M5,
- M1.

It represents:

- short-term fluctuations inside the external swing,
- micro-level liquidity engineering,
- stop hunts and inducement patterns,
- algorithmic manipulation before major moves.

Internal structure is where:

- frequent CHoCH/BOS patterns occur,
- Fair Value Gaps (FVGs) are created and filled,
- liquidity sweeps take place,
- execution models such as OB–FVG entries are found.

Internal structure provides **entry precision**, not overall trend direction. It is the *micro blueprint* inside the larger macro map.

External Structure Determines Bias, Internal Structure Provides Entries

The interaction between the two structure types can be summarized as:

- **External Structure** sets the directional bias,
- **Internal Structure** refines entries within that bias.

For example:

$$\begin{aligned}\textbf{Bias:}\quad & \text{External Bullish Trend}\\ \textbf{Trigger:}\quad & \text{Internal Bullish CHoCH}\\ \Rightarrow\quad & \text{High-Probability Long Setup}\end{aligned}$$

$$\begin{aligned}\textbf{Bias:}\quad & \text{External Bearish Trend}\\ \textbf{Trigger:}\quad & \text{Internal Bearish CHoCH}\\ \Rightarrow\quad & \text{High-Probability Short Setup}\end{aligned}$$

Internal structure should never be traded *against* external structure. Doing so places you directly into institutional liquidity traps.

How Institutional Algorithms Use Structure Layers

Institutional algorithms use external and internal structure in different ways:

External Structure

- Identifies long-term liquidity targets,
- Determines macro trend direction,
- Guides large-scale accumulation or distribution,
- Sets the framework for future manipulation.

Internal Structure

- Engineers inducement (fake direction),
- Constructs liquidity pools,
- Creates micro-level inefficiencies (FVGs),
- Allows precision execution inside the macro swing.

External structure shows institutional **intent**. Internal structure shows institutional **execution**.

A Step-by-Step Method for Reading Structure

Step 1: Identify External Swings

Mark the major highs and lows on HTF charts (D1 or H4).

Step 2: Determine the External Bias

Assess whether the market is creating:

- Higher highs and higher lows (bullish),
- Lower highs and lower lows (bearish).

Step 3: Drop to Lower Timeframes

Move to M15, M5, or M1 to observe internal structure.

Step 4: Wait for Internal CHoCH in the Direction of External Bias

This acts as confirmation that institutional algorithms are ready to align LTF with HTF intent.

Step 5: Execute Using Internal OB/FVG Signals

Use internal structure to refine entries:

- OB taps,
- FVG rebalances,
- Liquidity sweeps,
- Mitigation blocks.

Common Mistakes Retail Traders Make

Retail traders often:

- mistake internal pullbacks for trend reversals,
- chase every internal CHoCH without HTF context,
- ignore macro liquidity levels,
- trade inside manipulation zones,
- misinterpret algorithmic inducement as real movement.

Internal structure is highly manipulative and should always be interpreted through the HTF lens.

Key Differences

Feature	External Structure	Internal Structure
Timeframe	HTF (D1, H4, H1)	LTF (M15, M5, M1)
Purpose	Determine trend and bias	Provide precise entries
Stability	High	Low
Manipulation Risk	Low	Very High
Frequency of BOS/CHoCH	Low	High
Used For	Directional outlook	Execution refinement

Summary

- External structure defines the macro trend and liquidity objectives.
- Internal structure refines entries and reveals micro-level manipulation.
- Trading internal structure against external structure is a high-risk mistake.
- The optimal trading sequence is:

$$\text{External Bias} \rightarrow \text{Internal Confirmation} \rightarrow \text{Precision Entry.}$$

Understanding this dual-structure framework is a foundational skill for reading markets the way institutional algorithms do.

2.7 Fractals and Range Identification

Financial markets move in a hierarchical and self-similar fashion, producing repeating patterns across all timeframes. These repeating structural patterns are known as **fractals**, and they form the foundation for correctly identifying market ranges. Understanding fractals and ranges is critical for reading institutional intent, avoiding false signals, and anticipating where liquidity will be engineered and later targeted.

What Are Fractals?

Fractals are recurring structural patterns that represent local swing highs and swing lows. They appear on every timeframe and construct both internal and external market structure.

A fractal swing forms when:

- a swing high has two lower highs on each side, or
- a swing low has two higher lows on each side.

Fractals allow traders to:

- identify structure objectively rather than subjectively,
- detect valid swing points for BOS/CHoCH analysis,
- mark liquidity zones above highs and below lows,
- observe the nested nature of market movement across timeframes.

Fractals are the building blocks of both internal and external structure. Higher-timeframe fractals form large external swings, while lower-timeframe fractals create internal micro-swings.

Why Fractals Matter in Smart Money Concepts

Institutional algorithms interact with price at multiple levels simultaneously. To execute large orders, they must create:

- liquidity above highs and below lows,
- engineered inducement moves,
- micro structural shifts inside macro trends.

Fractals reveal these structural layers clearly. Without fractals, swing identification becomes inconsistent and leads to misreading BOS, CHoCH, or liquidity targets.

What Is a Range?

A **range** is a consolidation zone formed between a clearly defined fractal swing high and fractal swing low. It represents a state of equilibrium where institutions accumulate or distribute orders before initiating expansion.

A typical range consists of:

- **Range High**: a fractal swing high,
- **Range Low**: a fractal swing low,
- **Internal Structure**: micro swings forming liquidity within the range,
- **Liquidity Pools**: built above the high and below the low.

Ranges appear on all timeframes. Higher-timeframe ranges define institutional accumulation/distribution, while lower-timeframe ranges provide refined execution opportunities.

How Ranges Form (Institutional Logic)

Ranges are not random sideways movements. They serve specific purposes for institutional algorithms:

- They allow accumulation or distribution of large positions.
- They conceal directional intent prior to expansion.
- They engineer liquidity above/ below both ends of the range.
- They create inducement patterns to trap retail traders.

Inside a range, algorithms:

- sweep highs and lows repeatedly,
- generate internal CHoCH patterns,
- leave Fair Value Gaps (FVGs),
- form Order Blocks (OBs),
- induce premature entries.

Once the required liquidity is gathered, the algorithm breaks out via displacement.

Relationship Between Fractals and Ranges

Fractals define the boundaries of a range:

- The **Range High** forms from a fractal swing high.
- The **Range Low** forms from a fractal swing low.

Price then oscillates inside this zone, forming internal structure until either side is swept.

Thus, the sequence is:

$$\text{Fractal High} \rightarrow \text{Fractal Low} \rightarrow \text{Range Formation.}$$

Ranges are simply fractal-defined consolidation boxes.

Types of Ranges

1. Accumulation Range

Occurs at discount pricing in a bullish external trend. Characterized by:

- sweeping internal lows,
- internal CHoCH structure,
- formation of bullish OBs,
- displacement upward after liquidity collection.

2. Distribution Range

Occurs at premium pricing in a bearish external trend. Characterized by:

- sweeping internal highs,
- bearish micro-structure shifts,
- creation of bearish OBs,
- downside displacement after liquidity is collected.

3. Reversal Range

Forms after a macro liquidity sweep. Acts as the transition structure between old and new external trends.

4. Continuation Range

A mid-trend consolidation used for:

- rebalancing,
- mitigation,
- continuation setups.

How to Identify a Range in Real Time

Step 1: Identify a Fractal Swing High

A clean structural high forms with two lower highs on each side.

Step 2: Identify a Fractal Swing Low

A structural low forms with two higher lows on each side.

Step 3: Observe Price Behavior Between the Two Points

If price oscillates between the two fractal boundaries, a range is forming.

Step 4: Mark Liquidity Above the High and Below the Low

These liquidity pools represent future targets.

Step 5: Study Internal Structure

Watch for:

- mini BOS/CHoCH shifts,
- inducement patterns,
- FVGs forming and filling,
- OB creation.

Step 6: Wait for Sweep + Displacement

A true breakout occurs only when the algorithm:

- sweeps range liquidity,
- shows displacement,
- leaves an FVG,
- returns to mitigate before continuation.

Common Trading Mistakes

Retail traders often:

- misidentify ranges on very low timeframes,
- trade inside the range rather than at its boundaries,
- misinterpret internal CHoCH as trend reversal,
- confuse inducement with breakout,
- enter trades before liquidity is swept.

Ranges are manipulation zones. Precision trading begins after the sweep and displacement, not inside the noise.

Summary of Key Concepts

- Fractals define objective swing highs and lows.
- These swings create the boundaries for ranges.
- Ranges are zones of accumulation, distribution, manipulation, and inducement.
- Institutional algorithms engineer liquidity inside ranges before expansion.

- High-probability trades occur after a liquidity sweep and displacement.

Understanding fractals and range identification allows traders to read the market in a structured, institutional way, avoiding traps and aligning with algorithmic intent.

Chapter 3

Timeframe Analysis

In trading, context is everything. A single candlestick on a 5-minute chart tells only a tiny part of the story, while a daily or weekly chart reveals the broader market narrative. Understanding **timeframes** and how they interact is crucial for interpreting market structure, identifying high-probability setups, and aligning trades with institutional flows.

This chapter focuses on **Timeframe Analysis**, the practice of examining multiple layers of the market simultaneously to gain a comprehensive view of price action. By analyzing higher timeframes, traders can determine the dominant trend and institutional intent, while lower timeframes provide precision for entries, exits, and risk management.

Timeframe analysis is the bridge between understanding market structure and executing trades with precision. By mastering this skill, traders can see the "big picture" like institutions while identifying the exact points where high-probability trades emerge. In the sections that follow, we will dissect each concept in detail, providing practical frameworks, examples, and techniques to implement in real-world trading.

3.1 Top-Down Analysis: High → Low Timeframes

Top-Down Analysis is one of the most powerful tools in a trader's toolkit. It allows you to understand the market from the perspective of Smart Money, starting with the broader context and drilling down to the precise points for high-probability entries. This approach reduces noise, improves alignment with institutional flow, and enhances risk management.

Definition and Purpose

Top-Down Analysis involves examining multiple timeframes in a hierarchical manner:

- **Higher Timeframes:** (Weekly, Daily, 4H) — Determine the overall market bias, dominant trend, key support/resistance levels, and institutional intent.
- **Intermediate Timeframes:** (1H, 30M) — Identify potential liquidity zones, swing highs/lows, and order blocks.
- **Lower Timeframes:** (15M, 5M, 1M) — Fine-tune entries, exits, stop-loss placements, and observe micro-structural cues like fair value gaps or minor liquidity clusters.

By starting with higher timeframes, you ensure that your trades are in alignment with the broader market direction and Smart Money bias, avoiding conflicts that lead to unnecessary losses.

Step-by-Step Methodology

1. **Identify the Dominant Trend on Higher Timeframes:** Examine weekly and daily charts to determine whether the market is in an uptrend, downtrend, or sideways consolidation. This sets the foundation for all lower timeframe analysis.
2. **Mark Key Levels:** Identify major swing highs/lows, order blocks, and liquidity pools. These levels are where institutions are likely to act.
3. **Drill Down to Intermediate Timeframes:** Observe how price reacts around higher timeframe levels. Look for retracements, fair value gaps, and minor liquidity clusters that provide potential entry zones.
4. **Analyze Lower Timeframes for Precision:** Use short-term charts to refine your entry points. Look for retests, confirmations, and micro-structural cues. Ensure your trade aligns with the higher timeframe trend.
5. **Confirm Multi-Timeframe Alignment:** Only consider trades where the direction and bias on all relevant timeframes are in agreement. This maximizes probability and reduces risk.

Institutional Perspective

Institutions rarely make trades based on a single timeframe. Their operations are always grounded in a multi-timeframe approach:

- They observe long-term trends to identify where accumulation or distribution is likely occurring.
- Medium-term trends help them locate optimal zones to build or reduce positions.

- Short-term trends allow them to execute trades efficiently, often triggering retail stops to gather liquidity.

By mimicking this multi-layered view, retail traders can anticipate market movements and trade with the probability advantage that institutions enjoy.

Common Pitfalls for Retail Traders

- Trading only on low timeframes without context, leading to chasing noise.
- Ignoring higher timeframe structure, which often results in taking trades against institutional flow.
- Entering on early signs of a move without confirmation from multiple timeframes, increasing the likelihood of stop-outs.

Practical Tips

- Always start with the weekly or daily chart before moving to intraday charts.
- Highlight major liquidity zones and swing points on all timeframes for reference.
- Use lower timeframes only to optimize entry, stop-loss, and take-profit levels.
- Confirm that each timeframe supports the trade direction — a misalignment is a warning signal.
- Keep a journal noting how multi-timeframe analysis influenced trade decisions and outcomes.

Summary

Top-Down Analysis provides a structured roadmap for interpreting market action like Smart Money. By starting from higher timeframes and drilling down to lower ones:

- Traders can align with institutional bias.
- High-probability entry and exit points can be identified.
- Noise and impulsive retail decisions are minimized.
- Risk management becomes more precise and deliberate.

Mastering this approach is essential before exploring specific trading styles such as swing trading or intraday trading, which we will cover in the next section.

3.2 Swing Trading vs Intraday Trading

Different trading styles require different approaches to timeframes, risk management, and market analysis. Two of the most common styles are **Swing Trading** and **Intraday Trading**. Understanding their differences and how Smart Money operates in each context is critical for aligning trades with institutional flow.

Swing Trading

Definition: Swing trading involves holding positions over multiple days or weeks, aiming to capture medium- to long-term market moves. Trades are based on higher timeframe structures and key liquidity zones.

Characteristics:

- Timeframe: Daily, 4H, Weekly charts for analysis; 1H or 30M charts for entries.
- Trade Duration: Several days to weeks.
- Risk/Reward: Higher potential reward per trade; stops placed beyond major swing points.
- Institutional Alignment: Swing traders follow higher timeframe trends and liquidity zones, closely mimicking institutional positioning.
- Frequency: Fewer trades but each with greater significance.

Advantages:

- Reduced screen time.
- Trades are based on well-defined market structure.
- Lower sensitivity to intraday noise.

Challenges:

- Requires patience to wait for setups.
- Exposure to overnight and weekend gaps.
- Larger capital required due to wider stops.

Intraday Trading

Definition: Intraday trading, or day trading, focuses on capturing short-term price movements within a single trading session. Traders open and close positions the same day, avoiding overnight exposure.

Characteristics:

- Timeframe: 5M, 15M, 30M charts for analysis; 1M-5M charts for execution.
- Trade Duration: Minutes to hours within the same session.
- Risk/Reward: Smaller per-trade profits; tight stops relative to intraday volatility.
- Institutional Alignment: Intraday traders must be aware of session liquidity, market openings, and institutional flow that drives short-term volatility.
- Frequency: Multiple trades per day; requires constant monitoring.

Advantages:

- No overnight risk.
- Faster feedback and learning opportunities.
- Can capitalize on intraday volatility spikes.

Challenges:

- Requires intense focus and quick decision-making.
- Higher transaction costs due to frequent trading.
- Vulnerable to market noise and false breakouts.

Key Differences: Swing vs Intraday

	Swing Trading	**Intraday Trading**
Timeframe Focus	Daily, 4H, Weekly	1M, 5M, 15M, 30M
Trade Duration	Days to Weeks	Minutes to Hours
Frequency	Low	High
Stop Loss	Wider, beyond key swings	Tighter, based on intraday volatility
Risk/Reward	High per trade	Lower per trade
Screen Time	Minimal	Intensive
Institutional Alignment	Higher timeframe bias and Session liquidity	short-term order flow

Institutional Perspective

- Swing trades align with medium- to high-timeframe institutional positioning, capturing accumulation and distribution zones over days or weeks.

- Intraday trades must account for session-specific liquidity, order flow, and intraday manipulation by institutions to hunt stops or create favorable entry/exit conditions.
- Understanding which timeframe institutions favor in a given session helps traders avoid being caught in false moves and increases the probability of success.

Choosing the Right Style

Selecting between swing and intraday trading depends on:

- Capital availability and risk tolerance.
- Time commitment and personal schedule.
- Preferred level of market involvement and emotional tolerance.
- Alignment with higher timeframe structure and liquidity zones.

Summary

Both swing trading and intraday trading have advantages and challenges, but the key to success lies in aligning with **institutional bias** and multi-timeframe market structure:

- Swing trading emphasizes patience and strategic alignment with higher timeframe trends.
- Intraday trading leverages short-term liquidity flows and session dynamics.
- Combining top-down analysis with chosen trading style enhances probability and reduces exposure to retail traps.

In the next section, we will examine **Session Bias: London, New York, Asia**, exploring how different trading sessions affect liquidity, volatility, and institutional behavior, which is critical for timing trades accurately.

3.3 Session Bias: London, New York, Asia

The global forex and equity markets operate 24 hours a day, divided into three major sessions: **Asian, London, and New York**. Each session has distinct characteristics in terms of liquidity, volatility, and institutional activity. Understanding session bias is essential for timing trades, managing risk, and aligning with Smart Money behavior.

Asian Session (Tokyo/Sydney)

Characteristics:

- Timeframe: Typically 23:00–08:00 GMT.
- Market Participants: Primarily Asian banks, institutions, and regional traders.
- Liquidity: Relatively low compared to London and New York sessions.
- Volatility: Lower; price often moves in ranges with smaller swings.

Trading Implications:

- Best for range-bound strategies or monitoring accumulation zones.
- Breakouts often lack follow-through until London session begins.
- Institutions may quietly accumulate or distribute positions in preparation for the London session.

London Session

Characteristics:

- Timeframe: 07:00–16:00 GMT.
- Market Participants: Major European banks, hedge funds, and institutional traders.
- Liquidity: High; major market participants enter trades.
- Volatility: Medium to high; significant swings often occur, especially at session open.

Trading Implications:

- Key session for initiating trends, stop hunts, and liquidity grabs.
- Aligning trades with dominant London session flows increases probability of success.
- Watch for overlap with Asian close and New York open for enhanced liquidity and volatility.

New York Session

Characteristics:

- Timeframe: 12:00–21:00 GMT.
- Market Participants: US banks, hedge funds, corporate traders, and retail participants.
- Liquidity: High; overlaps with London session produce peak trading volume.
- Volatility: High, especially during economic news releases or major announcements.

Trading Implications:

- Ideal for executing trades around high-probability setups identified on London session.
- Provides follow-through or exhaustion signals for trends initiated earlier.
- Watch for liquidity hunting at key swing highs/lows and institutional order blocks.

Session Overlaps

- **London/Asian Overlap:** Moderate volatility; useful for testing swing points and minor liquidity zones.
- **London/New York Overlap:** Maximum liquidity and volatility; ideal for high-probability setups and Smart Money manipulations.
- **New York/Asian Overlap:** Low liquidity; price often consolidates, preparing for the next London session.

Institutional Perspective on Sessions

- Institutions exploit session overlaps for efficient order execution and liquidity accumulation/distribution.
- Stop hunts are often timed with session openings and key liquidity clusters.
- Understanding which session dominates allows traders to anticipate likely price behavior and avoid trading in low-probability conditions.

Practical Trading Tips

- Align trades with the session that matches your strategy and timeframe.
- Avoid initiating trades in low-liquidity sessions unless following specific setups.
- Use session-specific volatility ranges for stop-loss placement and position sizing.
- Observe institutional behavior during overlaps for clues on upcoming trend continuation or reversals.

Summary

Each trading session exhibits unique behavior, liquidity patterns, and institutional activity:

- **Asian Session:** Quiet accumulation and low volatility.
- **London Session:** High liquidity, trend initiation, stop hunts.
- **New York Session:** High volatility, trend continuation, and liquidity exploitation.

Recognizing session bias and timing trades accordingly allows retail traders to avoid unnecessary risks, anticipate institutional activity, and align entries and exits with high-probability market movements.
In the next section, we will explore **Multi-Timeframe Alignment and Context**, combining all the concepts of trend, structure, swing points, and session bias into a cohesive framework for precise, Smart Money-aligned trading.

3.4 Multi-Timeframe Alignment and Context

Multi-Timeframe Alignment is the art and science of analyzing multiple layers of the market simultaneously to make high-probability trading decisions. By combining insights from higher, intermediate, and lower timeframes, along with session bias and liquidity analysis, traders can align their trades with institutional activity and reduce the likelihood of entering low-probability setups.

The Concept of Multi-Timeframe Alignment

At its core, multi-timeframe alignment ensures that the market bias, trend direction, and key liquidity zones across all relevant timeframes support a single trading decision. Misalignment between timeframes often results in conflicting signals, which is a common cause of retail trading losses.

- **Higher Timeframes:** Weekly and daily charts establish the dominant trend, institutional bias, and major support/resistance levels.
- **Intermediate Timeframes:** 4H, 1H charts reveal liquidity clusters, order blocks, swing highs/lows, and fair value gaps for potential entries.
- **Lower Timeframes:** 30M, 15M, 5M charts allow precise entries, exits, stop-loss placement, and observation of micro-structural behavior.

Step-by-Step Alignment Process

1. **Assess Dominant Trend:** Begin with the weekly and daily charts. Identify whether the market is trending up, down, or consolidating. Mark major swing highs and lows, key liquidity zones, and institutional order blocks.
2. **Identify Intermediate Patterns:** Move to 4H and 1H charts to observe intermediate swings, break of structure (BoS), and change of character (CHoCH). Check if these patterns support the higher timeframe trend.
3. **Locate Precision Entry Zones:** On lower timeframes (15M–5M), refine entry points by examining retests of order blocks, fair value gaps, and swing liquidity clusters. Confirm alignment with higher timeframe trends and session bias.
4. **Incorporate Session Bias:** Determine which trading session is active and how institutional participants are likely to behave. Align trade timing with the session that offers optimal liquidity and volatility for your setup.
5. **Confirm Multi-Timeframe Confluence:** Only execute trades where all relevant timeframes and session context agree. This increases probability and reduces risk of false breakouts or stop hunts.

Institutional Perspective

Institutions operate with a multi-timeframe mindset:

- They accumulate or distribute positions gradually over days and weeks, respecting higher timeframe structure.
- Intermediate timeframes help them target liquidity pools efficiently.
- Short-term fluctuations are used to trigger retail stop-losses and execute orders with minimal market impact.

By adopting this approach, retail traders can anticipate institutional moves and position themselves advantageously.

Practical Trading Framework

1. Start with a **weekly chart** to determine overall market bias and institutional zones.
2. Analyze the **daily chart** for swing highs/lows, order blocks, and liquidity clusters that may influence the next moves.
3. Drill down to **4H and 1H charts** for intermediate liquidity, structure shifts, and retracement opportunities.
4. Use **15M–5M charts** to fine-tune entries, exits, stop-losses, and confirm confluence.
5. Check the **active session** (London, New York, or Asia) for volatility, liquidity, and institutional participation.
6. Enter trades only when **alignment exists across all relevant timeframes and session context**.

Common Pitfalls to Avoid

- Ignoring higher timeframe trends and trading solely on low-timeframe noise.
- Entering trades when intermediate and lower timeframes contradict the higher timeframe bias.
- Disregarding session dynamics, leading to ill-timed entries and exits.
- Overcomplicating analysis without clear hierarchy or structure.

Psychological Benefits

Multi-timeframe alignment not only improves trade probability but also enhances trader discipline and confidence:

- Reduces impulsive entries based on emotional reactions.
- Provides a structured, repeatable framework for analyzing markets.
- Builds patience by waiting for confluence across timeframes and sessions.

Summary

Multi-Timeframe Alignment is the culmination of all previous Market Structure and Timeframe Analysis concepts:

- Higher timeframe trends guide overall bias.

- Swing highs/lows, order blocks, BoS, CHoCH, and liquidity zones provide tactical trade opportunities.
- Session bias ensures optimal timing relative to institutional participation.
- Confluence across all levels maximizes probability and aligns trades with Smart Money flow.

By mastering multi-timeframe alignment and integrating it with market structure, liquidity analysis, and session bias, traders can approach the market with a probabilistic mindset, minimizing risk and trading with institutional efficiency.

3.5 Killzones Overview

In Smart Money Concepts (SMC) and ICT methodology, time plays a critical role in market behavior. Institutional algorithms do not operate uniformly throughout the trading day. Instead, they activate most aggressively during specific high-liquidity windows known as **Killzones**. These windows correspond to session opens, overlaps, and key institutional execution periods.

Killzones are the times when:

- liquidity is highest,
- volatility increases significantly,
- institutional algorithms initiate accumulation or distribution,
- stop hunts and liquidity sweeps occur,
- high-probability setups emerge.

Understanding Killzones enables traders to anticipate when the market is likely to produce meaningful moves.

Why Killzones Exist

Killzones exist due to the interaction of global banking sessions, economic data releases, and scheduled algorithmic execution cycles. Institutions require liquidity to execute large orders efficiently, and liquidity is highest when major markets overlap.

Institutional algorithms activate during Killzones to:

- rebalance portfolios,
- accumulate or distribute positions,
- sweep liquidity pools,

- engineer directional moves following inducement,
- react to or prepare for economic news releases.

Thus, Killzones represent the periods when Smart Money reveals intent through displacement and structural shifts.

Major ICT Killzones

ICT identifies several key Killzones throughout the trading day. Each has distinct behavior and plays a specific role in the daily liquidity cycle.

1. Asian Killzone (00:00–03:00 New York Time)

The Asian session typically provides:

- slow, controlled price action,
- tight consolidation ranges,
- low volatility,
- the initial liquidity pool for the day.

Price often forms the day's first significant range during this period. The highs and lows of the Asian session frequently become liquidity targets for London.

2. London Killzone (02:00–05:00 New York Time)

This is one of the most important Killzones. Characteristics include:

- sharp increases in volatility,
- sweeping of Asian highs or lows,
- formation of major intraday BOS/CHoCH,
- initiation of the day's primary directional move.

London often sets the **directional bias** for the session or even the entire trading day.

3. London Close Killzone (09:00–11:00 New York Time)

During London Close:

- positions from the London session are unwound,
- algorithms hedge exposure ahead of New York continuation,
- retracements or reversals are common.

It often produces sharp wicks or temporary corrections.

4. New York Killzone (07:00–10:00 New York Time)

New York Killzone is the most volatile and decisive session of the trading day. It coincides with the overlap of London and New York markets and includes many economic data releases.

Key behaviors:

- aggressive liquidity sweeps above/below London highs/lows,
- major displacement moves,
- formation of the day's high or low,
- entries into OB/FVG structures after sweeps.

This Killzone provides the highest-probability setups for intraday traders.

5. New York Lunch Killzone (11:30–13:00 New York Time)

Characterized by:

- reduced volatility,
- slower price action,
- engineered traps and false moves,
- narrow intraday ranges.

This period is generally avoided unless trading range-bound setups.

Daily Liquidity Cycle and Killzones

Killzones fit into a predictable intraday liquidity cycle:

1. The Asian session creates a range containing early liquidity.
2. London sweeps the Asian liquidity and initiates directional moves.
3. New York sweeps London highs/lows and confirms (or reverses) direction.
4. London Close or New York Lunch consolidates the move.

This pattern appears consistently across currency pairs, indices, and even commodities, because institutional behavior is time-driven, not market-driven.

Killzones in Practical Trading

Killzones refine the trader's understanding of:

- **Bias:** London sets the tone; New York confirms or reverses it.
- **Entries:** Optimal setups often occur after a liquidity sweep + CHoCH during a Killzone.
- **Targets:** Session highs and lows become predictable liquidity magnets.

For example, a common pattern is:

- Asian range forms,
- London sweeps Asian high,
- New York sweeps London high,
- New York displacement forms the true move of the day.

Killzones therefore help traders identify when structural shifts are meaningful and when price action is merely noise.

Common Mistakes Regarding Killzones

Retail traders often:

- trade heavily outside Killzones where liquidity is thin,
- misinterpret pre-Killzone inducement as real direction,
- enter positions before liquidity sweeps,
- ignore the session-based nature of institutional algorithms,
- expect volatility at times when institutions are inactive.

Recognizing when *not* to trade is just as important as knowing when to trade.

Summary

- Killzones are high-liquidity periods driven by institutional algorithmic activity.
- Asian range sets initial liquidity; London defines bias; New York confirms the day's direction.
- Liquidity sweeps and displacement moves are most likely to occur during Killzones.
- High-probability trades align with Killzone timing rather than random hours of the day.

Killzones bring structure to intraday trading by revealing **when** the market is likely to create opportunities aligned with institutional intent.

Part II

Core Smart Money Tools

Chapter 4

Order Blocks

Order Blocks are one of the most powerful tools in the Smart Money Concepts (SMC) and ICT methodology. They represent areas where institutions have placed large buy or sell orders, leaving footprints of accumulation or distribution in the market. Understanding order blocks allows traders to identify high-probability zones where price is likely to react, retrace, or reverse, effectively giving insight into institutional intentions.

Order blocks serve as a bridge between understanding market structure and executing precise trades. Institutions rarely move the market randomly; they act in specific zones that provide liquidity and minimize slippage. By learning to identify and trade these zones, retail traders can align their strategies with institutional behavior, increasing the likelihood of capturing significant moves with controlled risk.

In the sections that follow, we will break down each concept of order blocks, provide practical examples, and demonstrate how to integrate them into a complete Smart Money trading strategy. Mastery of order blocks not only enhances technical skill but also builds the probabilistic mindset required to think like the banks.

4.1 Definition & Types: Bullish/Bearish

Definition of Order Blocks

An **Order Block (OB)** is a price zone where large financial institutions (banks, hedge funds, and smart money participants) accumulate or distribute positions, causing observable imbalances in the market. These zones represent the footprints of institutional buying or selling and often act as future support or resistance levels.

Unlike typical retail support/resistance, order blocks are formed not merely by price extremities but by areas of concentrated order flow, where liquidity is available for institutions to execute their trades efficiently with minimal market impact.

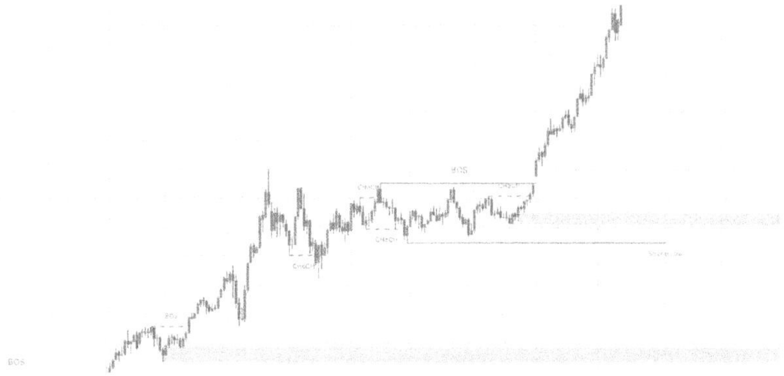

Figure 4.1: Bullish Order Block (OB): The last down-close candle before a strong upward expansion. This area represents institutional demand.

Bullish Order Blocks

A **Bullish Order Block** forms when institutions accumulate buy orders after a price retracement within a downtrend or at the early stages of an uptrend. Characteristics include:

- Typically appears at the last bearish candle before a strong bullish move.
- Represents an area where buyers overwhelmed sellers, causing a significant upward move.
- Serves as a potential support zone on future price retests.
- Often coincides with liquidity clusters such as previous swing lows.

Example: Imagine a market in a downtrend that briefly retraces upward. A strong bearish candle forms, followed by a sudden bullish rally. The bearish candle's range becomes a **bullish order block**, as it marks the zone where institutional buying absorbed selling pressure.

Bearish Order Blocks

A **Bearish Order Block** forms when institutions distribute sell orders after a price retracement within an uptrend or at the early stages of a downtrend. Characteristics include:

- Appears at the last bullish candle before a strong bearish move.

- Indicates that sellers overcame buyers, initiating a significant downward move.
- Acts as a potential resistance zone on future price retests.
- Often aligns with liquidity clusters such as previous swing highs.

Example: During an uptrend, a strong bullish candle is followed by a sudden drop. The bullish candle's range becomes a **bearish order block**, highlighting the area where institutions initiated selling.

Key Characteristics of Genuine Order Blocks

To differentiate real order blocks from minor price fluctuations:

- They usually precede strong impulsive moves (indicative of institutional participation).
- Often coincide with liquidity zones where retail stops accumulate.
- They retain significance even after multiple retests.
- True order blocks respect market structure; they do not form in random sideways noise.

Bullish vs Bearish Summary

Feature	Bullish OB	Bearish OB
Formation	Last bearish candle before upward impulse	Last bullish candle before downward impulse
Market Bias	Acts as support	Acts as resistance
Institutional Action	Accumulation (buying)	Distribution (selling)
Typical Location	Swing lows or retracements in downtrend	Swing highs or retracements in uptrend
Future Use	Entry for long trades	Entry for short trades

Institutional Perspective

Institutions operate in order blocks because:

- They provide high liquidity without causing excessive slippage.
- Concentrating orders in these zones allows accumulation or distribution while minimizing market disruption.
- Order blocks often align with key swing highs/lows, making them reliable for future reference.

Practical Tip for Traders

- Identify the last candle before a strong impulsive move to locate potential order blocks.
- Observe whether price revisits this zone; a retest often offers high-probability entry points.
- Combine order blocks with other SMC concepts like fair value gaps, liquidity pools, and market structure for confirmation.

By mastering bullish and bearish order blocks, traders can align with institutional positioning, anticipate high-probability zones, and execute trades with greater precision and confidence.

4.2 Identification Criteria & Examples

Correctly identifying genuine order blocks is critical to trading like Smart Money. Not all price zones preceding impulses qualify as order blocks. This section provides clear criteria, practical steps, and examples for spotting high-probability bullish and bearish order blocks.

Key Identification Criteria

1. **Impulsive Move Confirmation:** Identify a strong bullish or bearish impulse following a retracement. The candle or zone immediately preceding this impulse is the potential order block.
2. **Last Opposite Candle:** For a bullish order block, locate the last bearish candle before the upward impulse. For a bearish order block, locate the last bullish candle before the downward impulse.
3. **Market Structure Alignment:** Ensure that the order block aligns with higher timeframe structure. For example, bullish OBs should appear near swing lows in a trending up market, bearish OBs near swing highs in a downtrend.
4. **Liquidity Consideration:** Check if the zone is near clusters of retail stops (above swing highs for shorts, below swing lows for longs). True institutional OBs often coincide with liquidity zones.
5. **Retest Validation:** A valid order block often causes price to react on retest, either reversing or showing a strong reaction. Repeated retests strengthen the OB's significance.
6. **Size and Structure:** Genuine order blocks have defined ranges, not scattered candles. Avoid zones formed by small wicks or insignificant price action.

7. **Timeframe Confirmation:** Validate the order block across multiple timeframes. A higher timeframe OB carries more weight than a lower timeframe OB for strategic entries.

Step-by-Step Identification

1. Start with the higher timeframe (e.g., Daily or 4H) to determine the market bias and key swing points.
2. Locate impulsive candles with preceding retracements.
3. Identify the last opposite candle before the impulse; mark its high and low as the order block boundaries.
4. Check if the zone coincides with previous liquidity pools or swing highs/lows.
5. Zoom into lower timeframes to observe micro-retests for precision entry points.
6. Confirm that the OB aligns with overall market structure and session bias.

Illustrative Examples

Bullish Order Block Example:

- Price is in a downtrend.
- A strong bearish candle forms (potential OB zone).
- Immediately after, a large bullish candle appears, signaling institutional buying.
- The last bearish candle's high and low mark the bullish OB. Future retests of this zone are high-probability long entries.

Bearish Order Block Example:

- Price is in an uptrend.
- A strong bullish candle forms.
- Followed by a rapid bearish impulse, signaling institutional selling.
- The last bullish candle's high and low define the bearish OB. Retests of this zone offer shorting opportunities.

Common Mistakes in Identification

- Mistaking minor price wicks for OBs.
- Ignoring higher timeframe alignment and trading against the institutional bias.
- Failing to consider liquidity zones or swing points.
- Relying on a single timeframe without multi-timeframe confirmation.

Practical Tips

- Always mark order block ranges on your charts with horizontal zones for clarity.
- Combine OBs with other SMC tools such as fair value gaps and liquidity pools for confluence.
- Observe how price reacts on retests; consistent reaction strengthens the validity of the OB.
- Keep a trading journal noting OB identification, retest behavior, and trade outcomes.

By systematically applying these criteria, traders can reliably identify institutional footprints, anticipate market reactions, and improve the probability of executing successful trades.
The next section will cover **Trading Strategies: Retests, Breaker Blocks, Confluence**, showing how to translate these identified order blocks into actionable, high-probability trading setups.

4.3 Trading Strategies: Retests, Breaker Blocks, Confluence

Once genuine order blocks are identified, the next step is learning how to trade them effectively. Smart Money traders focus on high-probability strategies that exploit institutional footprints and liquidity. This section explores three essential trading techniques: retests, breaker blocks, and confluence.

Retests of Order Blocks

Concept: After price leaves an order block impulsively, it often revisits the zone to retest institutional interest. These retests provide high-probability entry points for traders aligning with Smart Money.

Key Guidelines:

- Wait for price to return to the OB range without breaking the market structure.
- Observe for candlestick patterns or micro-structure confirming institutional reaction.
- Confirm alignment with higher timeframe trends and session bias.

Example: Price creates a bullish OB at a swing low. After the impulsive bullish move, price retraces to the OB. A bullish engulfing pattern on a 15M chart indicates a strong long entry with tight stop-loss below the OB.

Breaker Blocks

Definition: A **Breaker Block** is a previous order block that has been violated and now acts as a potential entry in the opposite direction. Breaker blocks often form when price breaks a key structure and later retests it.

Key Points:

- Breaker blocks are typically formed after a change of character (CHoCH).
- They provide high-probability zones for counter-trend or continuation trades.
- Confirm with liquidity pools, fair value gaps, or session bias for optimal entries.

Example: Price breaks a bullish OB in an uptrend (change of character occurs). Later, price retraces to the broken OB, which now acts as support for a continuation trade.

Confluence Trading

Concept: Confluence occurs when multiple SMC elements converge in the same zone, increasing trade probability. Combining order blocks with other structures—such as fair value gaps, liquidity pools, swing highs/lows, and session bias—creates powerful setups.

Key Steps:

1. Identify an order block at a key swing high or low.
2. Look for overlapping fair value gaps or liquidity clusters.
3. Check alignment with market structure (trend, BoS, CHoCH).
4. Confirm session bias to ensure institutional participation.
5. Enter the trade when all conditions align, using appropriate stop-loss and risk management.

Example: A bullish OB aligns with a liquidity pool just above a swing low. The 1H chart shows a break of structure in favor of buyers, and the London session is active, providing strong institutional participation. This multi-layered confluence increases the probability of a successful long trade.

Practical Tips

- Never enter solely based on an order block; always seek confluence.
- Observe how price reacts to the OB on retests; hesitation may indicate weakening institutional interest.
- Combine with multi-timeframe alignment for precision entries and optimal trade management.
- Record each setup in a trade journal noting OB location, retest behavior, and session context.

Institutional Perspective

Institutions often leave footprints in these setups:

- Retests allow them to absorb liquidity without pushing price against their position.
- Breaker blocks exploit stop-hunting zones to trigger retail orders.
- Confluence setups show areas where multiple institutional strategies overlap, providing maximum probability and liquidity.

By mastering retests, breaker blocks, and confluence, traders can execute trades with higher confidence, aligning closely with Smart Money behavior, and significantly improving their edge in the markets.
The next section, **ICT Advanced Techniques: Optimal Trade Entry (OTE) with Fibonacci**, will build upon this knowledge to refine entry precision within order blocks for maximum efficiency.

4.4 ICT Advanced Techniques: Optimal Trade Entry (OTE) with Fibonacci

The **Optimal Trade Entry (OTE)** is an advanced technique popularized by Inner Circle Trader (ICT) methodology. OTE combines order block analysis, market structure, and Fibonacci retracement levels to pinpoint high-probability entry zones. This technique refines trade timing within institutional footprints, increasing reward-to-risk efficiency.

Definition of OTE

Optimal Trade Entry refers to entering a trade within a specific retracement range of an impulsive move, usually after the market has absorbed liquidity. The goal is to capture the next major move while minimizing exposure and maximizing alignment with institutional activity.

- Typically, the OTE zone lies between **61.8% and 79% Fibonacci retracement** of the previous impulse.
- This range often coincides with order blocks, fair value gaps, and liquidity clusters.
- OTE is most effective when combined with trend alignment, swing highs/lows, and session bias.

Steps to Calculate OTE

1. Identify the impulsive move: Determine the swing low and swing high (for bullish impulse) or swing high and swing low (for bearish impulse).
2. Apply Fibonacci retracement tool from start to end of the impulse.
3. Highlight the **61.8%–79% retracement zone**. This is the OTE zone.
4. Confirm alignment with a previously identified order block or liquidity cluster.
5. Look for price reaction patterns (candlestick structure, micro support-/resistance) within this zone for optimal entry.

Bullish OTE Example

- Market forms a swing low at 1.2000 and swings to 1.2200.
- Apply Fibonacci from 1.2000 to 1.2200.
- The OTE zone is approximately 1.2124–1.2182 (61.8%–79% retracement).
- A bullish order block exists at 1.2130–1.2150.
- Price enters the OTE zone, shows bullish reaction, and aligns with session bias.
- High-probability long entry can be taken with stop-loss just below the order block.

Bearish OTE Example

- Market forms a swing high at 1.3000 and falls to 1.2800.
- Apply Fibonacci from 1.3000 to 1.2800.
- The OTE zone is approximately 1.2864–1.2916.
- A bearish order block exists at 1.2880–1.2900.
- Price retraces into this zone and shows bearish reaction.
- High-probability short entry can be taken with stop-loss just above the OB.

Key Considerations for Traders

- **Market Structure Confirmation:** Only trade OTE setups that align with the higher timeframe trend and market bias.
- **Session Bias:** OTE entries are more reliable during sessions with active institutional participation (London or New York overlaps).
- **Confluence is Critical:** Combine OTE with order blocks, fair value gaps, liquidity zones, and swing points to maximize probability.
- **Stop Placement:** Place stops just beyond the opposite side of the OB or OTE zone to reduce false triggers.
- **Position Sizing:** Use proper risk management; OTE is high-probability but not foolproof.

Institutional Perspective

Institutions use OTE-like strategies implicitly:

- They often absorb liquidity in retracement zones before driving the next major move.
- OTE zones coincide with areas of low slippage and concentrated order flow.
- By waiting for price to enter OTE zones, traders mimic institutional precision and reduce exposure to erratic moves.

Practical Application

- Mark impulsive moves and calculate OTE on your chart before trading.
- Observe how price interacts with the zone; look for reversal candlestick patterns, confluence with OBs, and session context.
- Enter trades with disciplined stop-loss and take-profit planning.
- Record outcomes to refine OTE identification skills and improve probabilistic decision-making.

By mastering OTE in conjunction with order blocks, traders gain a precise entry framework that respects institutional footprints, aligns with Smart Money flow, and maximizes risk-to-reward efficiency in the markets.

4.5 Refinement of Order Blocks (Premium and Discount OB)

Order Blocks (OBs) form the foundation of Smart Money Concepts (SMC) execution models. However, not all OBs are equal in quality. Institutional algorithms refine OBs based on **premium and discount pricing models**, which determine where high-probability entries occur within the overall structure.

This section explains how to refine OBs for maximum precision, avoid weak zones, and align with institutional intent.

Understanding Premium and Discount Pricing

The concept of premium and discount is derived from the idea that institutional traders prefer to:

- buy at a **discount (below equilibrium)**, and
- sell at a **premium (above equilibrium)**.

Equilibrium is typically defined by the **50% midpoint** of a major swing range. Thus:

$$\text{Price } < 50\% \Rightarrow \text{Discount Zone (favorable for longs)}$$

$$\text{Price } > 50\% \Rightarrow \text{Premium Zone (favorable for shorts)}$$

Premium and discount pricing allow traders to filter OBs and focus only on those that align with institutional macro-bias.

Why OB Refinement Is Necessary

Raw OBs often cover large zones. Refinement helps:

- narrow the OB to the most efficient entry level,
- eliminate invalid or weak OBs,
- reduce stop-loss size,
- identify high-probability continuation or reversal points,
- align internal structure entries with the external discount/premium context.

Refining OBs ensures that entries occur only where institutions are likely to execute orders.

Types of OB Refinement

There are three primary OB refinement techniques:

1. Candle Body vs Wick Refinement

Some OBs require using:

- the entire candle (wick to wick),
- only the candle body,
- the wick of the candle as the most efficient entry.

Wick refinement is often used when a wick clearly sweeps liquidity before displacement.

2. Imbalance-Based Refinement (OB + FVG)

When an OB overlaps with a Fair Value Gap (FVG), the refined OB is:

$$\text{OB refined to the boundaries of the FVG}$$

This creates high-probability zones because institutions often use imbalance to mitigate their previous positions.

3. Premium/Discount Refinement

The most powerful refinement technique. It uses the Fibonacci 50% equilibrium of an external swing:

- Bullish OBs refined only within the **discount zone**.
- Bearish OBs refined only within the **premium zone**.

OBs outside the appropriate pricing zone are ignored.

Premium/Discount OB Logic

For a bullish trend:

- Identify the major swing range.
- Mark the 50% midpoint.
- Only consider OBs below the midpoint (discount area).

For a bearish trend:

- Identify the major swing range.
- Mark the midpoint.
- Only consider OBs above the midpoint (premium area).

This ensures that trades occur where institutions accumulate or distribute positions efficiently.

How to Refine OBs Step-by-Step

Step 1: Identify the External Swing Range

Use HTF data (H1, H4, D1) to mark:

- the swing high,
- the swing low,
- equilibrium (50% line).

Step 2: Determine Premium or Discount Zone

- Above 50%: Premium zone (favorable for shorts).
- Below 50%: Discount zone (favorable for longs).

Step 3: Identify OBs within the Correct Zone

Ignore all OBs located on the wrong side of equilibrium.

Step 4: Use Internal Structure for Precision Refinement

Drop to lower timeframes (M15, M5, M1) to:

- refine the OB to a smaller candle,
- find mitigation wicks,
- locate embedded FVGs,
- identify inducement before the OB tap.

Step 5: Wait for Displacement + Return to Refined OB

The refined OB is not valid until displacement confirms institutional intent.

Common Mistakes in OB Refinement

Retail traders often:

- use all OBs without filtering for premium/discount,
- select OBs on very low timeframes without HTF alignment,
- fail to wait for displacement before entry,
- trade OBs formed inside manipulation rather than structure,
- refine OBs too aggressively, missing the true institutional level.

Proper refinement reduces false signals and aligns trading with algorithmic behavior.

Summary

- Order Block refinement is essential for precise institutional-style entries.
- Premium and discount zones filter OBs according to market context.
- Only bullish OBs in discount zones and bearish OBs in premium zones should be considered.
- Refinement reduces stop-loss size and increases setup quality.
- The highest-probability setups occur when refined OBs align with displacement and internal confirmation.

Refining OBs using premium and discount logic transforms basic SMC understanding into a professional-level execution model.

Chapter 5

Supply & Demand Zones

Supply and demand zones are foundational concepts in understanding how price reacts to institutional activity. While order blocks highlight specific areas of accumulation or distribution, supply and demand zones provide a broader perspective on market imbalances. These zones represent areas where buying or selling pressure overwhelms the opposite side, often resulting in strong impulsive moves.

5.1 Definition and Drawing Techniques

Understanding Supply and Demand Zones

Supply and demand zones are not merely horizontal lines or abstract support and resistance; they are precise areas on the chart where imbalances between buyers and sellers create strong, impulsive price movements.

- A **Demand Zone** forms when buyers overwhelm sellers, leading to a sharp upward move. This area represents institutional accumulation or strong buying pressure.
- A **Supply Zone** forms when sellers dominate buyers, causing a rapid downward move. This area reflects institutional distribution or heavy selling pressure.

Unlike retail support and resistance levels, which are often psychological or arbitrary, supply and demand zones are rooted in **actual market behavior**—the footprints of smart money. By understanding these zones, traders can anticipate where price is likely to react, reverse, or accelerate.

Key Characteristics of Genuine Zones

1. **Impulsive Reaction:** The zone is defined by a strong, impulsive move away from the consolidation or base. Weak moves are often false zones.

2. **Base Formation:** Zones typically originate from a consolidation or tight range before the impulse. This shows where liquidity was gathered.
3. **Market Structure Alignment:** Demand zones align with swing lows or higher timeframe structure; supply zones align with swing highs.
4. **Volume Confirmation:** Strong volume or activity often accompanies the creation of these zones, indicating institutional participation.
5. **Longevity:** True zones retain significance even after multiple retests or price cycles.

Step-by-Step Drawing Techniques

Accurate drawing of supply and demand zones is critical for their effectiveness. Follow these steps:

1. **Identify the Impulse Move:** Locate a strong price move on the chart, either bullish or bearish, preceded by a base or consolidation.
2. **Determine the Base Range:**
    - For a **Demand Zone**, find the lowest wick of the consolidation before the bullish impulse. This defines the bottom of the zone.
    - For a **Supply Zone**, locate the highest wick of the consolidation before the bearish impulse. This defines the top of the zone.
3. **Draw the Horizontal Zone:** Extend the zone slightly to cover the entire area of buyer/seller activity, including minor price wicks that may have absorbed liquidity. Avoid overly narrow zones, as price often tests the edges.
4. **Validate on Higher Timeframes:** Zoom out to check if the zone aligns with larger swing highs/lows or key market structure points. Higher timeframe zones carry more significance.
5. **Observe Price Interaction:** On lower timeframes, monitor how price reacts when it returns to the zone. Look for rejection patterns, engulfing candles, or consolidation that indicates absorption of liquidity.

Institutional Perspective

Institutions rely on supply and demand zones to execute large orders without causing excessive slippage:

- They accumulate or distribute within these zones, allowing the market to absorb liquidity from retail participants.

- These zones often coincide with stop-loss clusters, providing the necessary liquidity for large trades.
- By mapping these zones, traders can anticipate institutional behavior and avoid trading against smart money.

Practical Tips for Traders

- Focus on zones that preceded strong impulsive moves; weak zones often fail on retests.
- Use multiple timeframes: draw zones on higher timeframes for context and refine entries on lower timeframes.
- Track reactions on retests: repeated reactions strengthen the zone's validity.
- Combine supply and demand zones with other SMC tools, such as order blocks, fair value gaps, and liquidity pools, for high-probability setups.
- Keep a visual record of active zones to monitor price interaction and institutional footprints.

Mastering the definition and drawing of supply and demand zones provides traders with a strategic map of where the market is likely to react. This understanding forms the foundation for high-probability setups, enabling traders to align with institutional activity and improve trade accuracy significantly.

5.2 Supply & Demand vs ICT Interpretation

Supply and demand zones and ICT order blocks are both key elements of Smart Money Concepts (SMC), but they serve different purposes and offer distinct perspectives on market behavior. Understanding their similarities, differences, and how to integrate them is critical for executing high-probability trades and aligning with institutional activity.

Traditional Supply and Demand Zones

Classical supply and demand zones are derived from the concept of market imbalances:

- A **demand zone** represents an area where buyers have historically dominated, causing a strong upward price move.
- A **supply zone** represents an area where sellers have historically dominated, causing a strong downward move.

These zones focus primarily on price reactions, highlighting areas where market participants either aggressively bought or sold. The methodology is often visual, relying on strong impulse moves and consolidation bases to draw zones.

Key Characteristics of Traditional Zones:

1. Zones are usually broader, covering an area where price previously reacted strongly.
2. They can be identified on any timeframe but carry more weight when validated on higher timeframes.
3. Focus is on observable market behavior rather than institutional order flow.

ICT Order Blocks and Interpretation

ICT (Inner Circle Trader) methodology refines supply and demand concepts by focusing on **institutional footprints**:

- An order block is a precise candle or zone where institutions have accumulated or distributed large orders.
- ICT order blocks are smaller and more precise than classical supply and demand zones, highlighting exact areas of institutional participation.
- The methodology considers market structure, liquidity, and fair value gaps, integrating multiple layers of SMC to create actionable zones.

Key Characteristics of ICT Order Blocks:

1. Derived from the last opposite candle before a strong impulse (bullish or bearish).
2. Emphasizes alignment with liquidity pools, stop hunts, and institutional market moves.
3. Often used with Optimal Trade Entry (OTE) and Fibonacci retracements for precision entries.
4. Smaller and more focused, offering tighter stop-loss placement and higher risk-to-reward ratios.

Comparing Supply/Demand Zones and ICT Order Blocks

Feature	Supply/Demand Zone	ICT Order Block
Definition	Broad area of price imbalance	Precise institutional accumulation/distribution zone
Formation	Strong price reaction from a base/consolidation	Last opposite candle before impulsive move
Size	Larger, can span several candles	Smaller, one to a few candles
Focus	Price reaction	Institutional order flow
Timeframe Significance	Higher timeframe for strength	Both higher and lower timeframes with multi-timeframe confirmation
Precision	Moderate, more subjective	High, rules-based identification
Trading Style	Useful for general zones and entries	High-probability setups, optimal trade entries

Integration of Concepts

The most effective Smart Money trading strategies integrate both classical supply/demand zones and ICT order blocks:

- Identify a supply or demand zone on a higher timeframe to locate areas of significant market imbalance.
- Zoom in to detect ICT order blocks within these zones for precise entry points.
- Use OTE and Fibonacci retracements to refine entries within the order block.
- Combine with liquidity pools, fair value gaps, and market structure for multi-layered confluence.

Institutional Perspective

From the institutional viewpoint:

- Supply and demand zones represent the general areas where institutions accumulate or distribute, helping them gauge potential market reaction.
- ICT order blocks reflect the precise execution points, where large players place orders to maximize efficiency and minimize slippage.
- Institutions often exploit the natural liquidity within supply/demand zones but execute with precision using smaller, focused order blocks.

Practical Implications for Traders

1. **Broader Context:** Use supply and demand zones to understand the market's overall balance of power.

2. **Precision Entries:** Use ICT order blocks for exact entries and tight risk management.

3. **Confluence is Critical:** High-probability trades often occur when an ICT order block aligns perfectly with a larger supply or demand zone.

4. **Stop-Loss and Take-Profit Planning:** Place stops just beyond the order block, while take-profit targets can consider the boundaries of the broader supply/demand zone.

5. **Avoid Over-Reliance on Either:** Supply/demand zones provide context; order blocks provide precision. Using both together improves trade quality.

Example Scenario

Imagine a market in an uptrend:

- A demand zone is identified on the daily chart between 1.2000–1.2100.

- Zooming into the 1H chart, an ICT bullish order block is detected between 1.2040–1.2050.

- Price retraces to 1.2050, showing bullish reaction. Entry within the ICT order block provides a precise, high-probability long trade.

- Stop-loss is placed below the order block, while take-profit considers the upper boundary of the daily demand zone.

This approach allows traders to combine the broader market context (supply/demand) with precise execution (ICT order block), aligning with institutional strategy and maximizing probability.

Conclusion

While classical supply and demand zones provide a macro-level understanding of market imbalances, ICT order blocks offer micro-level precision. Smart traders leverage both: using supply and demand for context, and ICT order blocks for actionable entries. By integrating these concepts, one can anticipate institutional moves, respect liquidity dynamics, and execute trades with enhanced confidence and probability.

5.3 Aligning Zones with Order Blocks for High-Probability Trades

High-probability trades in Smart Money Concepts (SMC) are rarely executed using a single tool in isolation. Combining supply and demand zones with ICT order blocks (OBs) allows traders to align broader market imbalances with precise institutional footprints. This integration creates a multi-layered confluence that increases the likelihood of trade success.

Why Alignment Matters

- Supply and demand zones provide the macro context, showing where institutions have historically created imbalances.
- Order blocks highlight exact points where institutions entered or exited positions.
- Aligning these elements ensures that traders enter trades in areas of both structural significance and precise liquidity, minimizing risk and improving reward-to-risk ratios.

Step-by-Step Alignment Process

1. **Identify the Zone:** Begin by locating a significant supply or demand zone on a higher timeframe (daily or 4H). Look for strong impulsive moves and clear consolidation bases as the origin of the zone.
2. **Locate Order Blocks Within the Zone:** Zoom into a lower time-frame (1H or 15M) to find ICT order blocks that exist inside or at the edge of the broader zone. These order blocks represent precise institutional activity within the macro imbalance.
3. **Check Market Structure Alignment:** Confirm that the identified OB within the zone aligns with market structure:
   - For bullish setups, ensure higher highs and higher lows support the trend.
   - For bearish setups, ensure lower highs and lower lows are present.
4. **Overlay Liquidity Pools and Fair Value Gaps:** Identify areas where stop-loss clusters, previous swing highs/lows, or fair value gaps coincide with the OB within the zone. These areas represent liquidity concentration where institutions may act.
5. **Time-of-Day Consideration:** Align the setup with active trading sessions (London, New York) to ensure institutional participation. Avoid low-liquidity periods where moves may be erratic.

6. **Define Entry, Stop, and Target:**
   - Entry: Within the OB in alignment with the zone.
   - Stop-Loss: Slightly beyond the OB, outside minor wicks or micro-structure.
   - Take-Profit: Can consider the opposite boundary of the zone or next key liquidity cluster.

Example Scenario

Consider a bullish example:

- On the daily chart, a demand zone exists between 1.3000 – 1.3100.
- Zooming to the 1H chart, a bullish order block is located at 1.3030 – 1.3050.
- A fair value gap exists at 1.3040, and a liquidity pool of stop-loss orders sits slightly below 1.3030.
- During the London session, price retraces to 1.3045, triggering the OB and interacting with the liquidity pool.
- This multi-layered confluence provides a precise entry with strong institutional alignment and high-probability bullish potential.

Practical Tips for Traders

- Never rely on a single tool; confluence is critical for high-probability trades.
- Confirm OBs are genuine by checking impulsive moves and prior market structure.
- Use multiple timeframes: zones for context, OBs for precision, and lower timeframes for entry timing.
- Keep a visual record or a trade journal noting zones, OBs, liquidity, session, and market reaction for continual refinement.
- Patience is key; wait for price to enter the OB within the zone and show reaction before committing.

Institutional Perspective

Institutions operate within this same framework:

- They exploit liquidity in broader supply/demand zones while executing precise entries through order blocks.

- By entering within the OB inside the zone, they minimize slippage and maximize the probability of capturing the next impulse move.
- Retail traders who align their entries with both the zone and the OB effectively trade alongside institutions rather than against them.

By consistently aligning supply and demand zones with ICT order blocks, liquidity pools, and fair value gaps, traders can build a systematic approach to high-probability trading. This multi-layered methodology respects the footprints of smart money and greatly improves trade execution and outcomes.

5.4 Avoiding False Zones

Not all supply and demand zones are created equal. Some zones appear strong but fail to produce meaningful price reactions when revisited. Trading false zones can lead to premature entries, stop-outs, and reduced confidence. In this section, we discuss how to identify false zones, the common traps retail traders fall into, and techniques for confirming genuine areas of institutional activity.

Characteristics of False Zones

False supply or demand zones often share certain traits:

- **Weak Impulse:** Zones that originate from small or indecisive price movements typically fail on retests.
- **Overcrowded Price Action:** Areas with frequent choppy movement, many overlapping candles, or sideways congestion may indicate indecision rather than institutional control.
- **Minimal Reaction:** Genuine zones cause strong, impulsive moves. If a zone previously produced only mild or slow price changes, it is likely weak.
- **Timeframe Misalignment:** Zones drawn on lower timeframes without higher timeframe context may lack significance.

Common Retail Mistakes Leading to False Zones

Retail traders often make mistakes that create the illusion of valid zones:

1. **Drawing Zones Too Narrow or Too Broad:** Extreme precision or overly broad zones reduce effectiveness. Too narrow may miss reaction, too broad may include noise.
2. **Ignoring Market Context:** Failing to consider the larger trend or higher timeframe structure often results in trading against the dominant market bias.

3. **Chasing Price:** Entering zones before confirmation of a reaction often triggers stop-losses.

4. **Relying on Visual Patterns Alone:** Assuming any consolidation or wick forms a valid zone without checking volume, impulsive moves, or institutional footprints.

Techniques to Confirm Genuine Zones

- **Check for Strong Impulsive Moves:** Confirm that the zone originated from a clear and decisive price movement.

- **Volume Validation:** Higher volume during the initial move adds credibility; it indicates strong participation by larger market players.

- **Multi-Timeframe Alignment:** Cross-check zones on higher timeframes. A zone that appears significant on a 15-minute chart but is minor on a 1-hour or daily chart may be unreliable.

- **Reaction on Retest:** Observe price reaction when the zone is revisited. Strong rejections, candlestick wicks, or engulfing patterns confirm validity.

- **Confluence with Order Blocks and Liquidity Pools:** Zones overlapping with ICT order blocks, fair value gaps, or liquidity clusters carry higher probability.

Case Study: False vs Genuine Demand Zones

Consider two potential demand zones in an uptrend:

- **Zone A:** Formed on a small consolidation with minimal upward impulse. When price retraces, the zone is breached without reaction. This is a **false zone**.

- **Zone B:** Originated from a strong swing low, with a 50-pip impulsive move upward, high volume, and alignment with an ICT bullish order block. On retest, price shows clear rejection and continues upward. This is a **genuine zone**.

Practical Tips for Traders

1. Focus on zones with clear impulsive origin; ignore minor consolidations.

2. Use higher timeframe validation for strength.

3. Wait for confirmation—price interaction and reaction are key before entering.

4. Combine with other SMC tools (order blocks, fair value gaps, liquidity pools) for confluence.
5. Maintain a trading journal documenting which zones worked, which failed, and why; this helps refine your detection and interpretation skills.

Institutional Perspective

Institutions rarely act in areas with weak imbalances. They target zones with strong liquidity, clear market structure, and predictable reactions. By filtering out false zones, retail traders can better align with institutional activity, reduce risk, and improve the probability of successful trades.

In summary, avoiding false supply and demand zones requires discipline, multi-timeframe analysis, volume confirmation, and confluence with other SMC tools. Mastering this process allows traders to focus only on the most significant zones, enhancing trade quality and aligning effectively with smart money flow.

Chapter 6

Liquidity Concepts

In the financial markets, liquidity is the lifeblood of price movement. Understanding where liquidity resides, how it is targeted, and how institutions manipulate it is crucial for traders who aim to align with smart money rather than fight against it. Unlike simple support and resistance or supply and demand zones, liquidity concepts reveal the underlying forces that drive markets—where institutions accumulate or distribute positions, trigger stops, and engineer price action to their advantage.

6.1 Liquidity Pools & Stop-Loss Clusters

Liquidity is the fuel that drives markets, and liquidity pools are the concentrated areas where it accumulates. In essence, a liquidity pool is a cluster of pending orders—buy or sell—that provides the necessary volume for institutions to execute large trades efficiently. Stop-loss clusters are a common component of these pools, representing points where retail traders have placed protective stops that can be exploited by smart money. Understanding and identifying these areas is critical for traders who aim to align with institutional activity rather than be caught on the wrong side of the market.

Definition

- **Liquidity Pool:** A price level or zone where a significant number of pending buy or sell orders are concentrated. These pools act as magnets for price because institutions require liquidity to execute large orders without causing undue slippage.

- **Stop-Loss Cluster:** A specific type of liquidity pool where retail stop-loss orders are concentrated, usually beyond obvious swing highs or lows, trend lines, or support/resistance levels. Institutions often target these clusters to absorb liquidity efficiently.

Why Liquidity Pools Matter

Institutions cannot move markets without sufficient liquidity. Retail traders often unknowingly provide this liquidity through their stops and pending orders. Liquidity pools thus serve multiple purposes:

1. **Execution Efficiency:** Large institutional orders require absorption of existing liquidity to avoid moving the market too aggressively.

2. **Market Manipulation:** By triggering retail stop-losses, institutions can engineer price swings that favor their accumulation or distribution strategy.

3. **Price Magnets:** Liquidity pools often attract price because the market tends to seek areas where orders can be filled.

Characteristics of Stop-Loss Clusters

- Located just beyond obvious swing highs or lows, key support/resistance, or technical levels.

- Often coincide with prior supply or demand zones, adding further confluence.

- Typically align with fair value gaps, mitigation zones, or other institutional footprints.

- Act as triggers for impulsive moves when reached, as clustered stops are absorbed.

How to Identify Liquidity Pools and Stop-Loss Clusters

1. **Swing Highs and Lows:** Identify areas where retail traders are likely to place stops just beyond key swing points.

2. **Support and Resistance Levels:** Pending orders often cluster around obvious structural levels.

3. **Price History:** Observe zones where prior reactions were strong; these are likely areas for future liquidity accumulation.

4. **Volume Analysis:** Zones with high volume during prior moves may indicate the presence of institutional liquidity.

Institutional Perspective

Institutions operate with significant capital and therefore require a deep understanding of liquidity dynamics:

- They target retail stop-loss clusters to absorb liquidity, which enables smoother execution of large orders.
- By moving price into these clusters, institutions can accumulate or distribute positions without revealing the full extent of their intentions.
- Recognizing these zones allows traders to align with institutional behavior, avoiding being prematurely stopped out and increasing the probability of entering in the direction of smart money.

Practical Applications for Traders

1. **Entry Timing:** Wait for price to reach or slightly penetrate a liquidity pool or stop-loss cluster before entering in the direction of the larger trend.
2. **Risk Management:** Place stop-losses in areas outside the cluster, reducing the risk of being caught in institutional manipulations.
3. **Confluence:** Combine liquidity pools with order blocks, fair value gaps, and market structure for multi-layered confirmation.
4. **Observation and Patience:** Monitor how price interacts with these zones. Strong rejection or absorption signals increase the probability of a successful trade.

By mastering the identification and interpretation of liquidity pools and stop-loss clusters, traders gain a crucial edge: the ability to anticipate institutional moves, avoid retail traps, and position themselves strategically in alignment with smart money. This understanding forms the foundation for higher-probability trades, particularly when combined with other SMC tools such as order blocks and fair value gaps.

6.2 Fair Value Gaps (FVG) and Mitigation Zones

Fair Value Gaps (FVG) and mitigation zones are essential concepts in Smart Money Concepts (SMC) that help traders identify areas where price imbalance exists due to institutional activity. These zones are closely tied to liquidity pools and order blocks and provide additional precision for high-probability trade setups.

Definition of Fair Value Gaps

- A **Fair Value Gap (FVG)** occurs when price moves sharply in one direction, leaving behind a void in the market where minimal trading occurred. Typically, this is visible as a gap or imbalance between two consecutive candles, where the market did not establish equilibrium.

- These gaps represent areas where institutions may return to fill liquidity, balance their positions, or trigger stops, creating opportunities for traders who understand the underlying dynamics.

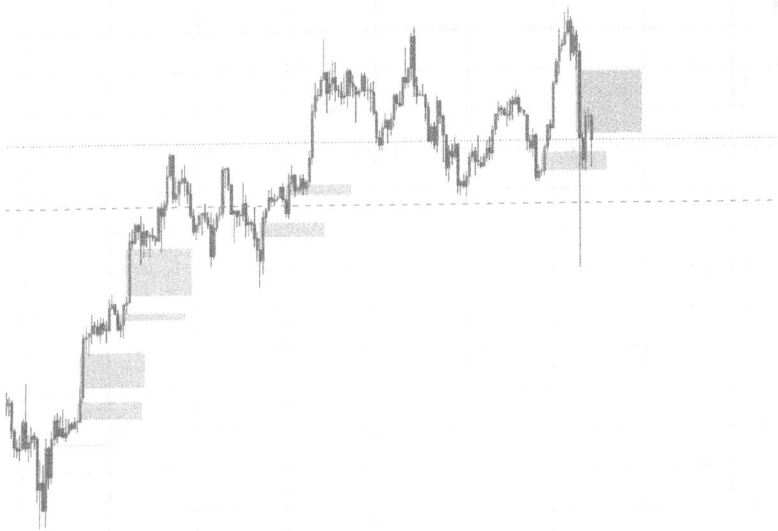

Figure 6.1: Fair Value Gap (FVG): An area of price inefficiency where the wick of the third candle fails to overlap the wick of the first candle, often acting as a high-probability reversal or continuation entry point.

Characteristics of FVGs

- Often appear after strong impulsive moves in either direction.
- Represent areas of unfilled orders or market inefficiency.
- Act as magnets for price retracements, providing potential entry points for traders.
- Can exist on multiple timeframes; higher timeframe FVGs carry more significance.

Mitigation Zones

A **mitigation zone** is a region where an institution seeks to balance or mitigate previously unfilled or inefficient trades. Mitigation often overlaps with fair value gaps:

- Price often returns to the FVG to "fill" the gap, allowing institutions to mitigate risk from overexposure or incomplete positions.

- Mitigation zones provide high-probability areas for entries in the direction of the original trend.
- They also act as confirmation for liquidity and order block confluence.

Integration with Liquidity Pools and Order Blocks

For high-probability setups, FVGs and mitigation zones should be aligned with liquidity pools and order blocks:

1. Identify a significant liquidity pool or stop-loss cluster.
2. Look for a nearby FVG or mitigation zone that overlaps or is within reach of that liquidity area.
3. Confirm that the order block aligns with the FVG and the broader market structure.
4. Wait for price to interact with the FVG or mitigation zone, providing a potential low-risk entry in the direction of institutional intent.

Practical Example

Consider a bullish market scenario:

- Price impulsively rises from 1.2000 to 1.2150, leaving a Fair Value Gap between 1.2030–1.2050.
- A bullish order block exists within the 1.2040–1.2050 range.
- A liquidity pool formed slightly below 1.2030 indicates stop-loss clusters from retail sellers.
- Price retraces to the FVG and order block, triggering the liquidity pool. Traders can enter long within this zone with tight stop-losses below the cluster, aligning with institutional flow.

Key Takeaways

- FVGs and mitigation zones highlight areas of market inefficiency and institutional interest.
- When combined with liquidity pools and order blocks, these zones offer precise, high-probability entries.
- Multi-timeframe confirmation and alignment with market structure increase the likelihood of successful trades.
- Patience is essential; traders should wait for price interaction and confirmation within these zones before executing trades.

Mastering Fair Value Gaps and mitigation zones equips traders with the ability to identify areas where institutions are likely to act, anticipate market moves, and execute trades with enhanced probability and reduced risk. This layer of precision, when combined with liquidity and order block analysis, forms a robust foundation for Smart Money-aligned trading strategies.

6.3 Smart Money Traps (SMT)

Smart Money Traps (SMTs) are deliberate price manipulations designed by institutions to exploit the predictable behavior of retail traders. These traps occur when the market appears to break a level of support, resistance, or trend, prompting retail traders to take positions that align against institutional intent. Understanding SMTs is crucial for avoiding false breakouts, stop hunts, and other manipulative moves that can erode capital.

Definition of Smart Money Traps

- **Smart Money Trap:** A market scenario in which price movement is engineered to lure retail traders into positions that are contrary to institutional objectives. These traps often occur near liquidity clusters, stop-loss zones, or fair value gaps.
- The goal of SMTs is to provide liquidity for institutions to execute their orders efficiently while minimizing slippage and maximizing profit.

Common Types of SMTs

1. **Stop Hunts:** Price moves briefly beyond swing highs or lows to trigger retail stop-loss orders, providing liquidity for institutions to enter or exit positions.
2. **Fake Breakouts:** Price appears to break a key support or resistance level, enticing retail traders to follow the breakout, only to reverse sharply in the opposite direction.
3. **Liquidity Sweeps:** Price targets known liquidity pools to accumulate or distribute positions before resuming the main trend.
4. **False Trend Reversals:** Short-term reversals engineered to mislead traders, inducing premature entries against the institutional bias.

Identifying Smart Money Traps

Recognizing SMTs requires combining market structure, liquidity analysis, and institutional footprint tools:

- **Look for Impulsive Moves and Retracements:** Genuine moves typically have clear structure and momentum; suspicious reversals or spikes may indicate a trap.
- **Analyze Liquidity Pools:** If price aggressively moves into areas of concentrated stop-losses or pending orders, it may be a liquidity hunt rather than a real breakout.
- **Check Market Structure:** Evaluate whether the apparent breakout aligns with the higher timeframe trend or breaks structure in an unnatural way.
- **Multiple Timeframe Confirmation:** Cross-check the move on higher and lower timeframes; institutional traps often show divergence between timeframes.

Practical Example

Consider a bearish scenario:

- Price is in an uptrend with a key swing low at 1.2500.
- Retail traders place stop-loss orders below 1.2500.
- Institutions push price down to 1.2490, triggering stops and creating a liquidity pool.
- Immediately after, the market reverses sharply upward, continuing the original uptrend.
- Traders who anticipated a breakdown are caught in the trap, while those aligned with institutional behavior can capitalize on the continuation.

Avoiding Smart Money Traps

1. **Wait for Confirmation:** Do not enter trades solely on breakouts; wait for reaction confirmation such as engulfing candles, structure alignment, or liquidity absorption.
2. **Respect Market Structure:** Trade with the institutional bias, not against it. Avoid contrarian positions near known liquidity clusters unless there is clear evidence of reversal.
3. **Use Confluence:** Align entry with order blocks, fair value gaps, and liquidity pools to increase probability.
4. **Patience and Discipline:** Resist the urge to chase price. Many traps succeed because retail traders act impulsively.
5. **Maintain a Journal:** Document suspected SMTs, trade outcomes, and reactions to refine detection skills.

Institutional Perspective

From an institutional standpoint, SMTs are strategic maneuvers:

- They provide the necessary liquidity for large trades without moving the market unfavorably.
- They exploit predictable retail behavior, such as stop placement and trend-chasing.
- By understanding SMTs, retail traders can align with institutional intent rather than being manipulated, improving entry timing and risk management.

Mastering the identification of Smart Money Traps is a critical skill in SMC trading. Recognizing these engineered moves, and knowing when to act or step aside, allows traders to protect capital, anticipate institutional behavior, and execute trades with higher probability of success.

6.4 Recognizing Institutional Manipulation

Markets are not random; they are driven by the intentions of large institutional players. Recognizing institutional manipulation is key to trading like smart money. Institutions have the capital and resources to move markets strategically, often creating patterns, traps, and liquidity sweeps that mislead retail traders. Understanding these manipulations allows traders to anticipate market behavior, avoid common pitfalls, and align with high-probability trade setups.

Signs of Institutional Activity

- **Stop Hunts:** Sudden price spikes that trigger retail stop-losses, often occurring near previous swing highs or lows.
- **Fair Value Gap Fills:** Price retraces to unfilled gaps, indicating institutional mitigation and position balancing.
- **Order Block Engagements:** Price frequently reacts at order block levels, confirming their relevance as institutional footprints.
- **Liquidity Sweeps:** Sharp moves into liquidity pools to absorb pending orders, followed by continuation in the institutional bias direction.
- **Unnatural Reversals:** Rapid reversals against the retail consensus, often engineered to mislead and capture liquidity.

Market Structure Clues

Institutions rarely act randomly. Observing market structure helps identify their influence:

1. **Break of Structure (BoS) and Change of Character (CHoCH):** These are often accompanied by liquidity hunts that confirm institutional bias.
2. **Swing Highs/Lows and Liquidity Pools:** Price tends to target clustered stops before reversing or continuing the trend.
3. **Multi-Timeframe Consistency:** Institutional manipulation often respects higher timeframe structure while exploiting lower timeframe liquidity.

Combining SMC Tools for Recognition

Recognizing manipulation is most effective when combining multiple SMC tools:

- **Order Blocks:** Identify areas of institutional accumulation or distribution.
- **Fair Value Gaps and Mitigation Zones:** Observe where price is likely to retrace for mitigation.
- **Liquidity Pools:** Anticipate stop hunts and liquidity sweeps.
- **Smart Money Traps (SMT):** Recognize engineered moves designed to mislead retail traders.

Practical Example

Consider a bearish institutional setup:

- Price is in a downtrend, approaching a liquidity pool below a key swing low.
- A bearish order block exists above the liquidity pool, and a fair value gap remains unfilled.
- Retail traders expect a minor retracement, placing stops just above the swing high.
- Institutions push price up slightly, triggering stops (liquidity sweep) before reversing strongly downward, filling the FVG and continuing the downtrend.
- Traders who recognize these signals and align with institutional manipulation can enter near the order block with favorable risk-to-reward.

Behavioral Insights

- **Predictable Retail Behavior:** Institutions rely on predictable retail responses, such as chasing breakouts or placing stops at obvious levels.
- **Patience and Timing:** Institutional moves are often precise and deliberate. Retail traders benefit by waiting for confirmation rather than anticipating moves prematurely.
- **Pattern Recognition:** Repeated observation of price interactions with liquidity, order blocks, and FVGs builds the ability to anticipate manipulation.

Practical Tips for Traders

1. Map liquidity pools, order blocks, and FVGs to identify potential manipulation zones.
2. Observe how price reacts to these zones; impulsive moves followed by sharp reversals often indicate institutional activity.
3. Use multi-timeframe analysis to confirm higher timeframe bias while executing trades on lower timeframes for precision.
4. Avoid trading against the institutional bias; instead, align entries with the anticipated smart money direction.
5. Maintain a journal tracking suspected manipulation events to refine detection skills and improve trade decision-making.

By mastering the recognition of institutional manipulation, traders gain the ability to see beyond surface-level price action, anticipate moves engineered by smart money, and execute trades with higher probability and lower risk. This understanding, combined with liquidity, order block, and FVG analysis, forms a comprehensive framework for trading in alignment with the true market movers.

6.5 Relative Equal Highs and Lows Manipulation Concept

One of the most important liquidity principles in Smart Money Concepts (SMC) is the idea of **Relative Equal Highs (REH)** and **Relative Equal Lows (REL)**. These formations are not accidental. Rather, they are intentionally engineered by institutional algorithms to accumulate liquidity before delivering a displacement move.

Relative equal highs/lows represent one of the clearest footprints of algorithmic manipulation and are essential for understanding how liquidity is built, trapped, and then harvested.

Definition of Relative Equal Highs and Lows

Relative Equal Highs (REH) occur when two or more highs form at nearly the same price level. **Relative Equal Lows (REL)** occur when two or more lows form at nearly the same price level.

They are characterized by:

- very small price deviation between swing highs or lows,
- flat or visually aligned levels on a chart,
- repeated rejection from the same level,
- clustering of liquidity above (for highs) or below (for lows).

Although retail traders commonly interpret these levels as "strong support" or "strong resistance," institutions treat them as **liquidity pools**.

Why Institutions Engineer Equal Highs and Lows

Institutions require liquidity to:

- enter large positions,
- exit positions efficiently,
- induce traders into taking opposite positions,
- fuel displacement moves in their preferred direction.

Relative equal highs and lows are perfect liquidity magnets because they contain:

- clusters of stop-loss orders,
- breakout trader entries (buy stops or sell stops),
- resting limit orders,
- retail expectations of support/resistance.

The more times price touches these levels, the more liquidity accumulates.

How Algorithms Manipulate REH and REL

Institutional algorithms typically follow a consistent pattern:

1. Creation of Equal Highs/Lows

Price rejects from a level repeatedly, forming an illusion of strong support or resistance.

2. Inducement Phase

The repeated touches entice retail traders to:

- buy near equal lows expecting a bounce,
- sell near equal highs expecting a reversal,
- place stop-losses tightly above/below the equal levels.

This builds a substantial liquidity pool.

3. Liquidity Sweep

The algorithm pushes price:

- above relative equal highs to collect buy stops and short stop-losses,
- below relative equal lows to collect sell stops and long stop-losses.

This sweep is deliberate and forms a critical part of the institutional execution cycle.

4. Displacement

After the sweep, the algorithm delivers a directional move away from the liquidity zone. Displacement confirms the sweep was intentional and reveals institutional intent.

Types of Relative Equal Highs/Lows

1. True Equal Highs/Lows

Almost identical highs or lows (same wick or body level).

2. Near Equal Highs/Lows

Slight deviation but visually equal on most timeframes.

3. Engineered Equal Highs/Lows

Created intentionally by the algorithm to build liquidity before expansion.

Engineered equal highs/lows often contain:

- inducement wicks,
- tiny internal CHoCH patterns,
- multiple rejections with low-volume candles.

Why REH and REL Are Not Support or Resistance

Retail education often labels equal highs/lows as "strong levels." However, in institutional logic, these are:

- liquidity shelves,
- resting points for algorithmic manipulation,
- predictable trap zones,
- areas where retail traders are repeatedly wrong.

Institutions use these levels to trigger mass participation before reversing or continuing the move.

How to Trade Around REH and REL

1. Expect a Sweep, Not a Hold

The algorithm will almost always:

- run above relative equal highs, or
- run below relative equal lows.

2. Wait for Displacement

A valid setup forms only when displacement occurs after the sweep:

- strong impulsive candles,
- Fair Value Gaps (FVG),
- Break of Structure (BOS).

3. Enter on the Mitigation

After displacement, price often returns to:

- the FVG,
- the Order Block (OB),
- the mitigation block left behind.

These retests offer high-probability entries.

Common Mistakes Traders Make

Retail traders often:

- trade reversals at equal highs/lows,
- place stops directly above/below them,
- mistake sweep candles as breakouts,
- fail to wait for confirmation via displacement,
- ignore that equal highs/lows are inducement structures.

These mistakes lead to immediate stop-outs during liquidity runs.

Summary

- Relative equal highs and lows represent liquidity pools, not support or resistance.
- They are engineered intentionally by institutional algorithms.
- A sweep of these levels is often the precursor to a major displacement move.
- The proper trade follows the sweep and waits for displacement before entry.
- Understanding REH and REL manipulation helps traders avoid traps and align with institutional execution logic.

Mastering this concept is essential for reading liquidity behavior and anticipating trend reversals or continuations.

Chapter 7

Entry & Exit Strategies

Successful trading is not just about identifying high-probability setups; it is equally about executing trades with precision and managing them effectively. While understanding market structure, liquidity, order blocks, and fair value gaps provides the framework for Smart Money-aligned trading, the way a trader enters and exits a position can make the difference between consistent profitability and repeated losses.

7.1 Entry Techniques: OB Retests, Breaker Blocks, OTE

Entry timing is one of the most critical aspects of trading. Even the best market analysis can fail if the trader enters at the wrong price. Smart Money Concepts (SMC) and Inner Circle Trader (ICT) methodologies provide structured approaches to entering trades that maximize the probability of success while minimizing risk. This section will cover three key techniques: Order Block (OB) Retests, Breaker Blocks, and Optimal Trade Entry (OTE) using Fibonacci retracements.

Order Block (OB) Retests

An **Order Block** is a price zone where institutions previously accumulated or distributed positions. These zones represent areas of high probability for reversals or continuations because institutional orders remain active and often control price behavior.

- **Entry Strategy:** Wait for price to retest the identified order block after an initial impulsive move. A successful retest indicates that the institutional orders are absorbing retail activity and preparing for the next directional move.

- **Confirmation Signals:** Look for bullish or bearish rejection candles, wicks that test the OB, or confluence with other SMC tools such as liquidity pools or fair value gaps.

- **Example:** In a bullish scenario, price rallies impulsively, then retraces to a previously identified bullish OB. Observing a rejection candle at this zone allows traders to enter long with tight stops below the OB.

Breaker Blocks

A **Breaker Block** forms when a previous order block is broken and then tested from the opposite side. It acts as a new level of support or resistance and provides high-probability trade entries aligned with institutional intent.

- **Formation:** Occurs when an initial order block fails to hold, price breaks through it, and then returns to test it as a new resistance or support.

- **Entry Strategy:** Enter trades when price reacts to the breaker block in alignment with the larger trend or institutional bias. This technique capitalizes on the change of market character (CHoCH) and institutional footprint.

- **Example:** A bearish breaker block forms after price breaks a bullish OB. Price retraces to test the broken OB as resistance, providing a short entry with favorable risk-to-reward.

Optimal Trade Entry (OTE) with Fibonacci

Optimal Trade Entry (OTE) is a technique that combines market structure and Fibonacci retracement levels to identify high-probability entry zones. The 61.8% to 79% Fibonacci retracement is commonly used to locate the OTE, aligning with the institutional footprint.

- **Entry Strategy:** Identify an impulsive move (leg), measure the retracement, and mark the OTE zone. Enter trades when price reaches this zone and shows confirmation via OB, breaker block, or liquidity cluster interaction.

- **Benefits:** Provides a structured entry with better risk-reward, aligning with the natural ebb and flow of institutional order execution.

- **Example:** Price makes a strong bullish leg from 1.2000 to 1.2200. The 61.8%–79% retracement zone (approximately 1.2060–1.2120) serves as the OTE. Price reaches this area and finds support at a bullish OB, signaling a high-probability long entry.

Practical Tips for Entry

1. Always align entries with the higher timeframe bias and market structure.
2. Combine multiple entry signals—OB retest, breaker block, OTE, and liquidity pools—for confluence.
3. Avoid chasing price; wait for confirmation within the identified zone.
4. Keep stops tight and logical, usually beyond the OB, breaker block, or liquidity cluster.
5. Document entries and outcomes to refine timing and improve trade accuracy over time.

By mastering OB retests, breaker blocks, and OTE entries, traders can approach the market with confidence, placing trades that are aligned with institutional intentions and structured to maximize probability while managing risk effectively. These techniques provide a practical framework for entering trades in high-probability zones, forming the foundation for disciplined and profitable trading.

7.2 Exit Techniques: Partial Profit-Taking, Trailing Stops

While precise entries set the stage for profitable trades, effective exits determine the ultimate outcome. Many traders fail not because they enter poorly, but because they exit prematurely or let winning trades turn into losses. In Smart Money Concepts (SMC) trading, exit strategies are closely linked to market structure, liquidity zones, and institutional footprints. This section explores partial profit-taking and trailing stops as key techniques for optimizing trade outcomes.

Partial Profit-Taking

Partial profit-taking involves closing a portion of a trade at predetermined levels to secure gains while leaving the remainder of the position open to capture further movement.

- **Purpose:** Reduces emotional stress and locks in profits, while still allowing the trade to benefit from larger market moves.
- **Identification of Levels:** Use market structure, liquidity pools, order blocks, and fair value gaps to identify logical exit points.

- **Practical Example:** Suppose a long trade enters at 1.2100 targeting 1.2250. A trader may close 50% of the position at 1.2180 (first liquidity pool) and let the rest ride toward 1.2250, using a trailing stop to protect profits.
- **Advantages:** Secures gains, reduces risk, and improves psychological comfort by realizing partial profits without exiting entirely.

Trailing Stops

A trailing stop is a dynamic exit mechanism that moves with price, locking in profits as the market progresses in your favor.

- **Fixed vs. Volatility-Based Trailing Stops:** Fixed trailing stops move a set number of pips, while volatility-based stops adjust according to market fluctuations, using ATR (Average True Range) or candle structure.
- **Placement Strategy:** Position trailing stops below key support zones, order blocks, or swing lows in bullish trades (above key resistance in bearish trades) to avoid being stopped prematurely.
- **Practical Example:** In a bullish trade from 1.2000 to 1.2200, set an ATR-based trailing stop that moves up with price, maintaining a buffer of 30–40 pips. This ensures that as price moves higher, profits are protected, while allowing for normal market retracements.
- **Advantages:** Maximizes profits, allows trades to capture extended moves, and reduces the need for constant monitoring.

Combining Partial Profit-Taking and Trailing Stops

Integrating both techniques provides flexibility and better risk management:

1. Take partial profits at logical zones (e.g., first liquidity pool, minor order block) to lock in gains.
2. Use a trailing stop on the remaining position to capture extended trends.
3. Adjust the trailing stop based on market volatility, session bias, and higher timeframe structure.
4. Avoid moving stops too tightly, which can result in premature exits.

Psychological Benefits

- Reduces anxiety and overtrading by securing incremental gains.
- Helps traders adhere to their plan without second-guessing.
- Encourages disciplined trade management, which is essential for long-term profitability.

Key Takeaways

- Exits are as critical as entries; planning them in advance increases the probability of profitable trades.
- Partial profit-taking balances security and opportunity, while trailing stops allow trades to capitalize on momentum.
- Always align exits with market structure, liquidity zones, and institutional activity for maximum effectiveness.
- Document trade exits to refine strategies and understand how market behavior affects stop placement and profit realization.

By mastering partial profit-taking and trailing stops, traders can protect gains, reduce risk, and maximize trade outcomes. These techniques, when applied in conjunction with SMC tools such as order blocks, fair value gaps, and liquidity pools, form a robust framework for disciplined and profitable trading.

7.3 Risk-to-Reward Ratios and Position Sizing

One of the most overlooked aspects of trading is proper risk management. Even with high-probability setups, poor risk-to-reward ratios and improper position sizing can lead to account depletion. In Smart Money Concepts (SMC) trading, understanding how to balance risk with potential reward and sizing positions appropriately is essential for long-term success.

Risk-to-Reward (R:R) Ratios

The risk-to-reward ratio measures the potential reward of a trade relative to the amount risked. It helps traders determine whether a trade offers sufficient upside to justify the risk.

- **Formula:**

$$R:R = \frac{\text{Potential Profit (Target} - \text{Entry)}}{\text{Risk (Entry} - \text{Stop Loss)}}$$

- **Optimal R:R:** A minimum of 1:2 is often recommended, meaning the potential reward is at least twice the risk. Higher R:R ratios (e.g., 1:3 or 1:5) further improve long-term profitability.
- **Example:** Entering a long trade at 1.2100 with a stop loss at 1.2050 (risk = 50 pips) and a target of 1.2200 (potential profit = 100 pips) yields an R:R of 1:2.

Position Sizing

Position sizing determines how many units (lots, shares, contracts) to trade based on account size, risk tolerance, and stop-loss distance. Proper sizing ensures that no single trade can damage the trading account.

- **Formula for Position Size:**

$$\text{Position Size} = \frac{\text{Account Risk Amount}}{\text{Trade Risk (Entry} - \text{Stop Loss)}}$$

- **Example:** With a $10,000 account and a maximum risk of 2% per trade ($200), if the stop loss is 50 pips, the position size should be calculated such that the total loss does not exceed $200 if stopped out.
- **Factors to Consider:** Volatility, market conditions, session bias, and proximity to liquidity pools or FVGs can influence optimal position size.

Combining R:R with Position Sizing

Integrating risk-to-reward analysis with position sizing allows traders to:

1. Ensure that each trade aligns with long-term profitability objectives.
2. Avoid overexposure, even on high-probability setups.
3. Maintain consistent account growth by risking a small percentage per trade while targeting larger rewards.
4. Adapt position size dynamically based on stop-loss distance and market volatility.

Advanced Risk Techniques

- **Kelly Criterion:** An advanced formula to calculate optimal position size based on win rate and R:R ratio.
- **Fixed Fractional Risking:** Risking a fixed percentage of the account per trade to maintain consistent exposure.
- **Scaling In and Out:** Adjusting position size incrementally as the trade progresses, combining partial profit-taking and trailing stops.

Practical Guidelines

1. Never risk more than a small percentage (1–3%) of the account on a single trade.
2. Adjust position size based on stop-loss distance and market volatility.
3. Prioritize trades with higher R:R ratios, even if they occur less frequently.
4. Maintain a trading journal to track actual versus planned risk and reward.
5. Combine with SMC tools—OBs, FVGs, liquidity pools—to ensure entries and stops are logically placed according to institutional behavior.

Key Takeaways

- Risk-to-reward ratios and position sizing are the backbone of long-term trading success.
- Proper calculation ensures that losing trades do not materially harm the account.
- Combined with high-probability Smart Money setups, disciplined risk management maximizes account growth while minimizing drawdowns.
- Traders who master these principles can navigate markets with confidence, knowing that each trade is aligned with probability, structure, and capital preservation.

7.4 Practical Trade Examples

Theory becomes powerful only when applied in practice. This section illustrates step-by-step examples of trades that integrate Smart Money Concepts (SMC) and ICT methodologies, including entry techniques, exit strategies, and risk management. Each example demonstrates how these elements work together to maximize probability and manage risk.

Example 1: Bullish Order Block Retest with OTE

1. **Setup:** Price is in an uptrend on the higher timeframe. A bullish order block (OB) is identified at 1.2000–1.2020, and a recent impulsive leg moved price to 1.2150.
2. **OTE Identification:** The retracement of the impulsive move between 1.2150 and the OB is measured using Fibonacci. The 61.8%–79% zone corresponds to 1.2060–1.2080.

3. **Entry:** Price retraces to 1.2070 within the OTE zone and touches the bullish OB. A bullish engulfing candle forms, confirming institutional rejection.
4. **Stop-Loss:** Placed just below the OB at 1.2045.
5. **Target / R:R:** Initial target at the previous swing high 1.2150. Risk-to-reward ratio = 1:2.
6. **Partial Profit-Taking:** 50% closed at 1.2120 (near minor liquidity zone), remainder left with trailing stop.
7. **Outcome:** Price reaches target, trailing stop protects the remaining position, resulting in maximized profits and minimal risk exposure.

Example 2: Breaker Block Short with Liquidity Sweep

1. **Setup:** Price is in a downtrend. A previous bullish OB at 1.2300–1.2320 is broken. Price retraces to test this OB as a breaker block.
2. **Entry:** Observe liquidity sweep above the breaker block, triggering retail stop-losses. Confirmed by a bearish pin bar rejection.
3. **Stop-Loss:** Placed just above the breaker block at 1.2330.
4. **Target / R:R:** Initial target at the next swing low 1.2200. Risk-to-reward ratio 1:3.
5. **Partial Profit-Taking:** 40% closed at minor liquidity cluster near 1.2250; trailing stop applied to remainder.
6. **Outcome:** Trade captures extended move, with partial profits secured and trailing stop protecting remaining position.

Example 3: Multi-Timeframe Confluence Trade

1. **Setup:** Higher timeframe indicates bullish bias. Mid-timeframe shows a fair value gap (FVG) at 1.3100–1.3120, aligning with a bullish OB.
2. **Entry:** Lower timeframe retracement reaches OTE zone at 1.3110 with rejection candle forming at the OB + FVG confluence.
3. **Stop-Loss:** Placed below OB at 1.3085.
4. **Target / R:R:** Swing high target 1.3200; risk-to-reward ratio 1:3.5.
5. **Partial Profit-Taking:** 50% at intermediate liquidity pool 1.3160; trailing stop applied to remaining position.
6. **Outcome:** Trade demonstrates multi-timeframe alignment, capturing maximum institutional moves with structured risk management.

Key Lessons from Examples

- Always wait for confirmation within OBs, breaker blocks, or OTE zones.
- Partial profit-taking reduces emotional stress and secures incremental gains.
- Trailing stops allow trades to capture extended moves while protecting profits.
- Align trades with higher timeframe bias and liquidity zones for higher probability.
- Risk-to-reward calculation and position sizing are integral to trade management and account preservation.
- Multi-timeframe confluence and SMC tools provide a comprehensive framework for anticipating institutional behavior.

These examples demonstrate that disciplined application of entry and exit techniques, combined with structured risk management, transforms theoretical Smart Money setups into actionable, high-probability trades. By practicing these strategies consistently, traders can improve timing, optimize outcomes, and align their decisions with the institutional flow of the market.

7.5 Refined Confirmation Entry Model

One of the most precise and reliable entry techniques in Smart Money Concepts (SMC) and ICT methodology is the **refined confirmation entry model**, built on the sequence:

$$\text{CHoCH} \rightarrow \text{FVG} \rightarrow \text{Order Block (OB)}$$

This model ensures that:

- the market has shifted away from inducement and manipulation,
- true institutional displacement has occurred,
- price retraces to a high-probability execution zone,
- entries are aligned with algorithmic intent rather than retail noise.

It is a three-step confirmation model designed to filter weak setups and deliver optimal precision.

Why This Entry Model Works

The CHoCH → FVG → OB sequence mirrors the algorithmic execution cycle:

1. **CHoCH** signals the first internal shift in market structure.
2. **FVG** confirms displacement by institutional algorithms.
3. **OB** provides the refined mitigation point for execution.

This means the model only triggers when:

- manipulation has ended,
- real institutional momentum has begun,
- price offers a retracement for optimal entry.

Step 1: CHoCH (Change of Character)

A **CHoCH** is the earliest sign that the market is shifting direction.

Requirements for a Valid CHoCH

- It must break the most recent internal swing.
- It must occur after liquidity inducement or a run on equal highs/lows.
- It must form with clear intent (strong candle body, wick sweep, or imbalance).

A CHoCH alone does not confirm a trend reversal; it only indicates that internal structure has transitioned from one side of liquidity to the other.

Step 2: Displacement and FVG Formation

After the CHoCH, we must see a **displacement leg** that confirms institutional participation. This displacement typically leaves behind one or more **Fair Value Gaps (FVGs)**.

Why the FVG Matters

- It proves that the CHoCH was meaningful.
- It shows that algorithmic buying or selling has entered the market.
- It creates an imbalance that price often returns to for mitigation.

The FVG is the second confirmation. Without displacement, the CHoCH may simply be liquidity inducement.

Step 3: Mitigation into the Refined Order Block

The final step is a retracement into the **refined Order Block (OB)** inside the displacement leg.

Key Conditions for the OB

- It must originate from the displacement that created the FVG.
- It should be refined to the smallest efficient candle (wick/body refinement).
- It must be located inside a discount zone for longs or premium zone for shorts.
- It should align with internal liquidity (inducement before tap).

This OB acts as the institutional mitigation point where algorithms:

- close hedges,
- re-enter the trend,
- complete unfilled orders.

A refined OB offers the highest-probability entry with the smallest stop-loss.

Putting It All Together: The Complete Sequence

A complete refined entry should follow this order:

1. **Liquidity sweep** (e.g., equal highs/lows, inducement).
2. **CHoCH** showing a break in internal structure.
3. **Displacement** confirming intent.
4. **FVG** created inside the displacement leg.
5. **Retracement** back into the refined OB that caused the move.
6. **Entry** at OB tap, targeting opposing liquidity.

This sequence prevents traders from entering:

- too early during manipulation,
- before displacement,
- without confirmation of direction.

Trade Logic for Long and Short Setups

Bullish Setup Logic

- Price sweeps a key low.
- CHoCH breaks minor bearish structure.
- Bullish displacement creates an FVG.
- Price retraces into the bullish OB inside the displacement.
- Enter long at OB; stop below inducement low.

Bearish Setup Logic

- Price sweeps a key high.
- CHoCH breaks minor bullish structure.
- Bearish displacement creates an FVG.
- Price returns into the bearish OB inside the displacement.
- Enter short at OB; stop above inducement high.

Common Mistakes Traders Make

- Taking CHoCH entries without waiting for displacement.
- Entering FVG-only setups without OB confirmation.
- Trading OB taps that did not originate from true displacement.
- Ignoring inducement before the OB tap.
- Trading OBs outside premium/discount zones.

The strength of this model comes from requiring **all three** confirmations. Skipping any step increases the likelihood of being caught in manipulation.

Summary

- CHoCH identifies the first structural shift.
- FVG confirms displacement and institutional intent.
- OB provides the refined and efficient entry point.
- The sequence CHoCH → FVG → OB filters out weak and manipulative setups.

- This entry model aligns trading with the algorithmic execution cycle used by institutions.

Mastering this refined confirmation model significantly improves precision, reduces losses from false setups, and enhances alignment with institutional order flow.

Part III

Advanced SMC & ICT Concepts

Chapter 8

Market Manipulation & Smart Money Techniques

Markets are not purely driven by supply and demand in isolation—they are heavily influenced by the strategic actions of large institutional players. Unlike retail traders, institutions operate with vast capital, sophisticated tools, and a deep understanding of market psychology. Their actions often create patterns that appear chaotic to the untrained eye but follow predictable principles when viewed through the lens of Smart Money Concepts (SMC).

This chapter explores the various ways institutions manipulate price to their advantage, capturing liquidity, inducing retail mistakes, and orchestrating high-probability moves. From stop hunts and liquidity sweeps to fake breakouts, false structure shifts, and smart money traps (SMT), understanding these techniques allows traders to anticipate market behavior rather than react blindly.

By mastering the mechanics of institutional manipulation and combining them with market structure, liquidity analysis, and order block strategies, traders can align their decisions with the true movers of the market. This chapter provides a detailed roadmap for recognizing, interpreting, and trading in sync with these manipulative actions, offering practical insights for building higher-probability setups while avoiding common pitfalls.

8.1 Stop Hunts and Liquidity Sweeps

One of the most powerful and frequently observed techniques employed by institutional traders is the **stop hunt** or **liquidity sweep**. Understanding this concept is essential for aligning retail trading strategies with the actions of smart money. Stop hunts occur when large players intentionally push the price to trigger stop-loss orders clustered around obvious levels, creating liquidity that institutions can use to enter or exit positions efficiently.

Mechanics of Stop Hunts

Stop hunts exploit the behavior of retail traders who typically place stop-loss orders around key support and resistance levels, previous swing highs/lows, or psychologically round numbers. When enough stops are accumulated, institutions move the market to trigger these orders:

- Retail traders' stop orders provide instant liquidity for institutions.
- Price temporarily moves against the prevailing trend to absorb this liquidity.
- Once stops are cleared, institutions reverse the price, capturing the larger move in the intended direction.

This mechanism is not random—it is a deliberate orchestration of market structure and psychology. By creating liquidity in predictable areas, institutions can enter positions at optimal levels with minimal slippage and maximum efficiency.

Liquidity Sweeps

Figure 8.1: Liquidity Sweep (LS): A strong move that briefly penetrates a previous high or low (a liquidity pool) with a wick before closing back inside, indicating a clear manipulation event prior to a reversal.

A **liquidity sweep** is closely related to stop hunts. It occurs when institutions target clusters of pending orders, which often include:

- Stop-loss orders above/below swing highs and lows.
- Limit orders placed at obvious breakout levels.
- Marginal retail positions at support/resistance zones.

The sweep temporarily pushes the price beyond these zones, triggering orders and creating a liquidity pool. Once the sweep is complete, the market reverses sharply, following the institutional bias. Recognizing these sweeps allows traders to avoid being "stopped out" prematurely and even position themselves to trade with the momentum that follows.

Identifying Stop Hunts and Liquidity Sweeps

- Look for sudden price spikes against the trend with quick reversion afterward.
- Monitor higher timeframe levels where retail stops are likely clustered.
- Observe wicks beyond support/resistance that do not break the overall trend—these often indicate liquidity sweeps rather than genuine reversals.
- Combine with SMC tools such as order blocks, liquidity pools, and fair value gaps to identify high-probability reaction zones.

Trading the Concept

1. **Wait for Confirmation:** Do not enter trades immediately during a sweep. Allow price to confirm the reversal or rejection from the liquidity zone.
2. **Align with Institutional Bias:** Ensure the overall trend and higher timeframe bias support the trade direction.
3. **Use Tight Risk Management:** Place stops logically beyond OBs or liquidity clusters to avoid being caught in noise.
4. **Capture Momentum:** Once the liquidity sweep completes, look for impulsive moves that provide favorable risk-to-reward trades.

Example Scenario

Consider a bullish market on the 4-hour timeframe with a recent swing low at 1.2000. Retail traders place stop-loss orders slightly below at 1.1980. Institutions push price down to 1.1975, triggering these stops and creating liquidity. Immediately after absorbing these orders, price reverses sharply upward, resuming the bullish trend. A trader who identifies this sweep and enters long near 1.1980 captures the move with minimal slippage and optimal position sizing.

Key Takeaways

- Stop hunts and liquidity sweeps are deliberate institutional techniques to capture liquidity efficiently.
- Retail traders often become victims due to predictable stop placement.
- Recognizing these maneuvers allows traders to avoid premature exits and even enter trades in alignment with institutional activity.
- Combining this knowledge with order blocks, fair value gaps, and market structure increases probability and confidence in trade decisions.

Mastering the identification and interpretation of stop hunts and liquidity sweeps is a critical skill for any trader aiming to think like institutions. It transforms what appears to be erratic market behavior into actionable, high-probability opportunities aligned with the flow of smart money.

8.2 Fake Breakouts and False Structure Shifts

Markets are designed to test and exploit the psychology of traders. One of the most common methods institutions use to manipulate retail traders is through **fake breakouts** and **false structure shifts**. These maneuvers can trap traders into poor entries, induce losses, and provide liquidity for larger players to execute their orders.

Fake Breakouts

A **fake breakout** occurs when price briefly breaches a key support or resistance level, only to reverse sharply in the opposite direction. Retail traders often interpret this as a genuine breakout and enter positions, while institutions use these moments to:

- Trigger stop-loss orders clustered around obvious levels.
- Accumulate or distribute positions at more favorable prices.
- Induce liquidity and create the illusion of trend continuation.

Identification of Fake Breakouts:

- Price breaches a major level (support/resistance) but lacks follow-through on higher timeframes.
- Sharp rejection candles or long wicks appear immediately after the breakout.
- Confluence with order blocks or liquidity pools indicates institutional absorption.

False Structure Shifts

A **false structure shift** occurs when price appears to break market structure (e.g., making a new high in a downtrend or a new low in an uptrend) but quickly reverses, returning to the original trend. These shifts are often used to:

- Shake out weak retail positions.
- Create liquidity for institutional entries or exits.
- Test supply and demand zones for absorption.

Example: In a bullish market, price makes a sudden lower low on the 1-hour chart, leading retail traders to short aggressively. Immediately afterward, price reverses strongly, absorbing these short positions, and continues the uptrend. This false shift allows institutions to enter long positions at optimal prices.

Trading Strategies Against Fakes

1. **Wait for Confirmation:** Avoid entering immediately on a breakout. Wait for rejection candles, retests, or confluence with higher timeframe zones.
2. **Align with Institutional Bias:** Analyze the overall trend and higher timeframe order blocks before trading the breakout.
3. **Use Liquidity Zones:** Identify where liquidity is likely to be swept. Trade after absorption, not during it.
4. **Tight Stops:** Place stop-loss orders logically beyond the order block or structural swing points to avoid being caught in fakes.

Practical Example

Consider a resistance zone at 1.3200 in an uptrend. Price breaches briefly to 1.3220, triggering retail stop orders. Institutions absorb these orders and reverse the price back to 1.3180, forming a rejection wick. Traders who recognize this as a fake breakout can enter long at 1.3180 with stops below the previous swing low, aligning with the institutional bias.

Key Takeaways

- Fake breakouts and false structure shifts are deliberate market manipulations to capture liquidity.
- Retail traders are often trapped due to predictable behaviors and poorly placed stops.

- Recognizing these setups allows traders to avoid premature entries, identify high-probability zones, and trade in harmony with institutional flows.

- Combining these insights with OBs, liquidity pools, and market structure analysis increases trade confidence and probability.

Understanding fake breakouts and false structure shifts equips traders to interpret market behavior more accurately, transforming deceptive movements into actionable trading opportunities aligned with the flow of smart money.

8.3 Smart Money Traps (SMT) in Depth

Smart Money Traps (SMT) are a cornerstone concept in institutional trading behavior. They occur when price action is deliberately designed to mislead retail traders into poor positions, creating liquidity for institutional players. Understanding SMT is essential for anticipating market moves, avoiding common retail pitfalls, and trading in alignment with Smart Money Concepts (SMC).

Definition of SMT

A Smart Money Trap is a scenario where price appears to behave in one direction, often suggesting a breakout, breakdown, or trend continuation, but in reality, it is engineered by institutions to trap retail participants. The goal is to:

- Capture stop-loss orders from retail traders.

- Accumulate or distribute positions at optimal prices.

- Create liquidity to facilitate large trades with minimal market impact.

SMTs exploit human psychology—retail traders' fear of missing out (FOMO), overconfidence, and tendency to follow obvious support/resistance levels.

Types of Smart Money Traps

1. **Stop-Loss Traps:** Institutions push price beyond obvious support/resistance to trigger retail stops, then reverse the market in their favor.

2. **Liquidity Grab Traps:** Price is moved toward clusters of pending orders (limits, stops) to collect liquidity before resuming the primary trend.

3. **False Breakout/Breakdown Traps:** Price briefly breaks key levels, luring retail traders into positions, only to reverse back into the main trend.

4. **Structural Traps:** Occur when price appears to shift market structure (e.g., a swing high is broken), tricking traders into premature entries or exits.

Mechanics of SMT

SMTs rely on the interplay between retail behavior, market structure, and institutional positioning:

- **Phase 1: Accumulation of Retail Orders** Retail traders cluster orders at obvious levels—e.g., round numbers, previous swing highs/lows, or trendline supports.
- **Phase 2: Liquidity Creation** Institutions manipulate price to trigger these clustered orders, creating the liquidity needed to enter or exit large positions.
- **Phase 3: Reversal** Once liquidity is captured, price moves in the intended institutional direction, often with strong momentum.

Identifying SMT in Charts

Recognition of Smart Money Traps requires careful observation and understanding of market structure:

- Look for sudden spikes or wicks that exceed key levels without follow-through.
- Compare with higher timeframe trends; SMT often occurs as temporary counter-moves against the prevailing bias.
- Check for alignment with order blocks, liquidity pools, and fair value gaps to identify likely trap zones.
- Observe the speed and volume of the move—sharp, impulsive moves followed by a swift reversal often indicate institutional activity.

Practical Trading Strategies Using SMT

1. **Wait for Confirmation:** Avoid entering trades during the trap itself. Enter after price shows clear rejection or confirmation from key zones.
2. **Align with Higher Timeframe Bias:** Ensure that the trade direction aligns with the primary trend or institutional bias.
3. **Position Sizing and Risk Management:** Place stops beyond the liquidity zone or order block to avoid being caught in trap noise.
4. **Use Multi-Timeframe Analysis:** Confirm trap signals on lower timeframes while validating bias on higher timeframes.

5. **Targeting Exits:** Use previous swing highs/lows, liquidity clusters, or Fibonacci extensions to plan profit-taking in coordination with trap behavior.

Example Scenario

Consider a bullish trend where price recently made a swing high at 1.3200. Retail traders place stops above this level at 1.3220. Institutions push price to 1.3230, triggering these stops. Immediately afterward, price reverses and continues the primary uptrend, leaving trapped retail sellers and capturing liquidity for institutional long positions. Traders who recognize the SMT can enter at 1.3210–1.3220 with confirmation candles and align risk appropriately.

Key Takeaways

- Smart Money Traps are deliberate manipulations to create liquidity and mislead retail traders.
- Recognizing SMT allows traders to avoid being trapped and to trade with institutional flow.
- Use market structure, order blocks, liquidity pools, and higher time-frame context to identify high-probability trap zones.
- Patience, confirmation, and disciplined risk management are critical when trading around SMT zones.

Mastering the identification and interpretation of Smart Money Traps empowers traders to see beyond retail patterns and align their strategies with the true movers of the market. This understanding transforms deceptive price action into high-probability trading opportunities.

8.4 Order Flow Manipulation Techniques

Order flow manipulation is a core tactic employed by institutional traders to control market movements and generate liquidity. Unlike retail traders who often react to price, institutions can actively shape price behavior by managing how orders are executed, absorbed, and distributed. Understanding these techniques allows traders to anticipate market moves rather than react to them blindly.

What is Order Flow Manipulation?

Order flow manipulation occurs when large players deliberately influence the execution of buy and sell orders in the market. By controlling the placement, timing, and absorption of these orders, institutions can:

- Create artificial price movements to trigger retail stops.
- Accumulate or distribute positions at optimal prices.
- Mask true market direction until sufficient liquidity is gathered.

The goal is to move the market efficiently while minimizing slippage and maximizing profit.

Common Techniques of Order Flow Manipulation

1. **Stop-Loss Sweeps:** Pushing price beyond obvious support/resistance levels to trigger retail stops and capture liquidity.
2. **False Breakouts and Breakdowns:** Creating temporary moves beyond key levels to induce retail entries or exits before reversing toward the institutional bias.
3. **Liquidity Pools Targeting:** Institutions identify areas with a concentration of pending orders and push price toward these zones to absorb liquidity.
4. **Layered Orders:** Placing multiple limit orders at staggered levels to create a perception of buying or selling pressure.
5. **Order Absorption:** Absorbing large market orders by using hidden liquidity, allowing institutions to enter or exit positions without causing significant price impact.

Identifying Manipulated Order Flow

While retail traders do not have direct access to institutional order books, several clues help identify manipulation:

- Rapid, sharp moves that reverse quickly near key levels.
- Price behavior inconsistent with higher timeframe trends.
- Large wicks or spikes without follow-through.
- Confluence with known liquidity zones, OBs, or fair value gaps.
- Volume anomalies indicating absorption or sudden execution of large orders.

Trading Strategies Using Order Flow Insight

1. **Trade with the Bias:** Align trades with higher timeframe institutional bias. Avoid fighting sudden spikes caused by manipulation.

2. **Wait for Confirmation:** Do not enter trades immediately on sudden price movements. Wait for rejections or confirmations within liquidity zones or order blocks.

3. **Position Sizing:** Adjust position size to account for potential volatility during manipulated moves.

4. **Use Confluence Zones:** Combine multiple SMC tools (OBs, liquidity pools, FVGs) to confirm high-probability setups.

5. **Partial Profit-Taking and Trailing Stops:** Lock in gains while allowing positions to benefit from the institutional trend continuation.

Practical Example

Consider a downtrend on the 4-hour chart, with price approaching a swing low at 1.2000. Retail traders place stops at 1.2020. Institutions push price to 1.2030, triggering these stops and absorbing liquidity. Price then reverses to continue the primary downtrend. By analyzing the move in conjunction with order blocks and liquidity pools, a trader can enter short positions at 1.2025 with a stop above the liquidity cluster, capturing the institutional flow.

Key Takeaways

- Order flow manipulation is a deliberate institutional strategy to move markets efficiently.

- Recognizing manipulated flows allows traders to avoid retail traps and enter trades aligned with smart money.

- Combining order flow analysis with SMC tools enhances trade probability and reduces risk.

- Patience and disciplined execution are essential—enter trades after confirmation, not during the manipulated moves.

Mastering order flow manipulation techniques provides traders with a critical edge. By observing how liquidity is gathered, stops are targeted, and market structure is exploited, traders can anticipate moves, avoid traps, and position themselves in alignment with the true market movers.

8.5 Anticipating Institutional Moves

Understanding the mechanics of stop hunts, liquidity sweeps, fake breakouts, Smart Money Traps (SMT), and order flow manipulation allows traders to anticipate institutional moves rather than merely react. This section explains how to synthesize these concepts into actionable insights and high-probability trading strategies.

The Importance of Anticipation

Retail traders often follow price, entering positions too late or exiting prematurely. Institutions, in contrast, plan moves in advance based on liquidity, market structure, and order flow. Anticipating institutional moves involves:

- Identifying potential liquidity zones where stops and limit orders are clustered.
- Recognizing order blocks and fair value gaps as areas of institutional interest.
- Observing price behavior that may indicate traps or manipulations.

By thinking ahead, traders can position themselves on the "right side of the market," aligning with the smart money rather than fighting it.

Step 1: Analyze Higher Timeframe Bias

Higher timeframes provide the context for institutional behavior:

- Identify the primary trend and key support/resistance levels.
- Highlight significant order blocks and liquidity pools.
- Note swing highs and lows that may act as stop clusters or target zones.

Anticipating moves begins with understanding where institutions are likely to accumulate or distribute positions.

Step 2: Map Liquidity Zones and Order Blocks

Combining order blocks with liquidity zones gives insight into where price might react:

- **Bullish zones:** Look for OBs below price with liquidity clusters around recent swing lows.
- **Bearish zones:** Look for OBs above price with liquidity around swing highs.

- **Fair value gaps (FVGs):** Mark areas where price moved impulsively, leaving gaps that institutions often revisit for liquidity absorption.

These areas act as magnets for price and provide high-probability entry points.

Step 3: Watch for Stop Hunts and SMT

Monitor price action near identified liquidity zones:

- Sudden spikes or wicks indicate stop hunts.
- Counter-trend moves may signal Smart Money Traps designed to mislead retail traders.
- Observe volume patterns to confirm institutional participation.

These setups often precede strong impulsive moves in the institutional direction.

Step 4: Confirm with Multi-Timeframe Analysis

Lower timeframes help refine entries:

- Look for OTE (Optimal Trade Entry) zones, breaker blocks, and retests of order blocks.
- Confirm that lower timeframe price action aligns with the higher timeframe bias.
- Watch for rejection candles, engulfing patterns, or other confirmation signals.

Step 5: Plan Entry, Stop, and Target

Use SMC tools to structure the trade:

- Enter near liquidity or OB confluence zones after confirmation.
- Place stop-loss orders logically beyond OBs or liquidity clusters to avoid being caught in traps.
- Set targets using swing highs/lows, liquidity clusters, or Fibonacci extensions.
- Consider partial profit-taking and trailing stops to optimize risk-to-reward.

Practical Example

Consider a market in an uptrend on the daily chart. A swing low at 1.2000 acts as a liquidity zone, with an OB identified at 1.2010–1.2030. Retail traders place stops below 1.2000. Observing a brief stop hunt to 1.1995, the price absorbs retail stops and reverses. Lower timeframe charts show a bullish retest candle at the OB + FVG confluence. Entering at 1.2020 with a stop below 1.1995 allows capturing the subsequent institutional push toward 1.2150, aligning perfectly with institutional strategy.

Key Takeaways

- Anticipating institutional moves requires synthesis of SMC tools: order blocks, liquidity zones, fair value gaps, SMT, and order flow analysis.
- Always start with higher timeframe context to understand institutional bias.
- Watch for stop hunts, traps, and liquidity sweeps as prelude to strong moves.
- Confirm entries on lower timeframes using retests, OTE, and rejection patterns.
- Proper risk management—stop placement, position sizing, and profit-taking—is crucial for trading in alignment with institutional flow.

By systematically anticipating institutional moves, traders shift from reactive, emotion-driven trading to strategic, high-probability decision-making, effectively trading alongside the smart money rather than against it.

8.6 Liquidity Inducement Model

A core principle in Smart Money Concepts (SMC) and ICT methodology is that the market often moves in the **wrong direction first** before delivering the real move. This behavior is not random. It is engineered by institutional algorithms to create the liquidity needed to execute large orders efficiently. This engineered process is known as the **Liquidity Inducement Model (LIM)**.

Liquidity inducement refers to the deliberate creation of structural patterns or price movements that *induce* traders into taking positions prematurely or in the wrong direction. The resulting accumulation of stop-losses and open positions becomes a liquidity source for institutions.

Why Liquidity Inducement Exists

Institutions cannot execute multi-million or multi-billion dollar positions without sufficient opposing orders. To ensure liquidity availability, institutional algorithms:

- manipulate price to lure traders into the market,
- generate false structural signals,
- accumulate stop-loss orders around engineered swing points,
- create visually convincing patterns of continuation or reversal.

Inducement is not a failure of technical analysis; it is a **necessary precursor** to institutional execution.

How Inducement Fits Into the Algorithmic Cycle

Liquidity inducement typically follows a consistent sequence:

1. Creation of an inducement structure (micro highs/lows, equal highs/lows, trendline touches).
2. Retail traders enter trades or place stop-losses near these levels.
3. Liquidity accumulates above or below the inducement zone.
4. The algorithm sweeps the inducement to capture liquidity.
5. True displacement begins in the intended direction.

This cycle ensures that institutions obtain the liquidity required for efficient market participation.

Forms of Liquidity Inducement

Inducement manifests in several recurring patterns:

1. Micro Highs and Micro Lows

Small swing points created immediately before the true entry zone. These attract:

- breakout traders,
- counter-trend traders,
- retail traders placing tight stops.

2. Relative Equal Highs and Lows

Engineered equal highs/lows create clusters of stop-losses. They serve both as liquidity targets and inducement traps.

3. Trendline Inducement

Each touch of a trendline encourages traders to enter with tight stops. The algorithm later sweeps both sides of the trendline before displacement.

4. Fake CHoCH or BOS

A minor internal structural break against the prevailing trend induces premature entries. After liquidity builds around the fake structure, the algorithm reverses sharply.

5. Shallow FVG Taps

A small mitigation into a Fair Value Gap lures traders into entering early. Price later returns deeper into the true Order Block.

Psychology Behind Inducement

Inducement exploits predictable retail behavior:

- chasing early reversals,
- entering at "strong" support or resistance,
- using tight stop-losses,
- reacting emotionally to small structural shifts.

The algorithm designs inducement patterns to create confidence and attract participation at the wrong moment.

How To Identify Liquidity Inducement

Several signals help identify inducement before it traps traders:

- A newly formed swing point directly ahead of an expected OB or FVG entry.
- Equal highs/lows near a key liquidity zone.
- A minor CHoCH forming during a pullback against HTF bias.
- A rapid rejection from a level that appears "too obvious."
- Internal structure forming inducement peaks before displacement.

Once identified, traders should **avoid entering** and instead anticipate a sweep of the inducement.

Trading the Liquidity Inducement Model

A high-probability trading approach using inducement follows these steps:

1. Recognize Inducement

Identify the inducement structure near the anticipated entry zone.

2. Wait for the Sweep

The algorithm must run above the inducement high (for shorts) or below the inducement low (for longs).

3. Confirm With CHoCH and Displacement

A meaningful CHoCH and FVG show institutional intent.

4. Enter at the Mitigating Order Block

Execution occurs when price returns to the refined OB inside the displacement leg.

Common Mistakes Traders Make

Retail traders often fall into inducement traps because they:

- enter trades as soon as price touches a support or resistance level,
- assume equal highs/lows are strong reversal points,
- take CHoCH signals without waiting for displacement,
- trade trendline touches without considering liquidity pools,
- place stop-losses in predictable locations.

Inducement explains why retail strategies fail consistently: they were never designed to withstand institutional liquidity engineering.

Summary

- Liquidity inducement is the algorithmic process of creating liquidity before a major move.
- Inducement forms through engineered highs/lows, trendlines, equal levels, and fake structural breaks.
- The sweep of inducement precedes true displacement, confirming institutional intent.

- Traders should wait for the sweep, CHoCH, and displacement before seeking OB entries.
- Mastering inducement improves precision, avoids traps, and aligns trading with institutional behavior.

Understanding the Liquidity Inducement Model transforms how traders perceive manipulation and helps them anticipate institutional execution with far greater accuracy.

Chapter 9

Mitigation & Optimal Trade Setups

Trading with Smart Money Concepts is not only about identifying where institutions are likely to act, but also about recognizing areas where prior moves have created structural inefficiencies and opportunities for high-probability entries. This chapter focuses on **mitigation blocks**, **liquidity reset zones**, and advanced techniques for combining order blocks, fair value gaps, and liquidity clusters to craft optimal trade setups.

Institutions rarely enter positions randomly—they often mitigate prior imbalances, fill gaps left by impulsive moves, and seek to capture liquidity efficiently. Understanding these mitigation behaviors allows traders to anticipate where price is likely to pause, reverse, or accelerate. By studying past institutional footprints and combining them with SMC tools, traders can construct trades that maximize reward while minimizing risk.

9.1 Mitigation Blocks and Liquidity Reset Zones

In institutional trading, price rarely moves in a perfectly smooth trend. Impulsive moves often leave inefficiencies, unfilled orders, or "gaps" in market structure. Institutions frequently return to these areas to mitigate risk, absorb remaining liquidity, or rebalance positions. Understanding **mitigation blocks** and **liquidity reset zones** is crucial for aligning trades with smart money behavior.

Definition of Mitigation Blocks

A **mitigation block** is an area where price previously moved impulsively, leaving orders unfilled or creating an imbalance between supply and demand. Institutions often revisit these zones to:

- Absorb residual liquidity.
- Re-enter positions at more favorable levels.
- Reduce risk from previous trades or large directional moves.

These zones are typically identifiable as previous order blocks or areas where price reacted strongly and left a visible footprint of institutional activity.

Liquidity Reset Zones

Liquidity reset zones are areas where accumulated stops, pending orders, or unfilled positions exist. They act as magnets for price when institutions need to capture liquidity efficiently. Key characteristics include:

- Occur near swing highs or lows, round numbers, or previous structural extremes.
- Often coincide with prior order blocks or fair value gaps.
- Price may "sweep" through these zones quickly before reversing, reflecting the liquidity grab.

Identification Techniques

Traders can identify mitigation and liquidity reset zones by:

1. **Analyzing previous order blocks:** Look for strong bullish or bearish reactions where price moved impulsively.
2. **Spotting unfilled gaps:** Fair value gaps and sudden wicks indicate areas where liquidity remains unabsorbed.
3. **Using higher timeframe context:** Zones on daily or 4-hour charts often have greater significance than those on lower timeframes.
4. **Observing liquidity clusters:** Swing highs/lows, round numbers, and stop-loss concentrations often overlap with reset zones.

Trading Strategies Around Mitigation Zones

- **Wait for Retest:** Enter trades when price revisits a mitigation block or liquidity reset zone and shows signs of rejection.
- **Confluence with OB/FVG:** Ensure the zone aligns with an order block or fair value gap to increase probability.
- **Proper Stop Placement:** Place stops beyond the mitigation zone to avoid being caught in temporary sweeps.
- **Risk-to-Reward Alignment:** Target price moves toward the next structural level or liquidity cluster, optimizing risk-to-reward.

Practical Example

Consider a bullish impulse that moved from 1.2000 to 1.2150, leaving a fair value gap between 1.2050–1.2070. Retail traders may have placed buy orders above 1.2070, and stops below 1.2050. Institutions often revisit this zone to absorb liquidity, mitigate risk, and prepare for continuation. A trader recognizing this mitigation zone can enter long near 1.2055–1.2060 with stops below 1.2045, riding the next leg toward 1.2150 with high-probability alignment with institutional flow.

Key Takeaways

- Mitigation blocks and liquidity reset zones reveal where institutions are likely to act.
- These zones provide high-probability areas for trade entry with defined risk.
- Combining mitigation zones with other SMC tools—OBs, FVGs, and liquidity clusters—increases precision and trade confidence.
- Patience, confirmation, and disciplined execution are essential when trading around these zones.

Mastering mitigation blocks and liquidity reset zones transforms the way traders approach the market, turning reactive trading into strategic, institution-aligned decision-making.

9.2 Breaker Blocks & Retest Strategies

Breaker Blocks are one of the most powerful tools in Smart Money Concepts (SMC) trading, combining market structure shifts with institutional footprints to highlight high-probability trade setups. When paired with retest strategies, they allow traders to enter trades in alignment with the dominant institutional bias while minimizing risk and optimizing reward.

Definition of Breaker Blocks

A **breaker block** is a previously established order block that has been broken and then retested as a support or resistance level. Essentially, the role of the block flips:

- A **bullish breaker block** forms when a bearish order block is broken by upward momentum and then retested as support.
- A **bearish breaker block** forms when a bullish order block is broken by downward momentum and then retested as resistance.

Breaker blocks represent areas where institutions have absorbed opposing liquidity and are likely to continue the dominant move after a retest.

Mechanics of Breaker Blocks

1. **Initial Impulse:** Price breaks through a prior order block or structural level with strong momentum.
2. **Mitigation of Liquidity:** Institutions absorb residual liquidity and stop orders around the broken block.
3. **Retest:** Price revisits the broken block, now acting as a support (bullish) or resistance (bearish).
4. **Continuation:** Price reacts to the retest and continues in the direction of the institutional bias.

Identifying High-Probability Breaker Blocks

To recognize effective breaker blocks:

- Look for strong breaks of previous order blocks with clear impulsive momentum.
- Identify areas where liquidity has been absorbed (stop-loss clusters, fair value gaps filled).
- Confirm retest patterns on lower timeframes: rejection candles, wicks, or engulfing patterns indicate institutional confirmation.
- Ensure the breaker block aligns with the higher timeframe bias for maximum probability.

Retest Strategies

The retest is the most critical component of a breaker block setup. Traders should consider:

1. **Patience:** Wait for price to fully retest the breaker block and show clear rejection rather than entering immediately after the break.
2. **Confluence:** Combine the retest with other SMC tools such as fair value gaps, liquidity zones, or mitigation blocks.
3. **Entry Triggers:** Use price action signals such as pin bars, engulfing candles, or OTE levels within the breaker block for precise entries.
4. **Stop Placement:** Place stops slightly beyond the breaker block or liquidity clusters to avoid being caught in minor sweeps.

Practical Example

Consider a bearish order block at 1.2200–1.2220. Price breaks above this block impulsively to 1.2280, absorbing liquidity above 1.2220. Later, price retraces and retests the former order block between 1.2200–1.2220, now acting as a support. Observing a bullish rejection candle within this zone, a trader can enter long at 1.2210, place a stop below 1.2195, and target 1.2280–1.2300. This setup aligns perfectly with institutional behavior and provides

9.3 Combining OB + FVG + Liquidity Zones for Precision

While each Smart Money Concept (SMC) tool—Order Blocks (OB), Fair Value Gaps (FVG), and Liquidity Zones—offers individual insights, the highest-probability trades arise when these tools are used in combination. Integrating multiple layers of institutional information increases precision, reduces risk, and aligns trades with the true market movers.

The Principle of Confluence

Confluence occurs when multiple SMC elements converge at a single price zone. Institutions rarely act randomly—they often require liquidity, structural validation, and favorable price levels. By trading in zones where:

- An Order Block indicates previous institutional activity,
- A Fair Value Gap highlights unfilled market inefficiencies, and
- Liquidity clusters or stop-loss concentrations exist,

traders position themselves alongside institutional intent, maximizing the probability of a successful trade.

Step-by-Step Approach

1. **Identify Higher Timeframe OBs:** Locate bullish or bearish order blocks on daily or 4-hour charts that reflect major institutional footprints.

2. **Overlay Fair Value Gaps:** Look for impulsive moves that left gaps within or near the OBs. FVGs indicate unfilled orders and potential areas for price to return.

3. **Mark Liquidity Zones:** Identify swing highs/lows, previous extremes, or round-number levels where retail orders accumulate. These often coincide with OBs and FVGs.

4. **Determine Confluence Zones:** Highlight areas where OB, FVG, and liquidity zones overlap. The more elements that converge, the higher the trade probability.

5. **Wait for Retest & Confirmation:** Monitor lower timeframes for rejection candles, OTE levels, or retests of the confluence zone before entering a trade.

6. **Define Risk & Targets:** Place stops just beyond the confluence zone or liquidity cluster. Set profit targets using the next structural level or liquidity pool.

Practical Example

On a bullish trend in the Forex market:

- Higher timeframe (4H) shows a bullish order block at 1.3050–1.3070.
- A Fair Value Gap exists at 1.3060–1.3075 from a prior impulsive move.
- Liquidity pools are identified around 1.3065, coinciding with previous swing lows.

The confluence of OB + FVG + liquidity zone between 1.3060–1.3070 becomes a high-probability entry zone. Waiting for a lower timeframe bullish retest candle, a trader enters at 1.3065, sets a stop at 1.3045, and targets 1.3150. This trade aligns with institutional intent, optimizes risk-reward, and leverages multiple SMC tools.

Key Takeaways

- Combining OBs, FVGs, and liquidity zones creates precise, high probability trade setups.
- Confluence zones reflect areas of institutional interest where price is likely to react favorably.
- Patience and confirmation are essential—never enter purely on the presence of a confluence zone without validating price action.
- Clear risk management and defined targets transform confluence-based setups into disciplined trades with consistent edge.

By mastering the integration of OBs, FVGs, and liquidity zones, traders move from reactive trading toward a strategic, institution-aligned approach, significantly increasing their probability of success and minimizing unnecessary risk.

9.4 Premium/Discount Logic for Manipulation

A central concept in Smart Money Concepts (SMC) and ICT methodology is the idea that the market trades within two pricing zones relative to a defined range: **premium** and **discount**. These zones are not only used by institutions to determine where to buy or sell, but also to engineer manipulation and inducement.

Understanding how institutional algorithms exploit premium and discount pricing allows traders to avoid false signals, anticipate liquidity sweeps, and align with the true direction of institutional intent.

Defining Premium and Discount

Premium and discount zones are derived from the midpoint (50% level) of a major swing range.

Let:

$$\text{Range High} = H, \quad \text{Range Low} = L$$

$$\text{Equilibrium} = \frac{H + L}{2}$$

Then:

- Price above equilibrium is the **premium zone**.
- Price below equilibrium is the **discount zone**.

Institutions prefer:

- to **sell** at premium,
- to **buy** at discount.

This simple framework becomes the foundation for complex manipulation patterns.

The Role of Premium/Discount in Manipulation

Institutional algorithms use premium and discount levels to:

- engineer inducement before a major move,
- trap traders into poor entries,
- sweep liquidity pools at premium or discount extremes,
- create false structural signals within the wrong pricing zone.

Retail traders often mistake these engineered moves as legitimate breakouts or reversals.

Manipulation in the Premium Zone

When price moves into the premium zone, institutions typically:

- create higher-timeframe or internal bearish setups,
- engineer equal highs or micro highs (liquidity shelves),
- induce breakout buying above swing highs,
- accumulate sell-side liquidity above reaction levels.

Common characteristics of premium manipulation:

- False breakouts above a prior high,
- CHoCH/BOS formed after sweeping liquidity,
- Displacement to the downside after inducement,
- Rapid return into an unmitigated bearish Order Block.

The goal is to entice buyers into paying too high of a price while institutions fill short positions cheaply.

Manipulation in the Discount Zone

In discount zones, price manipulation occurs in reverse:

- engineered equal lows encourage premature selling,
- fake breakdowns entice retail traders to sell the low,
- stop-loss clusters accumulate below the swing,
- price sweeps liquidity and rapidly reverses upward.

Key characteristics of discount manipulation:

- running sell-side liquidity below a swing low,
- bullish CHoCH after the sweep,
- bullish displacement leaving FVGs,
- mitigation into a refined bullish OB.

Here, retail traders sell at the worst price while institutions accumulate long positions at a discount.

Premium/Discount as a Framework for Inducement

Inducement almost always forms near the boundaries of premium or discount.

Examples:

- A swing high forms just under premium to induce breakout buying.
- A small swing low forms near discount as a target for liquidity sweeps.
- Trendline touches near the premium zone create false bullish signals.
- CHoCH or BOS inside premium often acts as a fake reversal.

Institutions exploit the psychological anchor of “cheap” vs “expensive” pricing.

Premium/Discount Combined With Liquidity

The premium/discount framework interacts with liquidity principles as follows:

- **Premium** becomes the zone where buy-side liquidity builds above highs.
- **Discount** becomes the zone where sell-side liquidity builds below lows.

Price naturally gravitates toward these liquidity shelves before reversing.

Thus, premium and discount zones define:

- where liquidity rests,
- where inducement forms,
- where the algorithm performs sweeps,
- where high-probability reversals occur.

Correct Use of Premium/Discount in Trading

A disciplined trader should:

1. Avoid Selling in the Discount Zone

Any bearish signal in discount is likely inducement or manipulation.

2. Avoid Buying in the Premium Zone

Any bullish pattern in premium is likely a trap designed to build liquidity.

3. Wait for the Sweep + CHoCH

Confirmation requires:

- liquidity sweep at premium or discount,
- a CHoCH indicating structural reversal,
- displacement creating an FVG,
- return to the OB for mitigation.

Premium/discount without structural confirmation is incomplete.

Practical Examples of Manipulation

Example 1: Premium Trap

1. Price enters the premium zone of a higher-timeframe range.
2. Retail buys a "breakout" above a previous high.
3. The algorithm sweeps the high.
4. Bearish displacement forms.
5. Price returns to a bearish OB for entry.

Example 2: Discount Trap

1. Price dips below a range low in discount.
2. Retail sells the breakdown.
3. Algorithm sweeps liquidity.
4. Bullish displacement occurs.
5. OB mitigation provides a long entry.

Summary

- Premium and discount zones guide institutional accumulation and distribution.
- Price in premium is more likely to induce liquidity for shorts.
- Price in discount is more likely to induce liquidity for longs.
- Manipulation often forms near zone boundaries as equal highs/lows, fake breakouts, or trendline taps.
- The true move occurs after liquidity inducement, sweep, and displacement.

Premium/discount logic is not only a pricing tool but also a blueprint for recognizing and avoiding institutional manipulation.

9.5 Imbalance Stacking Model

In Smart Money Concepts (SMC) and ICT methodology, imbalances—often identified as **Fair Value Gaps (FVGs)**—represent areas where price moved too quickly because one side of the market dominated liquidity. While a single imbalance can signal institutional displacement, the presence of **multiple imbalances stacked in sequence** provides a much stronger indication of institutional momentum and intent. This concept is known as the **Imbalance Stacking Model**.

The Imbalance Stacking Model is essential for understanding trend continuation, momentum strength, and high-probability entry points within a directional expansion.

What Is an Imbalance?

An imbalance occurs when the market leaves a price range with insufficient trading activity between two consecutive candles. It reflects an aggressive institutional move, typically caused by:

- algorithmic execution of large orders,
- directional liquidity seeking,
- repricing due to a shift in institutional sentiment.

Formally, an FVG is created when:

$$\text{Candle}_1(\text{low}) > \text{Candle}_3(\text{high}) \quad \text{or vice versa}$$

This gap reflects inefficiency that the algorithm may later return to mitigate.

What Is Imbalance Stacking?

Imbalance stacking occurs when multiple consecutive displacement legs leave behind a series of imbalances, each partially or completely unmitigated. These stacked imbalances signal:

- strong directional conviction,
- institutional dominance over the opposing liquidity,
- a multi-stage repricing event,
- reduced likelihood of deep pullbacks.

Stacked imbalances create a roadmap of institutional activity and serve as dynamic support/resistance zones.

Why Institutions Create Stacked Imbalances

Institutional algorithms create stacked imbalances when they must:

- move price rapidly toward a liquidity target,
- outrun opposing order flow,
- reprice to a new valuation level,
- capitalize on high-impact news or economic events,
- exploit retail attempts to fade the move.

Multiple imbalances indicate that the market is in a **repricing phase** rather than a simple correction or continuation.

Types of Imbalance Stacking

There are several forms of imbalance stacking used in institutional analysis:

1. Vertical Stacking

Multiple FVGs form one after another in a straight impulsive leg. This typically indicates:

- a powerful trend,
- institutional urgency,
- minimal retracement opportunities.

2. Layered Stacking (Stair-Step Imbalances)

Imbalances form with small pauses in between, producing a stair-step structure. Each pause often forms:

- a small internal consolidation,
- minor BOS signals,
- refined OBs before another impulse.

3. Overlapping Stacking

When one imbalance partially overlaps another, signaling heavy order flow. This structure often leads to:

- shallow pullbacks,
- aggressive continuation,
- reduced likelihood of deep OB mitigation.

How to Use Imbalance Stacking in Trading

Imbalance stacking provides multiple advantages for identifying directional intent and entry refinement.

1. Identifying Trend Strength

The more imbalances present in a sequence:

- the stronger the trend,
- the more committed institutions are,
- the less likely a reversal becomes without a major liquidity event.

2. Defining High-Probability Entry Zones

Stacked imbalances often serve as:

- retracement targets,
- mitigation levels,
- continuation zones.

When price retraces, it often reacts at:

- the first unmitigated imbalance,
- the midpoint of stacked imbalances,
- the OB that caused the first imbalance.

3. Measuring Displacement Quality

A single imbalance may be caused by short-term volatility. Stacking imbalances confirm:

- real displacement,
- institutional participation,
- sustained repricing.

Stacking Model: Bullish and Bearish Logic

Bullish Imbalance Stacking

In a bullish context:

1. Price sweeps sell-side liquidity.
2. Bullish CHoCH occurs.

3. Bullish displacement produces multiple FVGs.
4. Price retraces into a refined OB or unmitigated FVG.
5. Continuation occurs toward buy-side liquidity.

Bearish Imbalance Stacking

In a bearish context:

1. Price sweeps buy-side liquidity.
2. Bearish CHoCH is formed.
3. Bearish displacement creates stacked imbalances.
4. Price retraces into the bearish OB above.
5. Continuation moves toward sell-side liquidity.

Interpreting Stacked Imbalances as Support or Resistance

Stacked imbalances act as dynamic support and resistance zones:

- Bullish stacks become support zones on retracement.
- Bearish stacks become resistance zones on pullback.

The more imbalances stacked:

- the stronger the zone,
- the more likely price will respect the area.

Common Mistakes When Using Imbalance Stacking

Retail traders often:

- assume every imbalance will be filled immediately,
- ignore the context of displacement,
- misinterpret single imbalances as trend strength,
- take entries inside stacks without CHoCH confirmation,
- overlook the role of OBs in validating stacked FVGs.

Imbalance stacking is not a standalone signal—it must be paired with:

- liquidity analysis,
- CHoCH/BOS,
- refined OBs,
- time-of-day context.

Summary

- Imbalance stacking occurs when multiple FVGs form in sequence during strong displacement.
- Stacked imbalances reflect institutional dominance and repricing behavior.
- They provide reliable continuation zones and help filter high-quality entries.
- Stacking must be interpreted within liquidity and structure context.
- Mastering the Imbalance Stacking Model enhances precision in identifying strong trends and high-probability retracement zones.

The Imbalance Stacking Model is a powerful lens for reading institutional momentum and anticipating continuation in both bullish and bearish market environments.

Chapter 10

Confluence & High-Probability Trades

Trading is as much an art of synthesis as it is an analysis of individual signals. While understanding Smart Money Concepts (SMC) like Order Blocks (OB), Fair Value Gaps (FVG), and liquidity zones provides traders with powerful tools, the true edge comes from combining these signals into a cohesive framework. This is the principle of **confluence**—layering multiple signals to increase the probability of success and align trades with institutional behavior.

10.1 Layering Signals: Market Structure + OB + FVG + Liquidity Pools

Layering multiple Smart Money Concepts (SMC) signals is the essence of high-probability trading. Individual signals such as Order Blocks (OB), Fair Value Gaps (FVG), or liquidity pools may provide an edge, but their predictive power increases exponentially when combined with market structure analysis. This section explores how traders can synthesize these signals to align with institutional behavior and identify zones where price is most likely to react favorably.

The Role of Market Structure

Market structure sets the context for all trades. Understanding whether the market is in an uptrend, downtrend, or range allows traders to determine the dominant bias. For example:

- In an **uptrend**, bullish order blocks and fair value gaps that align with higher lows serve as potential entry zones.

- In a **downtrend**, bearish OBs and gaps near swing highs become high-probability short opportunities.
- In a **sideways market**, liquidity pools near support and resistance extremes offer controlled, range-bound setups.

By analyzing structure first, traders avoid taking trades against the dominant institutional flow and significantly improve the probability of success.

Integrating Order Blocks (OBs)

Order blocks represent areas where institutions accumulated positions. Layering OBs with market structure helps traders:

- Confirm the validity of swing highs/lows as zones of institutional activity.
- Time entries at levels where price is likely to react after retests.
- Avoid entering trades in weak or broken structural zones.

Fair Value Gaps (FVG) Alignment

FVGs indicate inefficiencies left by impulsive moves. When combined with OBs:

- They highlight unfilled orders that institutions may revisit to complete their positions.
- They provide secondary confirmation of entry zones identified via OBs and market structure.
- Multi-timeframe FVG alignment strengthens the confluence by showing that both lower and higher timeframe inefficiencies exist.

Liquidity Pools Integration

Liquidity pools—concentrated clusters of stop-losses or pending orders—are essential for anticipating institutional moves. Layering liquidity zones with OBs and FVGs helps traders:

- Predict where price is likely to pause, reverse, or accelerate.
- Understand potential stop hunts or sweeps before continuation.
- Improve risk-to-reward by placing stops beyond known liquidity clusters.

Creating High-Probability Confluence Zones

The process of layering signals involves:

1. **Identifying the dominant market structure** on the higher timeframe to determine bias.
2. **Marking Order Blocks** that coincide with the structure and likely institutional activity.
3. **Overlaying Fair Value Gaps** left by impulsive moves within or near the OBs.
4. **Locating Liquidity Pools** such as swing highs/lows, round numbers, or stop clusters.
5. **Highlighting Confluence Zones** where OB + FVG + liquidity align with the structural bias.
6. **Waiting for confirmation** on lower timeframes—rejection candles, OTE levels, or retests—before entry.

Practical Example

Consider a bullish trend in EUR/USD:

- Market structure shows higher highs and higher lows on the 4-hour chart.
- A bullish order block exists at 1.1200–1.1210.
- A fair value gap from a previous impulsive move resides at 1.1205–1.1215.
- Liquidity pool identified near 1.1208 (previous swing low and stop cluster).

The convergence of these signals creates a high-probability entry zone between 1.1205–1.1210. Waiting for a lower timeframe bullish retest candle, a trader can enter with confidence, set stops below 1.1195, and target the next structural high around 1.1280.

Key Takeaways

- Layering multiple SMC signals enhances precision and increases the probability of trade success.
- Market structure provides context; OBs indicate institutional footprints; FVGs show inefficiencies; liquidity pools highlight potential reaction zones.

- High-probability trades emerge when all these elements converge and align with institutional bias.
- Patience and confirmation on lower timeframes are critical—confluence without validation can still result in false entries.

By mastering the art of layering signals, traders shift from reactive trading to strategic, institution-aligned decision-making, significantly improving consistency and long-term profitability.

10.2 Time-of-Day Bias (London/New York Sessions)

In addition to understanding market structure and confluence, timing is a crucial factor in high-probability trading. The Forex, commodities, and indices markets are not equally active throughout the 24-hour cycle. Institutional participation, volatility, and liquidity vary depending on the session, creating **time-of-day biases** that traders can exploit. Among the most significant sessions are the **London** and **New York** sessions, which collectively account for the bulk of daily market volume.

London Session

The London session is the first major European trading session and often sets the tone for the day. Key characteristics include:

- **High liquidity and volatility:** Especially at the session open, price tends to move aggressively, providing opportunities for capturing institutional flows.
- **Overlap with Asia:** Early London overlaps with the tail end of the Asian session, allowing continuation of trends or liquidity sweeps left by Asian traders.
- **Optimal for structural analysis:** Impulsive moves and order block formation are often more reliable due to the participation of major European banks.

New York Session

The New York session overlaps with London for a few hours, creating one of the most active and liquid periods of the day. Key points include:

- **Continuation or reversal of London trends:** Institutions in New York may accelerate moves or trigger retracements depending on liquidity needs.

- **Volatility spikes near news events:** US economic releases frequently occur during this session, creating high-probability setups for liquidity capture.
- **High-probability retest zones:** Breaker blocks, FVGs, and liquidity pools identified during London often get tested or filled during New York.

Applying Time-of-Day Bias to Trading

Traders can increase probability by aligning trades with session-specific characteristics:

1. **Identify confluence zones before the session begins:** Highlight OBs, FVGs, and liquidity clusters on higher timeframes.
2. **Monitor session open reactions:** Price tends to move impulsively in the first hour of London or New York; patience is required to avoid premature entries.
3. **Use overlap periods strategically:** The London/New York overlap often creates explosive moves, ideal for executing trades near confluence zones with strong confirmation.
4. **Avoid low-activity hours:** Late New York or early Asia often see reduced liquidity and increased noise, decreasing trade quality.

Practical Example

Suppose EUR/USD is in a bullish structure on the 4-hour chart, with a confluence zone (OB + FVG + liquidity pool) at 1.1250–1.1260.

- During the London session open, price approaches 1.1255, creating a minor retest of the zone.
- Liquidity above the OB attracts a stop hunt.
- Once the New York session begins, institutional orders accelerate the move upward, confirming the confluence zone and providing a high-probability entry at 1.1255–1.1260.

This approach demonstrates the importance of timing alongside technical confluence,ensuring trades are executed when institutional activity is strongest.

Key Takeaways

- Time-of-day bias significantly affects market behavior and liquidity distribution.

- London and New York sessions provide the highest-probability windows for executing SMC-based trades.
- Aligning confluence zones with session dynamics increases the likelihood of smooth entries, reduced slippage, and more predictable price action.
- Patience and observation of session-specific patterns are essential to avoid premature or low-quality trades.

Mastering time-of-day bias allows traders to layer institutional activity, market structure, and confluence with precise timing, creating trades that are not only high-probability but also optimally executed.

10.3 Multi-Timeframe Confirmation

Multi-timeframe analysis is a cornerstone of professional trading. While a single timeframe may reveal a local bias, higher and lower timeframes provide context, precision, and validation for trade setups. Combining multiple timeframes allows traders to align with institutional intent, filter noise, and execute trades with higher probability.

The Principle of Multi-Timeframe Alignment

Market behavior differs across timeframes. Higher timeframes reflect institutional positioning and broader market trends, while lower timeframes show micro-structure and entry opportunities. Multi-timeframe alignment involves:

- **Higher Timeframe Bias:** Establish the dominant trend or structural bias using daily, 4-hour, or 1-hour charts.
- **Intermediate Timeframe Refinement:** Use 1-hour or 15-minute charts to locate confluence zones, fair value gaps, and liquidity clusters.
- **Lower Timeframe Execution:** Employ 5-minute or 1-minute charts for precise entry timing, observing price action signals such as rejection candles or OTE levels.

Benefits of Multi-Timeframe Confirmation

1. **Enhanced Probability:** Trades aligned with higher timeframe trends are more likely to succeed.
2. **Better Risk Management:** Stops and targets can be placed using structural levels across timeframes, reducing the risk of premature stop-outs.

3. **Noise Reduction:** Lower timeframe fluctuations often mislead traders; multi-timeframe context filters out irrelevant signals.

4. **Clearer Confluence Zones:** Overlapping signals across timeframes create robust zones for high-probability entries.

Practical Example

Consider GBP/USD:

- **Daily Chart (Higher Timeframe):** Shows a bullish order block at 1.3100–1.3120, forming the dominant trend.

- **1-Hour Chart (Intermediate Timeframe):** Reveals a fair value gap at 1.3110–1.3120, overlapping with the OB and a liquidity pool near previous swing lows.

- **5-Minute Chart (Lower Timeframe):** Displays a bullish retest candle at 1.3115, confirming entry precision.

By entering at the lower timeframe confirmation level (1.3115), a trader aligns with higher timeframe bias, targets structural highs, and places stops just below the OB/ liquidity pool. This multi-timeframe approach maximizes probability while controlling risk effectively.

Implementation Tips

- Always start with the higher timeframe to determine trend and institutional bias.

- Use intermediate timeframes to refine entry zones and identify potential confluence areas.

- Reserve lower timeframes solely for precision timing; avoid overanalyzing minor movements that conflict with higher timeframe bias.

- Confirm that all timeframes support the same directional bias before committing capital.

Key Takeaways

- Multi-timeframe confirmation bridges institutional context (higher timeframe) with entry precision (lower timeframe).

- It increases confidence, reduces false entries, and improves the risk-to-reward ratio.

- Combining OBs, FVGs, liquidity zones, and market structure across multiple timeframes creates a disciplined, methodical approach to trading.

Mastering multi-timeframe confirmation enables traders to see the market as institutions see it, aligning structural bias with precise entries for high-probability trades.

10.4 Examples of High-Probability Trades

To fully understand how confluence, session bias, and multi-timeframe analysis combine, it is essential to study real-world trade examples. These examples illustrate how Smart Money Concepts (SMC) and ICT principles guide decision-making, improve trade quality, and increase the probability of success.

Example 1: EUR/USD Bullish Setup

Market Context:

- **Higher Timeframe (4H):** Uptrend confirmed with higher highs and higher lows. Bullish Order Block identified at 1.1200–1.1210.
- **Intermediate Timeframe (1H):** Fair Value Gap between 1.1205–1.1215 overlapping with OB. Liquidity pool identified at 1.1208.
- **Session Bias:** London session open, high liquidity and volatility expected.
- **Lower Timeframe (5M):** Bullish rejection candle forms at 1.1210.

Trade Execution:

- Entry: 1.1210 (after retest confirmation)
- Stop: 1.1195 (below liquidity pool and OB)
- Target: 1.1280 (next structural high)

Analysis: This trade aligns higher timeframe bias with OB + FVG + liquidity confluence, executed during a high-liquidity session, maximizing the probability of success.

Example 2: GBP/USD Bearish Setup

Market Context:

- **Higher Timeframe (Daily):** Downtrend confirmed. Bearish Order Block at 1.3100–1.3120.
- **Intermediate Timeframe (1H):** Fair Value Gap at 1.3110–1.3118 and liquidity pool near prior swing high at 1.3115.

- **Session Bias:** New York session overlapping London, providing liquidity and momentum.
- **Lower Timeframe (5M):** Bearish retest candle forms at 1.3112.

Trade Execution:

- Entry: 1.3112 (after confirmation candle)
- Stop: 1.3130 (above liquidity cluster and OB)
- Target: 1.3050 (next swing low)

Analysis: This short trade demonstrates how aligning structure, OB, FVG, liquidity, and session bias creates a high-probability setup, minimizing risk and enhancing reward.

Example 3: USD/JPY Range-Based Trade

Market Context:

- **Higher Timeframe (4H):** Sideways structure between 148.50–149.20. OB at 149.10–149.15.
- **Intermediate Timeframe (1H):** Liquidity pools identified near swing extremes 148.55 and 149.15.
- **Session Bias:** Late London session, moderate liquidity.
- **Lower Timeframe (5M):** Pin bar rejection at 149.14 near OB and liquidity cluster.

Trade Execution:

- Entry: 149.13 (short after rejection candle)
- Stop: 149.25 (above OB and liquidity cluster)
- Target: 148.55 (lower swing extreme)

Analysis: Even in a range market, combining OB, liquidity zones, and lower timeframe confirmation allows for precise, high-probability trades. Understanding session bias helps avoid trading during low liquidity periods.

Key Takeaways

- High-probability trades are rarely based on a single signal; they emerge from the convergence of multiple SMC elements.
- Aligning trades with higher timeframe bias, session dynamics, and lower timeframe confirmation dramatically improves success rates.

- Risk management—through stops beyond OBs, liquidity clusters, or structural extremes—is critical to protecting capital.
- Studying real examples reinforces the application of theory, helping traders internalize the decision-making process used by institutions.

By practicing these examples and applying the principles of confluence, session bias, and multi-timeframe alignment, traders develop the ability to identify, execute, and manage high-probability trades consistently, moving closer to professional, institution-aligned trading.

10.5 HTF Liquidity Roadmap → LTF Entry

A core strength of Smart Money Concepts (SMC) and ICT methodology is the ability to combine high-timeframe (HTF) liquidity analysis with precise low-timeframe (LTF) execution. Institutions operate across multiple layers of structure simultaneously, but their true objectives are clearest on higher timeframes. The lower timeframes simply offer refined entry opportunities once the higher-timeframe roadmap is understood.

This section outlines how traders can build a **HTF liquidity roadmap** and then translate that bias into high-probability, low-risk entries on lower timeframes.

Why HTF → LTF Analysis Matters

HTF analysis provides:

- the macro directional bias,
- the key liquidity targets,
- the structural context for the day/week,
- clarity on premium vs. discount pricing,
- major OBs, FVGs, and imbalance zones.

LTF analysis provides:

- precision entries,
- tighter risk-to-reward ratios,
- confirmation through displacement,
- refined OB, FVG, and CHoCH signals.

Combining the two produces a framework that mirrors institutional execution.

Step 1: Identify the HTF Liquidity Roadmap

The liquidity roadmap begins on the higher timeframes such as:

- Daily (D1),
- 4-Hour (H4),
- 1-Hour (H1).

On these timeframes, identify:

- external liquidity pools (previous highs/lows),
- internal liquidity clusters,
- unmitigated Order Blocks,
- Fair Value Gaps (FVGs),
- premium/discount arrays,
- major displacement candles,
- macro CHoCH or BOS.

The goal is to determine:

Where is the HTF liquidity target?

Is price seeking buy-side or sell-side liquidity?

This HTF target becomes the directional anchor for all LTF decisions.

Step 2: Determine HTF Bias

Bias is derived from:

- structure direction (HH/HL for bullish, LH/LL for bearish),
- HTF displacement legs,
- the location of price relative to equilibrium (50%),
- HTF OBs and mitigation levels,
- the nearest liquidity target.

Examples:

If HTF is bullish and targeting buy-side liquidity, look only for LTF longs.

If HTF is bearish and targeting sell-side liquidity, look only for LTF shorts.

This prevents countertrend trading and aligns the trader with institutional flow.

Step 3: Drop to LTF for Internal Structure and Confirmation

Once the HTF roadmap is identified, shift to lower timeframes such as:

- M15,
- M5,
- M1.

On LTF charts, seek:

- internal liquidity sweeps,
- refined OBs,
- internal CHoCH,
- displacement with FVGs,
- inducement structures.

The LTF should show:

$$\text{HTF bias} \quad \Rightarrow \quad \text{LTF confirmation and precision entry.}$$

Step 4: Sequence for Execution (HTF $\rightarrow$ LTF)

The ideal execution follows a consistent multi-timeframe sequence:

1. **HTF identifies the liquidity target** (e.g., previous day's high).
2. **HTF structure confirms directional bias.**
3. **HTF OB/FVG defines the higher-timeframe context.**
4. **LTF forms inducement inside premium/discount zone.**
5. **LTF sweeps internal liquidity.**
6. **LTF confirms CHoCH.**
7. **LTF displacement creates FVG.**
8. **LTF retraces to OB/FVG for refined entry.**

This process ensures entries are made **after liquidity is collected** and **after institutions reveal their intent.**

Step 5: Entry Criteria

A valid LTF entry requires all of the following:

- alignment with HTF bias,
- inducement swept,
- LTF CHoCH,
- displacement with clear imbalance,
- retracement into a refined OB or FVG,
- entry at the edge of inefficiency for minimal stop-loss.

This aligns with the refined CHoCH → FVG → OB entry model.

Illustration of HTF → LTF Logic

Bullish Example

1. HTF (H4) shows bullish structure and targets previous week's high.
2. Price enters HTF discount zone.
3. LTF (M5) creates a sweep of internal lows (inducement).
4. LTF CHoCH forms.
5. LTF displacement creates a bullish FVG.
6. Retracement fills the FVG and taps a refined OB.
7. Entry long with target: HTF buy-side liquidity.

Bearish Example

1. HTF (H4) shows bearish trend targeting sell-side liquidity.
2. Price enters HTF premium zone.
3. LTF (M1) sweeps short-term highs (inducement).
4. LTF CHoCH confirms reversal.
5. LTF displacement forms FVG.
6. Retracement returns into refined OB above the FVG.
7. Entry short with target: HTF sell-side liquidity.

Common Mistakes Traders Make

- Taking LTF entries against HTF bias.
- Entering before inducement is swept.
- Trading CHoCH without displacement confirmation.
- Ignoring premium/discount context.
- Using HTF OBs without refining on LTF.
- Entering based on single timeframe signals.

Multi-timeframe alignment is mandatory for consistent results.

Summary

- HTF analysis defines directional bias and liquidity targets.
- LTF analysis provides refined, low-risk entries.
- Inducement must occur before execution.
- Entries require CHoCH → displacement → OB/FVG retracement.
- HTF → LTF alignment prevents countertrend mistakes.
- This framework mirrors institutional algorithmic decision-making.

Mastering the HTF Liquidity Roadmap → LTF Entry model allows traders to operate with institutional precision and avoid common retail traps.

Chapter 11

Advanced Technical Integration

Once a trader has mastered the core Smart Money Concepts—Order Blocks, Fair Value Gaps, Liquidity Zones, and confluence—they gain a strong edge in identifying high-probability setups. However, integrating these concepts with advanced technical tools can further refine entries, optimize risk-to-reward ratios, and provide deeper insight into market dynamics. This chapter explores how traditional technical analysis, when combined with SMC and ICT methodologies, enhances precision and offers a professional-level perspective on market behavior.

11.1 Fibonacci Retracements & Extensions with OB/OTE

Fibonacci tools are widely used in trading due to their ability to highlight potential reversal and continuation zones. When combined with Smart Money Concepts (SMC) and the ICT methodology, Fibonacci retracements and extensions provide a precision layer for trade entries, especially within Order Blocks (OB) and Optimal Trade Entry (OTE) setups.

Understanding Fibonacci Levels

Fibonacci retracement levels (commonly 23.6%, 38.2%, 50%, 61.8%) are used to measure potential pullback areas within a trend, while extensions (127%, 161.8%, 261.8%) identify potential price targets for impulsive moves. Within the context of institutional trading:

- **Retracements** often coincide with OBs or liquidity clusters, indicating high-probability entry zones.

- **Extensions** help forecast target levels based on the measured impulsive move, aligning with structural highs/lows and FVGs.

Optimal Trade Entry (OTE) Integration

OTE is an ICT technique that identifies high-probability entry points within retracement zones. Typically, OTE occurs between the 61.8% and 79% retracement of the previous impulsive swing. When layered with OBs:

- The OB provides institutional footprint confirmation.
- The OTE Fibonacci zone pinpoints the most favorable entry within that OB.
- Lower timeframe price action can be used to fine-tune exact entry levels.

Combining Fibonacci with Order Blocks

Integration involves:

1. Identifying a clear market structure trend (uptrend or downtrend) on a higher timeframe.
2. Locating the nearest bullish or bearish OB that aligns with the structural bias.
3. Measuring the impulsive swing preceding the OB to apply Fibonacci retracement levels.
4. Identifying the OTE zone within the OB and retracement levels for precise entry.
5. Confirming confluence with liquidity pools, FVGs, and session bias before executing.

Practical Example

Suppose EUR/USD is in a bullish structure:

- Higher timeframe OB: 1.1200–1.1210
- Previous impulsive swing: 1.1180–1.1230
- Fibonacci retracement levels applied: 38.2% = 1.1216, 50% = 1.1205, 61.8% = 1.1194
- OTE zone: 61.8%–79% retracement of swing, i.e., 1.1194–1.1200

The OTE zone overlaps with the bullish OB at 1.1200, creating a strong confluence area. Traders can look for lower timeframe confirmation (rejection candle, bullish engulfing) to enter with high probability, set stops just below the OB, and target the next structural high.

Key Considerations

- Always confirm that Fibonacci levels align with OBs, liquidity pools, or FVGs for maximum probability.
- Use higher timeframes for trend and OB identification; lower timeframes for entry precision.
- Remember that Fibonacci levels alone are not sufficient; they gain power only when combined with SMC context.
- Adjust targets based on session bias, risk-to-reward preferences, and volatility conditions.

Integrating Fibonacci retracements and extensions with OBs and OTE zones allows traders to enter trades with precision, minimize risk, and align with institutional behavior, transforming a simple technical tool into a professional-grade trading advantage.

11.2 Harmonic Patterns + SMC Integration

Harmonic patterns are advanced geometric formations in price action that rely on precise Fibonacci relationships to forecast potential reversal or continuation zones. While widely used in technical analysis, their true power emerges when combined with Smart Money Concepts (SMC) and ICT methodologies. This integration allows traders to align pattern-based predictions with institutional footprints, liquidity dynamics, and high-probability entry zones, transforming harmonic patterns from theoretical constructs into actionable trade setups.

Overview of Key Harmonic Patterns

The most commonly used harmonic patterns include:

- **Gartley Pattern:** Typically forms within a retracement of 61.8% of the previous impulse move and signals trend continuation.
- **Bat Pattern:** Characterized by deeper retracements, often around 88.6%, providing strong reversal potential with precision PRZs (Potential Reversal Zones).
- **Butterfly Pattern:** Projects reversals beyond the origin of the prior swing, capturing extreme institutional moves or stop hunts.
- **Crab Pattern:** Identifies extreme extensions and reversals, often coinciding with high liquidity clusters, making it ideal for capturing institutional activity.

Each pattern has specific Fibonacci ratios that define key points (X, A, B, C, D) and structure the PRZ, where price is most likely to react. Understanding these ratios is crucial, but alone they are insufficient for consistently high-probability trades.

Why SMC Integration Matters

Institutions rarely trade purely based on harmonic geometry. They operate around liquidity zones, order blocks, and market structure. Integrating SMC ensures that harmonic patterns:

- **Align with institutional activity:** PRZs that overlap with order blocks or liquidity pools indicate areas where banks and smart money participants are likely to enter.
- **Avoid false signals:** Patterns without confluence from OBs, FVGs, or structural bias often fail due to insufficient institutional participation.
- **Provide higher probability entries:** Layering SMC principles with harmonic PRZs refines entry zones and risk management.

Integrating Harmonics with Key SMC Tools

To maximize the probability of success, harmonic patterns should be evaluated alongside:

1. **Order Blocks (OBs):** Check if the PRZ coincides with a bullish or bearish OB, ensuring institutional alignment.
2. **Liquidity Pools and FVGs:** Confirm the presence of liquidity clusters or Fair Value Gaps, which institutions often target for stop hunts or rapid fills.
3. **Market Structure:** Align patterns with higher timeframe trends and structural bias to trade in the direction of smart money intent.
4. **Session Timing:** Consider time-of-day bias to ensure trades occur during periods of high liquidity and institutional participation.

Practical Example

Consider a bullish Gartley pattern on GBP/USD:

- PRZ: 1.3100–1.3120
- Overlapping bullish OB: 1.3110–1.3120
- Liquidity cluster: 1.3105
- Fair Value Gap: 1.3112–1.3115

The PRZ aligns perfectly with OB, FVG, and liquidity pool, forming a confluence zone. Lower timeframe price action can confirm the entry (e.g., bullish rejection candle), with stop-loss placed just below the OB and liquidity cluster, and profit targets set using previous swing highs or Fibonacci extensions.

Key Takeaways

- Harmonic patterns gain reliability when combined with SMC context OBs, liquidity, FVGs, and market structure.
- Multi-timeframe analysis enhances pattern precision, confirming higher timeframe bias with lower timeframe entry opportunities.
- Risk management is critical: stops should be placed beyond OBs or liquidity clusters, while profit targets consider structural highs/lows and Fibonacci projections.
- Integration of harmonic patterns with SMC transforms geometric structures into professional-grade trade setups that mirror institutional behavior.

By marrying harmonic pattern recognition with Smart Money Concepts, traders achieve a probabilistic edge, entering trades with precision, understanding institutional intent, and managing risk effectively. This integration moves trading beyond simple pattern recognition into a disciplined, high-probability methodology.

11.3 Pivot Points, VWAP, Moving Averages Context

While Smart Money Concepts (SMC) provide a structural and liquidity-based approach to understanding the market, traditional technical indicators like Pivot Points, VWAP (Volume Weighted Average Price), and Moving Averages remain valuable tools when interpreted through the lens of institutional behavior. By integrating these tools with market structure, order blocks, and liquidity zones, traders can gain additional confirmation, refine entries, and improve trade management.

Pivot Points: Identifying Key Levels

Pivot Points are calculated based on the previous period's high, low, and close and provide potential support and resistance levels for the current period. Institutional traders often observe these levels because:

- They represent areas where significant orders may accumulate.
- Price reactions around pivots can indicate market sentiment shifts.

- They often overlap with OBs, FVGs, or liquidity zones, enhancing confluence.

Example: Suppose EUR/USD is in an uptrend and approaches a daily pivot resistance (R1) at 1.1200. If this R1 also coincides with a previously identified bullish OB and liquidity pool, it becomes a high-probability reversal or breakout area.

VWAP: Understanding Institutional Average Price

VWAP calculates the average price weighted by volume and is widely used by institutions to gauge whether they are buying or selling relative to their average cost:

- Price above VWAP: indicates institutional buying pressure.
- Price below VWAP: indicates institutional selling pressure.
- VWAP often acts as dynamic support or resistance and aligns with OBs or liquidity zones.

Practical Application: A trader can use VWAP in conjunction with an OB. For instance, if price retraces to a bullish OB that also coincides with VWAP support during the London session, it provides a strong confluence for long entries with favorable risk-to-reward ratios.

Moving Averages: Trend and Dynamic Support/Resistance

Moving Averages (MAs), including Simple (SMA) and Exponential (EMA), help identify trend direction and dynamic support/resistance:

- **Trend Confirmation:** Align price above EMA 50/200 for bullish bias, below for bearish bias.
- **Dynamic Support/Resistance:** MAs often overlap with OBs or previous swing levels, reinforcing potential entry zones.
- **Crossover Signals:** EMA crossovers (e.g., 50 EMA crossing 200 EMA) may indicate institutional positioning shifts.

Example: In GBP/USD, price retraces to a bullish OB while the 50 EMA aligns beneath it, reinforcing support. Simultaneously, the VWAP indicates strong institutional buying. Together, this multi-layered confirmation increases entry probability.

Integrating Traditional Indicators with SMC

The key to using Pivot Points, VWAP, and MAs effectively lies in contextual integration:

1. Identify market structure and trend on higher timeframes.
2. Locate OBs, FVGs, and liquidity clusters to define institutional zones.
3. Overlay Pivot Points, VWAP, and relevant MAs to identify additional confluence.
4. Confirm trade timing with lower timeframe price action (rejection candles, OTE entries).

Key Takeaways

- Traditional indicators gain predictive power when interpreted through SMC and market structure.
- VWAP reflects institutional cost levels, helping to confirm entry zones.
- Pivot Points and Moving Averages can serve as additional confluence layers, especially when aligned with OBs, FVGs, and liquidity pools.
- Integration of these tools allows traders to execute trades with higher confidence, better timing, and more precise risk management.

By combining Pivot Points, VWAP, and Moving Averages with Smart Money Concepts, traders bridge classical technical analysis with professional institutional level insights, achieving a structured, probabilistic approach to high-probability trading.

11.4 Intermarket Correlations: Forex ↔ Commodities ↔ Indices

Markets do not operate in isolation. Currency pairs, commodities, and equity indices are often interlinked through macroeconomic factors, liquidity flows, and institutional positioning. Understanding these intermarket correlations allows traders to anticipate moves, align trades with smart money, and reduce risk while increasing probability of success. This section explores the key relationships and how they can be integrated into Smart Money Concepts (SMC) trading.

Why Intermarket Correlations Matter

Institutional participants often trade multiple markets simultaneously to hedge exposure, optimize risk, or capitalize on cross-market signals. Recognizing these relationships provides traders with:

- Early warning signals of potential market shifts.
- Confirmation of bias derived from SMC setups.
- Better risk management through alignment of correlated instruments.

Ignoring correlations can result in counterintuitive trades, false breakouts, or unexpected liquidity sweeps orchestrated by institutions across markets.

Forex and Commodities

Certain currencies are strongly correlated with commodities:

- **USD and Gold:** Gold often moves inversely to USD. A weakening USD can support bullish gold moves and vice versa.
- **AUD and Copper:** Australia is a major copper exporter; hence AUD/USD often follows copper price trends.
- **CAD and Crude Oil:** The Canadian Dollar is heavily influenced by oil prices, given Canada's energy exports.

Practical SMC Application: If an OB forms on AUD/USD in alignment with a bullish copper breakout, the trade has higher probability since institutional buying pressure is likely mirrored in both markets.

Forex and Indices

Major equity indices can influence currency pairs:

- Strong US equity performance (S&P 500, Nasdaq) often strengthens USD due to increased capital inflows.
- European indices (DAX, Euro Stoxx 50) can impact EUR pairs and correlated commodity flows.

Example: A bullish OB in EUR/USD coinciding with a strong Eurozone index rejection near support suggests institutional hedging between equities and FX, reinforcing trade probability.

Commodities and Indices

Equities and commodities often move together due to macroeconomic correlations:

- Rising oil prices may negatively impact indices dependent on oil importing nations.
- Precious metals like gold often act as a hedge against equity volatility.

SMC Integration: Observing liquidity clusters across commodities and indices can indicate where institutions are hedging positions, allowing Forex traders to anticipate correlated moves.

Practical Strategy for Traders

To effectively integrate intermarket correlations:

1. Identify primary market of interest (e.g., a currency pair with a clear OB and liquidity zone).
2. Check correlated commodities or indices for alignment in trend, OB, or liquidity clusters.
3. Confirm trade entries only when multiple correlated markets support institutional direction.
4. Adjust risk management considering potential cross-market divergences.

Key Takeaways

- Intermarket correlations reveal how institutions manipulate and hedge across multiple markets.
- Combining SMC setups with correlated instruments increases probability and reduces false signals.
- Traders should maintain a multi-market watchlist to align Forex trades with commodity and index flows.
- Understanding correlations allows for better timing, improved entries, and more accurate risk assessment.

By mastering intermarket correlations, traders elevate their SMC strategy from a single-market perspective to a holistic view of global liquidity and institutional behavior, gaining a professional edge in both entry precision and trade management.

11.5 Volume Profile and Market Profile

Although Smart Money Concepts (SMC) traditionally focus on price structure, liquidity, and algorithmic inefficiencies, institutional traders also rely heavily on volume-based auction tools such as **Volume Profile** and **Market Profile**. These tools provide insight into how the market distributed its trading activity, revealing areas of value, rejection, and imbalance from an auction theory perspective.

Integrating Volume Profile and Market Profile into an SMC framework enhances the understanding of institutional intent, particularly during consolidation, accumulation, and distribution phases.

What Is Volume Profile?

Volume Profile is a horizontal histogram plotting the amount of traded volume at each price level over a specified period. It highlights:

- **High Volume Nodes (HVNs)** — areas of heavy activity where institutional transactions are concentrated,
- **Low Volume Nodes (LVNs)** — areas of inefficiency or rejection,
- **Point of Control (POC)** — the price level with the highest volume,
- **Value Area (VA)** — the range containing a predefined percentage of volume (typically 70%).

Where SMC emphasizes liquidity, Volume Profile emphasizes **where the market accepted or rejected price**.

What Is Market Profile?

Market Profile organizes time-based transactions into a bell-shaped distribution. It segments the market into:

- **TPOs** (Time Price Opportunities),
- **Value Area High (VAH)**,
- **Value Area Low (VAL)**,
- **Point of Control (POC)**,
- **Initial Balance (IB)** for the first hour of trading.

While Volume Profile analyzes **volume at price**, Market Profile analyzes **time spent at price**. Both tools reflect institutional behavior through the auction process.

Why Institutions Use Profile Tools

Institutions utilize profile tools to assess:

- where liquidity is concentrated,
- where market participants are trapped,
- where imbalances exist between buyers and sellers,
- where price is likely to be revisited or rejected,
- where future mitigation or expansion may occur.

From an SMC perspective, profile tools provide a **deeper understanding of liquidity distribution** and often align with OBs, FVGs, and premium/discount zones.

Key Components of Volume Profile

1. High Volume Nodes (HVNs)

Areas where the most volume traded. These zones represent:

- institutional accumulation or distribution,
- strong acceptance of price,
- areas likely to act as magnet levels.

HVNs typically correspond to:

- consolidated OBs,
- mitigation zones,
- previous session value areas.

2. Low Volume Nodes (LVNs)

Areas with minimal volume. These reflect:

- imbalance,
- rejection,
- zones where price moved quickly.

LVNs often align with FVGs or displacement candles.

3. Point of Control (POC)

The price level with the highest traded volume. It is a benchmark for:

- fair value,
- institutional interest,
- potential reversion zones.

4. Value Area (VAH and VAL)

The upper and lower bounds of the value area. Price tends to oscillate between VAH and VAL unless strong imbalance occurs.

Key Concepts in Market Profile

1. Initial Balance (IB)

The price range formed during the first hour of trading. The IB often serves as:

- a benchmark for range expansion,
- a trap zone for early liquidity,
- a signal for New York session direction.

2. Single Prints (SPs)

Thin profile areas created by fast directional moves. They indicate:

- strong momentum,
- inefficiency similar to FVGs,
- probable retracement targets.

3. Profile Shapes

Profile shapes reflect market behavior:

- **D-profile** — balanced market,
- **P-profile** — bullish continuation with trap at bottom,
- **b-profile** — bearish continuation with trap at top.

Integration of Profile Tools with SMC Concepts

1. Profile and Liquidity

Profile tools help confirm whether liquidity above highs/lows is:

- weak and easy to sweep (LVN zones),
- strong and deeply auctioned (HVN zones),
- aligned with institutional accumulation/distribution.

2. Profile and FVG/Imbalances

LVNs often correspond directly to:

- FVGs,
- imbalance zones,
- displacement candles.

These become high-probability retracement or continuation levels.

3. Profile and Order Blocks

OBs located near:

- HVNs are stronger (institutions traded heavily here),
- LVNs are weaker (thin liquidity environment).

How to Use Profile Tools for Entry and Bias

1. Determining Bias

If price is:

- above POC: bullish environment,
- below POC: bearish environment.

2. Entry Refinement

Combine:

- HTF liquidity targets,
- LTF CHoCH,
- OB/FVG levels,
- profile-based levels (POC, HVN, LVN),

to refine execution into the highest-probability zones.

3. Take Profit Targets

Targets can be structured using:

- session VAH/VAL levels,
- LVN inefficiencies,
- prior-day POC.

Common Mistakes When Using Profile Tools

- Treating profile levels as fixed support or resistance.
- Ignoring SMC structure and using profile tools alone.
- Entering trades based on POC without displacement confirmation.
- Overfitting multiple profiles across too many sessions.

Profile tools must complement—not replace—SMC principles.

Summary

- Volume Profile highlights the price levels with the most institutional activity.
- Market Profile provides insight into auction behavior and value distribution.
- HVNs, LVNs, POC, and Value Area levels align naturally with SMC concepts such as OBs, FVGs, and liquidity pools.
- Profile tools enhance bias determination, entry refinement, and target setting.
- Used correctly, they add a powerful auction-theoretic dimension to SMC execution.

Integrating Volume Profile and Market Profile with SMC gives traders a deeper and more complete understanding of market structure and institutional intent.

Chapter 12

Portfolio & Risk Optimization

While mastering Smart Money Concepts (SMC) and ICT methodologies allows traders to identify high-probability setups, consistent success in trading ultimately depends on how risk is managed across the portfolio. Without proper risk and portfolio optimization, even a series of winning trades can be wiped out by a single poorly managed position. This chapter focuses on the principles and techniques that professional traders use to preserve capital, maximize returns, and maintain consistency over time.

12.1 Advanced Position Sizing: Kelly Criterion, Fixed Fraction

Position sizing is arguably the most critical component of trading success. Even with high-probability Smart Money Concept (SMC) setups, entering a trade with the wrong size can either expose the trader to excessive risk or underutilize potential edge. Advanced position sizing techniques, such as the Kelly Criterion and Fixed Fraction method, provide systematic approaches to determine optimal trade size relative to account equity and statistical edge.

The Kelly Criterion

The Kelly Criterion is a formula that calculates the optimal fraction of capital to risk on a trade based on probability of winning (W) and risk-reward ratio (R). The general formula is:

$$f^* = \frac{W \cdot (R+1) - 1}{R}$$

where:

- f^* = Fraction of capital to risk
- W = Probability of winning the trade (decimal form, e.g., 0.6 for 60%)
- R = Average risk-to-reward ratio of the trade

Example: A trader identifies an SMC setup with a 60% chance of winning ($W = 0.6$) and an expected risk-to-reward ratio of 1:2 ($R = 2$):

$$f^* = \frac{0.6 \cdot (2+1) - 1}{2} = \frac{0.6 \cdot 3 - 1}{2} = \frac{1.8 - 1}{2} = \frac{0.8}{2} = 0.4$$

This calculation suggests risking 40% of the trading capital on this trade. In practice, traders often use a fraction of the Kelly percentage (e.g., 50% of Kelly) to reduce volatility and drawdowns, known as the *fractional Kelly* method.

Fixed Fraction Position Sizing

The Fixed Fraction method is a simpler, more conservative approach. Traders risk a predetermined percentage of their account equity per trade, regardless of probability or edge. Typical risk ranges from 1–3% per trade for professional accounts.
Example: A trader with a $50,000 account risks 2% per trade:

$$Risk\_per\_trade = 50,000 \times 0.02 = \$1,000$$

This risk is then used to calculate position size based on stop-loss distance:

$$Position\_Size = \frac{Risk\_per\_trade}{Entry\ Price - Stop\ Loss}$$

Advantages of Fixed Fraction:

- Simple and easy to implement.
- Reduces risk of large drawdowns.
- Works well with multiple trades and correlated positions.

Comparing Kelly vs Fixed Fraction

- **Kelly Criterion** maximizes growth by accounting for edge and probability but can produce high volatility if used at full size.
- **Fixed Fraction** is more conservative, easier to manage psychologically, and often preferred by retail traders who prioritize drawdown control.
- Fractional Kelly bridges the gap, using statistical edge while controlling risk exposure.

SMC Context

In Smart Money Concepts trading, risk management is particularly critical because institutional moves often create sudden volatility. By combining OBs, FVGs, and liquidity zones with position sizing techniques:

- Traders can scale into high-probability zones with appropriate risk.
- Adjusting size according to confidence in confluence increases probabilistic edge.
- Avoids overexposure during stop hunts or liquidity sweeps.

Key Takeaways

- Position sizing protects capital and leverages statistical edge for long-term growth.
- Kelly Criterion provides a mathematically optimal approach but should be used conservatively (fractional Kelly).
- Fixed Fraction is simple, effective, and aligns well with multi-trade portfolio management.
- Integrating position sizing with SMC setups enhances trade precision, risk control, and confidence during high-volatility institutional moves.

12.2 Hedging Across Correlated Instruments

Hedging is a fundamental risk management technique used by professional traders and institutions to reduce exposure to adverse market moves. In the context of Smart Money Concepts (SMC), hedging becomes particularly powerful when applied across correlated instruments—currencies, commodities, or indices—that often move in tandem due to macroeconomic factors, liquidity flows, or institutional positioning. Understanding these relationships allows traders to protect their capital, maintain portfolio balance, and exploit high-probability setups while mitigating risk.

Why Hedging Matters

Even with high-probability SMC setups, unexpected liquidity sweeps, stop hunts, or news-driven volatility can lead to losses. Hedging allows traders to:

- Limit drawdowns during volatile periods.
- Lock in profits without exiting core positions.
- Exploit arbitrage opportunities between correlated markets.
- Maintain overall portfolio balance while taking multiple trades.

Identifying Correlated Instruments

Successful hedging begins with identifying instruments with high correlation, either positive or negative:

- **Positive correlation:** Instruments that tend to move in the same direction (e.g., EUR/USD and GBP/USD, or crude oil and CAD/USD). - Hedging may involve reducing exposure in one instrument when the other moves against you.
- **Negative correlation:** Instruments that move inversely (e.g., USD/JPY and Nikkei Index, or USD and Gold). - Hedging can involve opening offsetting positions in the negatively correlated instrument to neutralize risk.

Practical Hedging Strategies

1. Direct Hedging: Open an opposite position in a correlated instrument to offset risk. For example:

- Long EUR/USD with OB alignment.
- Short GBP/USD to partially hedge exposure if both pairs have positive correlation and USD risk is dominant.

2. Partial Hedging: Hedge only a portion of your position to reduce risk while still capturing potential upside. This is particularly effective when confidence in the SMC setup is high but market uncertainty exists.
3. Portfolio-Level Hedging: Instead of hedging individual trades, manage total portfolio exposure. For instance:

- Calculate net exposure to USD across all open trades.
- Open offsetting trades in negatively correlated instruments (e.g., Gold or JPY pairs) to reduce net risk.

Timing and Execution

Hedging is most effective when executed with awareness of liquidity and session timing:

- Align hedges with high-probability SMC zones (OBs, FVGs, liquidity clusters).
- Avoid over-hedging during low liquidity sessions, which can trigger slippage or sudden price moves.
- Use correlation strength and historical volatility to determine hedge size.

Example: Forex and Commodity Hedge

Consider a trader long CAD/USD based on an OB retest. Since CAD/USD is positively correlated with crude oil:

- If crude oil suddenly drops due to geopolitical news, the trader's long CAD/USD is at risk.
- Opening a short crude oil hedge reduces potential losses while maintaining the core USD exposure.
- Adjust hedge size based on correlation coefficient and account risk tolerance.

Key Takeaways

- Hedging across correlated instruments reduces risk without abandoning high-probability SMC setups.
- Understanding correlations—both positive and negative—is essential for effective portfolio protection.
- Partial and portfolio-level hedging allows traders to balance risk and reward while navigating uncertainty.
- Integrating hedging strategies with OBs, FVGs, liquidity pools, and market structure ensures alignment with institutional behavior and increases trade confidence.

By mastering hedging across correlated instruments, traders gain a systematic way to protect capital, optimize risk, and exploit high-probability setups while remaining aligned with Smart Money Concepts and institutional flows.

12.3 Managing Multiple Trades Simultaneously

Professional traders rarely execute a single trade at a time. Instead, they maintain multiple positions across different instruments, timeframes, and market sessions. Managing multiple trades simultaneously requires careful portfolio allocation, correlation awareness, and rigorous risk management to prevent overexposure and ensure consistent performance. This section explores how to handle multi-trade portfolios effectively while integrating Smart Money Concepts (SMC) strategies.

Challenges of Multiple Trades

Managing several trades introduces complexity and risk:

- **Overexposure:** Too many positions in correlated instruments can amplify losses during adverse moves.
- **Cognitive Load:** Tracking multiple OBs, FVGs, and liquidity zones simultaneously increases mental strain and error probability.
- **Position Conflicts:** Opposing trades within the same portfolio can reduce overall effectiveness if not carefully managed.

The key to successful multi-trade management is structured planning, precise sizing, and continuous monitoring.

Portfolio Allocation and Risk Distribution

Proper allocation ensures no single trade can significantly damage the account. Key principles include:

- **Risk Per Trade:** Use fixed fraction or fractional Kelly sizing to determine exposure for each trade.
- **Maximum Portfolio Risk:** Set a total risk threshold for all open trades (e.g., 5–10% of account equity) to prevent catastrophic drawdowns.
- **Diversification Across Markets:** Balance trades across Forex, commodities, and indices to reduce correlation risk.

Example: A trader has a $100,000 account. Risking 2% per trade on four positions would be $8,000 total. If two trades are positively correlated, the effective risk may be higher, so the trader adjusts position sizes accordingly.

Correlation Awareness

Understanding intermarket correlations is essential for managing multiple trades:

- Identify instruments that move together (positive correlation) or inversely (negative correlation).
- Reduce exposure on trades that amplify each other's risk.
- Use negatively correlated instruments to naturally hedge portfolio risk.

Example: A long GBP/USD trade may correlate positively with a long EUR/USD trade. To manage portfolio risk, the trader may reduce the size of one trade or offset exposure with a short USD/JPY trade.

Trade Prioritization and Timing

Not all trades require equal attention. Traders should prioritize based on:

- High-probability OB or FVG setups.
- Trades aligning with session liquidity (London/New York).
- Instruments with stronger institutional bias or confirmed multi timeframe alignment.

By staggering entries and exits, traders reduce cognitive overload and avoid simultaneous conflict between trades.

Monitoring and Adjustment

Active monitoring is crucial:

- Track open trades against market structure, liquidity zones, and institutional cues.
- Adjust stop-losses, take profits, and positions in response to evolving market conditions.
- Maintain a journal to review correlations, performance, and risk management efficacy.

Key Takeaways

- Multi-trade management requires disciplined portfolio allocation and strict risk limits.
- Awareness of correlations and market structure prevents overexposure and conflicting trades.
- Prioritization, monitoring, and adjustment are essential to maintain high-probability edges across multiple positions.
- Integrating these practices with Smart Money Concepts ensures trades are aligned with institutional behavior, enhancing consistency and long-term profitability.

Effectively managing multiple trades simultaneously transforms SMC strategies from isolated setups into a structured, probabilistic portfolio approach, allowing traders to scale strategies while controlling risk and maximizing edge.

12.4 Trade Journaling & Statistical Analysis

Maintaining a disciplined trading journal and performing statistical analysis are critical components of professional trading. Even with a strong understanding of Smart Money Concepts (SMC), failure to record trades and analyze performance systematically often leads to repeated mistakes, overlooked patterns, and inconsistent results. This section explores how to effectively document trades, analyze data, and apply insights to optimize future performance.

The Importance of Trade Journaling

A trade journal serves as both a record and a learning tool. Key benefits include:

- **Accountability:** Tracking trades ensures adherence to your strategy and risk management rules.
- **Pattern Recognition:** Identifying recurring mistakes or successful setups allows refinement of SMC strategies.
- **Confidence Building:** Reviewing past successes reinforces probabilistic thinking and patience.

Components of a Trade Journal:

- Trade date and instrument
- Entry and exit prices
- Trade rationale (OB, FVG, liquidity zones, session bias)
- Stop-loss and take-profit levels
- Position size and risk
- Outcome and profit/loss
- Observations and lessons learned

Integrating SMC Concepts

For SMC traders, journals should capture institutional cues:

- Alignment of OBs, FVGs, and liquidity pools.
- Multi-timeframe confirmation and session-specific biases.
- Notes on stop hunts, liquidity sweeps, and mitigation zones.

By recording these factors, traders can analyze which setups consistently outperform and which conditions signal increased risk.

Statistical Analysis of Trades

Quantitative evaluation provides objective insight into trading performance. Key metrics include:

- **Win/Loss Ratio:** Percentage of profitable trades.
- **Risk-to-Reward Ratio:** Average reward relative to average risk.
- **Expectancy:** Average amount gained or lost per trade, calculated as:

$$\text{Expectancy} = (W \times \text{Average Win}) - (L \times \text{Average Loss})$$

  where W is the win probability and $L = 1 - W$.
- **Drawdown Analysis:** Maximum percentage decline in account equity to measure risk exposure.
- **Edge Quantification:** Performance of trades based on specific setups (OB retests, FVG entries, SMT traps) to determine which setups yield the highest probability of success.

Using Data to Improve Performance

Once trades are logged and metrics calculated, traders can:

- Identify high-probability SMC setups and focus capital allocation accordingly.
- Adjust risk management strategies based on drawdown trends.
- Detect psychological patterns, such as overtrading or revenge trading, and implement corrective measures.
- Refine entry and exit techniques by reviewing outcome patterns in different market conditions and sessions.

Key Takeaways

- Trade journaling ensures accountability, pattern recognition, and learning from both wins and losses.
- Statistical analysis turns subjective trading observations into objective, actionable insights.
- Combining journaling with SMC-specific data enhances probabilistic decision-making and trade precision.
- A disciplined journaling and analysis routine is a cornerstone of consistent long-term profitability and professional trading behavior.

By rigorously documenting trades and performing statistical analysis, traders transform experience into measurable skill, allowing Smart Money Concepts strategies to be executed with confidence, precision, and repeatable success.

12.5 Drawdown Control System

One of the most critical components of professional trading is the ability to manage and limit drawdowns. While strategy development and technical execution determine profitability, **drawdown control** determines longevity, survivability, and scalability. In institutional trading, the primary goal is not to maximize returns, but to **minimize uncontrolled loss exposure**.

A well-designed Drawdown Control System (DCS) ensures that the trader remains within acceptable risk boundaries, protects capital during unfavorable conditions, and maintains psychological composure during losing streaks.

Understanding Drawdown

Drawdown (DD) is defined as the reduction in account equity from a peak to a trough during a series of losing trades.

Formally:

$$\text{Drawdown} = \frac{\text{Peak Equity} - \text{Trough Equity}}{\text{Peak Equity}} \times 100\%$$

Key types of drawdowns:

- **Equity Drawdown** — based on closed trades only,
- **Balance Drawdown** — based on running balance including open trades,
- **Relative Drawdown** — based on percentage of equity decline,
- **Absolute Drawdown** — difference between initial deposit and lowest equity point.

A trader may withstand poor win rates, inconsistent performance, or temporary losing periods, but cannot survive outsized drawdowns that erode psychological and financial stability.

Why Drawdown Control Is Essential

A robust drawdown control system:

- prevents catastrophic losses,
- protects the trader from emotional decision-making,
- ensures long-term growth and consistency,

- stabilizes risk exposure during volatility,
- enables compounding by preserving equity.

Institutions prioritize **risk preservation** over raw returns; retail traders must adopt the same mindset.

Maximum Drawdown (Max DD) Rules

Max DD is the predefined limit beyond which trading activity must be stopped or significantly reduced.

A typical Max DD rule is:

$$\text{Stop Trading If Drawdown Reaches } 10\%\text{–}12\%$$

However, Max DD levels vary depending on:

- risk appetite,
- strategy volatility,
- account size,
- professional or retail constraints.

Common institutional drawdown limits:

- Prop firms: 5% daily DD / 10% total DD,
- Hedge funds: typically 8%–15%,
- Conservative traders: 5%–8%,
- Medium-risk traders: 10%–15%.

Drawdown Control System Components

A professional drawdown control system includes the following elements:

1. Hard Max DD Limit

A strict equity level acting as the final stop:

$$\text{If Equity} \leq \text{Max DD Threshold} \Rightarrow \text{Stop Trading}$$

This prevents emotional trading during stress.

2. Soft DD Threshold

A buffer zone before the hard stop is hit:

$$\text{Soft DD (Warning Zone)} = 50\% \text{ of Max DD}$$

Example:

- Max DD = 12%
- Soft DD = 6%

At soft DD:

- reduce risk by 50%,
- avoid new positions against the bias,
- take only A+ setups.

3. Daily Drawdown Cap

Limits the maximum damage possible in one day:

$$\text{Daily DD Cap} \approx 2\% - 3\%$$

If hit:

- shut down trading for the day,
- avoid revenge trading,
- reset psychologically.

4. Losing Streak Rule

A predefined number of consecutive losses triggers a trading pause:

$$\text{If 3–4 consecutive losses occur} \Rightarrow \text{Stop and re-evaluate}$$

This protects against psychological deterioration during streaks.

5. Equity-Based Position Sizing

Position size should scale down automatically when equity falls:

$$\text{Risk per Trade} = \text{Fixed } \% \text{ of Equity}$$

As equity decreases, risk decreases proportionally.

The Equity Protection Model

A strong equity protection system contains:

- **Kill Switch**: Auto-stop trading after Max DD.
- **Cooling Period**: Mandatory break from markets.
- **Review Phase**: Diagnose what caused the DD.
- **Reduced-Risk Restart**: Begin trading at 50% of usual risk.

This ensures that traders recover conservatively, not aggressively.

Methods to Detect Drawdown Early

Techniques include:

- Equity curve monitoring,
- Rolling 20-trade performance analysis,
- Weekly expectancy review,
- Session-by-session win/loss clustering,
- Volatility-adjusted risk (reduce size during high volatility).

Cutting drawdown early is far more effective than recovering from deep losses.

Psychological Principles Behind Drawdown Control

Effective drawdown control stabilizes:

- emotional discipline,
- consistency of execution,
- avoidance of revenge trading,
- confidence in the system.

A trader who avoids deep drawdowns also avoids:

- stress-driven errors,
- impulsive trades,
- self-sabotage,
- strategy abandonment.

Summary

- Drawdown control is essential for long-term trading survival.
- Max DD limits protect traders from catastrophic loss.
- Soft DD thresholds allow time for risk reduction and analysis.
- Daily DD caps prevent emotional trading spirals.
- Losing streak rules reduce psychological pressure.
- Consistent drawdown management enables compounding and longevity.

A disciplined Drawdown Control System transforms trading from a high-stress activity into a scalable, risk-governed professional operation.

Part IV

Practical Implementation

Chapter 13

Trade Planning & Checklists

Consistent trading success is not only the result of mastering Smart Money Concepts (SMC) and technical tools—it is equally dependent on discipline, preparation, and systematic execution. The most profitable traders treat trading as a process rather than a series of random decisions. Trade planning and checklists are critical components of this process, providing structure, minimizing errors, and ensuring that every decision aligns with a high-probability setup.
This chapter focuses on building a professional-grade routine that integrates SMC strategies into daily trading practice. By implementing checklists for pre-trade preparation, live execution, and post-trade review, traders can:

13.1 Daily Routine for Analysis and Trade Prep

A disciplined daily routine is the backbone of consistent trading success. Professional traders treat each trading day as a structured workflow, ensuring that all setups are aligned with Smart Money Concepts (SMC), institutional behavior, and high-probability zones. Without a systematic routine, even well-understood strategies can fail due to oversight, emotional decisions, or market noise.

Step 1: Pre-Session Preparation

Before the market opens (or before your trading session begins), allocate dedicated time to prepare:

- **Review Economic Calendar:** Identify high-impact news events, central bank announcements, or geopolitical developments that could create volatility. Avoid entering trades during uncertain conditions unless your strategy accounts for it.

- **Assess Market Sentiment:** Examine key indices, commodities, or currencies for directional bias. Understanding overall market sentiment helps contextualize SMC setups.

- **Check Overnight Moves:** Analyze price action from previous sessions to identify liquidity sweeps, stop hunts, or breakouts that may influence the current market structure.

Step 2: Chart Analysis and Multi-Timeframe Review

Multi-timeframe analysis is crucial to align high-probability SMC setups:

- **Higher Timeframe (HTF) Analysis:** Identify the overarching trend, significant order blocks (OBs), supply and demand zones, and liquidity clusters. Determine institutional bias.

- **Intermediate Timeframe (ITF) Analysis:** Refine zones, watch for potential retests, fair value gaps (FVGs), and liquidity sweeps.

- **Lower Timeframe (LTF) Analysis:** Look for precise entries, break of structure (BoS), and optimal trade entry (OTE) confirmations.

Tip: Mark all significant OBs, FVGs, and liquidity zones using clear labels and color codes to maintain clarity across multiple charts.

Step 3: Identifying High-Probability Setups

Using SMC principles, highlight setups where multiple confluences occur:

- OB retests aligned with HTF bias.

- FVGs coinciding with liquidity pools.

- Time-of-day bias (London/New York sessions) supporting entry direction.

- Multi-timeframe confirmations indicating structural alignment.

Prioritize trades where multiple factors converge, increasing the probability of success and minimizing exposure to false breaks or traps.

Step 4: Risk Assessment and Position Sizing

For each identified setup:

- Calculate stop-loss placement relative to OBs, swing highs/lows, or mitigation zones.
- Determine position size using advanced techniques such as fractional Kelly or fixed fraction sizing.
- Assess overall portfolio risk to avoid overexposure, especially when multiple correlated trades are planned.

Step 5: Trading Plan Documentation

Document each potential trade in your journal before execution:

- Entry and exit levels.
- Risk-to-reward ratio.
- Reason for trade based on SMC zones, liquidity, and market structure.
- Contingency plan if price violates your OB or FVG.

Having a pre-documented plan prevents impulsive decisions and ensures adherence to probabilistic thinking.

Step 6: Mindset and Focus Preparation

Trading is as much mental as it is technical:

- Perform a brief mindfulness or focus exercise to center attention.
- Set realistic expectations for the session.
- Prepare to detach emotionally from individual trades, focusing on the process and probabilistic outcomes rather than short-term results.

Key Takeaways

- A structured daily routine reduces errors, ensures high-probability setups, and aligns trades with institutional behavior.
- Multi-timeframe analysis, OB/FVG identification, and session awareness are critical components of preparation.
- Documenting potential trades, calculating risk, and setting position sizes beforehand improves discipline and probabilistic execution.

- Mental and focus preparation ensures consistency, emotional control, and the ability to wait for optimal setups.

By following a disciplined daily routine, traders can approach each session with clarity, confidence, and a systematic framework for executing Smart Money Concept strategies while minimizing unnecessary risk.

13.2 Pre-Trade Checklist: Structure, Zones, Confluence

Before executing any trade, professional traders rely on a rigorous pre-trade checklist to ensure alignment with high-probability Smart Money Concept (SMC) setups. This checklist acts as a safeguard against impulsive decisions, emotional bias, and trades that violate market structure or liquidity principles. By systematically verifying each element, traders increase their chances of entering trades that are consistent with institutional behavior.

Step 1: Market Structure Verification

Every trade should start with an assessment of market structure:

- Identify the current trend: uptrend, downtrend, or sideways.
- Confirm break of structure (BoS) or change of character (CHoCH) to validate directional bias.
- Check swing highs and lows for potential liquidity zones and previous institutional interest.
- Ensure your intended trade aligns with higher timeframe bias to increase probability.

Checklist:

Trend correctly identified.

BoS / CHoCH confirmed.

Swing highs/lows marked as liquidity zones.

Trade direction aligned with HTF bias.

Step 2: Order Block and Supply/Demand Zone Alignment

Order blocks (OBs) and supply/demand zones form the core of SMC entries:

- Identify bullish or bearish OBs in the vicinity of intended entry.

- Check for overlapping supply/demand zones or fair value gaps (FVG) to strengthen confluence.
- Ensure the OB has not already been mitigated or absorbed by prior price action.
- Verify that the zone aligns with liquidity clusters to maximize institutional edge.

Checklist:

OB type confirmed (bullish/bearish).

Zone not previously mitigated.

Supply/demand/FVG overlap verified.

Liquidity clusters present.

Step 3: Confluence and Multi-Factor Confirmation

High-probability trades emerge from the convergence of multiple factors:

- Align trade with multiple timeframes for confirmation (HTF → LTF).
- Confirm time-of-day session bias (London/New York/Asia) supports intended move.
- Look for confluence with Fibonacci levels, harmonic patterns, or pivot points if applicable.
- Ensure no conflicting signals from correlated instruments or overall portfolio exposure.

Checklist:

Multi-timeframe alignment confirmed.

Session bias supports trade.

Technical confluence (Fibonacci, harmonic patterns) present.

Correlation risk checked.

Step 4: Risk and Position Assessment

Before executing, verify that risk parameters are appropriate:

- Confirm stop-loss placement respects OB, swing low/high, or mitigation zone boundaries.
- Calculate position size using pre-determined risk-per-trade limits.

- Evaluate risk-to-reward ratio (minimum 1:2 recommended) for potential trade.
- Ensure total portfolio risk remains within acceptable thresholds.

Checklist:

Stop-loss level validated.

Position size calculated.

Risk-to-reward ratio acceptable.

Portfolio risk within limits.

Step 5: Final Mental Confirmation

Even with all technical criteria met, a final mental check improves discipline:

- Ensure emotional state is calm and focused.
- Confirm adherence to trading plan and strategy rules.
- Mentally visualize trade execution, stop-loss, and take-profit scenarios.

Checklist:

Emotionally prepared.

Trading plan confirmed.

Trade visualization complete.

Key Takeaways

- A pre-trade checklist ensures every trade aligns with institutional market behavior and high-probability SMC setups.
- Verifying market structure, OBs, supply/demand zones, and liquidity clusters reduces risk of false entries.
- Multi-factor confluence and risk assessment further strengthen probabilistic edge.
- The checklist also reinforces discipline, emotional control, and consistent execution over time.

By rigorously applying this pre-trade checklist, traders convert analysis into actionable, disciplined trades, maximizing the likelihood of success while adhering to the principles of Smart Money Concepts.

13.3 Post-Trade Checklist: Review, Journaling, Improvement

The post-trade process is just as important as preparation and execution. Without systematic review and journaling, traders risk repeating mistakes, overlooking key patterns, and failing to refine their probabilistic edge. The post-trade checklist ensures that every trade, whether winning or losing, becomes a learning opportunity and a step toward consistent mastery of Smart Money Concepts (SMC).

Step 1: Immediate Trade Review

After closing a trade, perform an immediate assessment:

- Record actual entry, stop-loss, and take-profit levels.
- Note trade outcome (profit, loss, breakeven) and compare with expected result.
- Identify if trade execution adhered to the pre-trade plan.
- Highlight any deviation from intended OBs, FVGs, or liquidity zones.

Checklist:

Entry, stop-loss, and exit levels recorded.

Outcome noted.

Adherence to trade plan verified.

Deviations and observations logged.

Step 2: Detailed Journaling

Journaling transforms raw trade data into actionable insight:

- Document the rationale behind each trade, including market structure, session bias, and multi-timeframe alignment.
- Record emotions, confidence level, and any impulsive tendencies observed.
- Highlight institutional cues such as liquidity sweeps, stop hunts, or mitigation blocks.
- Track patterns across multiple trades to identify recurring mistakes or high-probability setups.

Checklist:

Trade rationale fully documented.

Emotional and psychological notes included.

Institutional cues captured.

Patterns and lessons noted.

Step 3: Statistical Analysis and Metrics

Analyze cumulative trade data to quantify performance and edge:

- Update win/loss ratios and risk-to-reward averages.
- Track expectancy per setup type (OB retest, FVG entry, SMT trap).
- Measure drawdowns and volatility of account equity to evaluate risk management effectiveness.
- Identify setups with the highest probability and refine focus accordingly.

Checklist:

Win/loss ratio updated.

Risk-to-reward ratios calculated.

Expectancy metrics reviewed.

Drawdowns analyzed.

Step 4: Learning and Improvement

Every post-trade review should feed forward into strategy refinement:

- Adjust entry, exit, and risk parameters based on observed outcomes.
- Refine identification of OBs, FVGs, and liquidity zones using recent trade data.
- Address psychological patterns like overtrading, FOMO, or revenge trading.
- Set actionable goals for the next session, focusing on process over outcome.

Checklist:

Strategy adjustments identified.

Zone and setup refinements noted.

Psychological improvements planned.

Goals for next session defined.

Key Takeaways

- Post-trade review and journaling transform experience into measurable skill.
- Statistical metrics allow objective evaluation of setups, risk management, and probabilistic edge.
- Continuous improvement through lessons learned enhances long-term consistency and profitability.
- Integrating post-trade analysis with Smart Money Concepts ensures trades evolve from isolated events into a structured, repeatable, and scalable system.

By rigorously following a post-trade checklist, traders convert every trade into a learning opportunity, steadily improving their understanding of market structure, institutional behavior, and high-probability Smart Money Concept setups. This disciplined approach is a cornerstone of professional trading and sustainable success.

Chapter 14

Backtesting & Replay

Understanding Smart Money Concepts (SMC) and executing trades in real-time is one aspect of trading, but the ability to consistently identify high-probability setups requires rigorous practice and validation. Backtesting and replaying historical market data provide traders with the tools to refine strategies, build confidence, and quantify the probabilistic edge of their trades without risking capital.
This chapter focuses on the systematic process of evaluating past market behavior, simulating trades, and learning from both successes and mistakes. By revisiting historical charts, traders can identify recurring patterns, test order block retests, fair value gaps (FVGs), liquidity zones, and other institutional cues.

14.1 Historical Chart Validation

Historical chart validation is the cornerstone of systematic trading. Before risking real capital, traders must rigorously test their strategies against past market behavior to determine whether setups, patterns, and techniques consistently offer a probabilistic edge. For Smart Money Concepts (SMC) and ICT-based strategies, understanding how institutional players interact with price across multiple timeframes is critical.

Step 1: Selecting the Right Data

- Choose high-quality historical price data for the instrument you intend to trade. This should include open, high, low, close (OHLC) values and, if available, tick-level data for precise analysis.
- Select a timeframe relevant to your strategy (e.g., daily charts for swing trading, 15-minute charts for intraday setups).

- Ensure the dataset covers various market conditions: trending, ranging, high volatility, and low liquidity periods.

Step 2: Identifying Key SMC Elements

Once the dataset is selected, systematically identify and mark critical SMC elements:

- **Order Blocks (OBs):** Identify bullish and bearish OBs and mark their boundaries. Observe how price reacts when revisiting these zones.
- **Liquidity Pools and Stop-Loss Clusters:** Highlight areas where institutional activity likely created liquidity sweeps or stop hunts.
- **Fair Value Gaps (FVGs):** Track unfilled gaps in price action and note how price behaves when approaching these levels.
- **Market Structure:** Label swing highs, swing lows, break of structure (BoS), and change of character (CHoCH) points.

Step 3: Testing Strategy Rules

Apply your trading rules to historical data as if executing trades in real-time:

- Check entry conditions, including OB retests, FVG fills, and confluence factors.
- Apply your pre-defined stop-loss and take-profit criteria.
- Record whether the trade would have met your risk-reward expectations.
- Note deviations, false signals, and price behaviors that challenge your assumptions.

Step 4: Statistical Evaluation

Quantifying your results transforms qualitative observations into measurable performance:

- Track win/loss ratios and average risk-to-reward for each setup.
- Analyze expectancy per setup type (OB retest, FVG entry, liquidity sweep response).
- Identify patterns in failures to adjust criteria for false breaks, mitigated zones, or poor confluence.
- Compare performance across different timeframes, market sessions, and instruments.

Step 5: Refinement and Optimization

Historical validation is not just about verifying past success—it is a learning tool:

- Refine zone identification techniques (OB, FVG, liquidity clusters) based on observed reactions.
- Adjust entry, exit, and risk management parameters to improve overall probabilistic outcomes.
- Document insights in your trading journal for future reference and pattern recognition.
- Repeat this process periodically to adapt to evolving market conditions.

Key Takeaways

- Historical chart validation allows traders to observe SMC patterns, institutional behavior, and market structure without financial risk.
- Properly executed, it highlights high-probability setups, identifies weaknesses in strategy, and builds confidence in probabilistic decision-making.
- Consistent validation and refinement create a feedback loop that transforms raw analysis into systematic, repeatable trading processes.
- Traders who rigorously validate historical data gain an edge by understanding how price truly behaves under institutional influence, improving accuracy and execution in live markets.

By dedicating time to historical chart validation, traders convert theory into actionable skill, laying the foundation for disciplined, confident, and profitable application of Smart Money Concepts in real-time trading.

14.2 Simulated Trading for Skill Refinement

Simulated trading, often referred to as paper trading or replay trading, is an essential step in converting theoretical understanding of Smart Money Concepts (SMC) into actionable skill. By practicing in a controlled environment without risking real capital, traders can refine entries, exits, and risk management strategies while reinforcing discipline and probabilistic thinking.

Step 1: Setting Up the Simulation Environment

- **Choose a Trading Platform:** Use platforms that allow historical data replay (e.g., TradingView, NinjaTrader, MT5) to recreate live market conditions.

- **Select Relevant Timeframes:** Simulate the same timeframes used in your live strategy to ensure consistency in analysis.
- **Use Realistic Conditions:** Incorporate spreads, slippage, and execution delays to mimic actual trading scenarios.
- **Focus on High-Probability Setups:** Concentrate on OB retests, FVG fills, liquidity zones, and SMC-specific signals to maximize learning efficiency.

Step 2: Practicing Trade Execution

- Execute trades as if they were real, applying all pre-defined entry rules, stop-losses, and take-profit levels.
- Observe price reactions to order blocks, supply/demand zones, liquidity pools, and fair value gaps.
- Note timing of entries relative to session bias (London, New York, Asia) and market structure.
- Avoid shortcutting the process; treat each simulation with the same discipline as a live trade.

Step 3: Evaluating Performance

- Record each simulated trade in your journal with details on entry, exit, rationale, and emotional state.
- Analyze win/loss ratios, risk-to-reward, and adherence to your trade plan.
- Identify patterns of mistakes such as premature entries, overtrading, or misinterpretation of zones.
- Compare simulated results against historical validation to verify consistency and reliability of setups.

Step 4: Skill Reinforcement

- Repeat simulations regularly to build muscle memory and internalize institutional behaviors reflected in SMC setups.
- Gradually increase complexity by simulating multiple correlated instruments, overlapping sessions, and volatile conditions.
- Focus on mastering the process, not just the outcome, ensuring probabilistic thinking guides every decision.
- Use simulation to experiment with new strategies or variations while maintaining risk-free learning.

Step 5: Bridging to Live Trading

- Once consistently profitable in simulations, transition to live trading with minimal capital and strict risk limits.
- Continue journaling and reviewing trades to maintain the feedback loop established in simulation.
- Recognize that psychological pressures differ in live markets; use simulated experience to mitigate fear, FOMO, and emotional errors.

Key Takeaways

- Simulated trading is a critical bridge between theoretical SMC knowledge and live execution skill.
- Practicing with realistic conditions improves timing, discipline, and confidence without financial risk.
- Regular simulation reinforces understanding of OBs, FVGs, liquidity zones, and market structure across multiple timeframes.
- A structured simulation process establishes procedural consistency, emotional control, and probabilistic decision-making that can be directly applied to real trading.

By systematically incorporating simulated trading into your routine, you develop the precision, discipline, and confidence necessary to execute Smart Money Concept strategies effectively in live markets, while reducing errors and reinforcing probabilistic thinking.

14.3 Improving Accuracy & Confidence

Accuracy and confidence are the pillars of successful trading. Mastery of Smart Money Concepts (SMC) requires not only understanding market structure, order blocks, liquidity, and fair value gaps, but also the ability to apply this knowledge consistently under real-time market conditions. This section focuses on practical steps to enhance trade accuracy, build confidence, and develop a disciplined, probabilistic approach.

Step 1: Measuring Accuracy

To improve accuracy, traders must quantify their performance objectively:

- Track the number of trades that meet your entry and exit criteria precisely.

- Record instances of false signals, premature entries, or missed opportunities.
- Analyze the success rate of individual setups such as OB retests, FVG fills, or liquidity sweeps.
- Evaluate multi-timeframe alignment accuracy and session bias adherence.

Checklist:

Entry precision evaluated.

Exit accuracy assessed.

Success rate of setup types recorded.

Multi-timeframe and session alignment verified.

Step 2: Identifying Improvement Areas

Accuracy improves when traders systematically identify weaknesses:

- Highlight patterns of mistakes: entering too early, overtrading, or ignoring liquidity zones.
- Review misinterpretations of OBs, FVGs, and market structure changes.
- Determine if emotional reactions (fear, FOMO, impatience) contributed to errors.
- Prioritize recurring issues for targeted practice in simulation and historical validation.

Step 3: Reinforcing Probabilistic Thinking

Confidence comes from trusting your process rather than outcomes:

- Focus on executing high-probability setups consistently, regardless of individual trade outcomes.
- Emphasize the importance of risk-to-reward and position sizing over "winning every trade."
- Recognize that even the best setups fail occasionally; consistency over time creates expected positive returns.
- Use journals, statistics, and backtesting results to reinforce process-driven confidence.

Step 4: Skill Reinforcement Through Repetition

Repetition under controlled conditions strengthens both accuracy and confidence:

- Replay historical charts and simulate trades regularly, incorporating lessons from past mistakes.
- Increase complexity gradually: multiple instruments, overlapping sessions, volatile markets.
- Apply probabilistic reasoning to every setup—focus on edge identification and risk management.
- Celebrate process-based successes, not just profitable outcomes.

Step 5: Mental and Emotional Conditioning

Confidence is inseparable from psychological preparedness:

- Develop routines for pre-trade mental focus and post-trade reflection.
- Practice mindfulness, visualization, or flow-state techniques to maintain composure during live trading.
- Condition yourself to detach from individual trade outcomes and reinforce trust in your strategy.
- Regularly review journals and metrics to internalize patterns of success and failure objectively.

Key Takeaways

- Accuracy is built through objective measurement, repeated practice, and targeted improvement.
- Confidence is strengthened by consistent execution of process-driven, high-probability setups rather than by individual trade results.
- Probabilistic thinking allows traders to focus on expected value and risk management, reducing emotional impact.
- Combining technical skill, disciplined routine, and psychological preparedness produces sustainable mastery of Smart Money Concepts in real-time markets.

By systematically improving accuracy and cultivating confidence, traders develop the capability to make disciplined, high-probability decisions, reinforcing their edge and preparing them to execute Smart Money Concept strategies with consistency, precision, and composure.

Chapter 15

Case Studies & Real-World Examples

Theory and methodology provide the foundation for successful trading, but true mastery comes from observing and analyzing how these principles manifest in real markets. Case studies and real-world examples bridge the gap between conceptual understanding of Smart Money Concepts (SMC) and practical application, offering insights into how institutional behaviors influence price action across different instruments.

This chapter explores a variety of markets—including Forex, Cryptocurrencies, Commodities, and Stocks—highlighting high-probability setups, market manipulations, and trade dynamics. By studying concrete examples, traders can learn to recognize recurring patterns, validate their own analysis, and refine strategies under diverse market conditions.

15.1 Forex, Crypto, Commodities, Stock Examples

One of the most effective ways to internalize Smart Money Concepts (SMC) is through real-world examples across different markets. Each instrument exhibits unique characteristics, yet the principles of liquidity, order blocks, fair value gaps, and institutional behavior remain consistent. By studying diverse markets, traders can learn to adapt strategies while recognizing universal patterns of market manipulation and high-probability setups.

Forex Examples

Forex markets are highly liquid and operate 24 hours a day, making them an ideal environment to observe institutional activity. Key SMC setups include:

- **Order Block Retests:** Major banks often create large bullish or bearish order blocks around central bank announcements. For example, EUR/USD may exhibit a bearish OB retest after an ECB interest rate decision.
- **Liquidity Sweeps:** Stops above recent swing highs or lows are frequently targeted during volatile news sessions. Observing these sweeps allows traders to enter in alignment with institutional bias.
- **Multi-Timeframe Confirmation:** Higher timeframe trends (daily/4H) provide context for lower timeframe entries (15m/1H) in alignment with market structure and liquidity zones.

Cryptocurrency Examples

Cryptocurrency markets, while more volatile, display institutional footprints similar to Forex:

- **Liquidity Pools:** Exchanges like Binance or Coinbase often exhibit stop clusters around psychological levels (e.g., BTC $30,000). Smart Money Concepts identify these as potential entry/exit zones.
- **False Breakouts:** Rapid pump-and-dump movements are common. Recognizing stop hunts and FVG fills helps traders avoid traps and align with genuine market momentum.
- **Extended Sessions:** Crypto trades 24/7, so session bias must be adapted; monitoring global liquidity flows becomes essential for accurate entries.

Commodities Examples

Commodities like Gold, Oil, and Copper reflect both retail sentiment and institutional hedging strategies:

- **Mitigation Zones:** Large commercial traders create liquidity resets to enter or exit positions without causing major disruptions in price.
- **Fair Value Gaps:** Price often revisits FVGs created by large institutional orders before resuming trends. Recognizing these zones increases the probability of successful trades.
- **Correlation Awareness:** For instance, Gold often reacts inversely to the USD index. Understanding intermarket correlations enhances confluence for commodity SMC setups.

Stock Market Examples

Stock markets demonstrate the interplay of retail and institutional participants:

- **Earnings Releases:** Institutions accumulate or distribute positions around earnings announcements, creating clear order blocks and liquidity zones.
- **Stop Hunts and Breakouts:** Stocks frequently exhibit fake breakouts to trigger retail stops. Recognizing these allows disciplined entries aligned with institutional flow.
- **Volume-Weighted Analysis:** High-volume nodes often indicate institutional accumulation or distribution, which can be integrated with OBs and FVGs for precision entries.

Key Takeaways

- SMC principles are universal; liquidity, order blocks, FVGs, and market manipulation appear across Forex, Crypto, Commodities, and Stocks.
- Market-specific nuances—such as volatility, session timing, and correlation—must be understood and adapted for consistent execution.
- Studying real examples builds intuition, reinforces probabilistic thinking, and develops the ability to anticipate institutional moves.
- Cross-market analysis enhances flexibility, allowing traders to apply SMC setups in multiple environments with confidence and accuracy.

By examining concrete examples across diverse instruments, traders learn to identify patterns, confirm high-probability setups, and refine their approach to align with institutional behavior—creating a systematic, repeatable edge in all markets.

15.2 Step-by-Step Trade Breakdowns

Understanding Smart Money Concepts (SMC) in theory is important, but the ability to execute trades successfully comes from dissecting real examples step by step. This section provides detailed breakdowns of trades across different markets, highlighting how institutional behavior, liquidity, and market structure dictate high-probability setups.

Step 1: Identifying Market Context

Before considering any trade, determine the overall market structure:

- **Trend Analysis:** Establish whether the market is in an uptrend, downtrend, or range. Use higher timeframe charts to identify primary bias.
- **Swing Highs and Lows:** Mark recent swing highs and lows to locate potential liquidity pools.
- **Session Consideration:** Take note of London, New York, and Asian session dynamics for timing entries.

Step 2: Locating High-Probability Zones

High-probability trades rely on confluence zones created by institutional activity:

- **Order Blocks (OBs):** Identify bullish or bearish OBs and anticipate potential retests.
- **Fair Value Gaps (FVGs):** Highlight gaps where price moved rapidly, leaving unfilled zones that institutions often revisit.
- **Liquidity Pools:** Mark stop-loss clusters above swing highs or below swing lows to anticipate stop hunts.

Step 3: Planning Entry and Exit

Once high-probability zones are identified, refine entry and exit strategy:

- **Entry:** Look for confirmation via OB retests, breaker blocks, or Optimal Trade Entry (OTE) levels.
- **Stop-Loss Placement:** Position stops beyond key liquidity pools or swing points to avoid being prematurely stopped out.
- **Take-Profit:** Target FVG fills, mitigation blocks, or previous structural levels to maximize risk-reward ratio.

Step 4: Trade Execution

Execute the trade with discipline and follow pre-defined rules:

- Enter only when confluence conditions align (OB + FVG + liquidity pool + trend bias).
- Confirm multi-timeframe alignment to ensure entries are in line with higher timeframe market direction.
- Monitor price action post-entry to adapt stops and partial profits if required.

Step 5: Post-Trade Analysis

After the trade, evaluate performance to improve future execution:

- Record trade in journal, including entry, exit, rationale, and observed institutional behavior.
- Analyze whether the setup met all pre-defined criteria and if deviations impacted the result.
- Identify lessons: what worked, what failed, and why certain price reactions occurred.

Example Trade Breakdown: EUR/USD

Context: Daily chart shows uptrend; recent 4H OB aligned with swing low.

1. **Identify OB:** Bullish OB on 4H chart near 1.0950.
2. **Locate FVG:** Unfilled gap between 1.0940–1.0945.
3. **Check Liquidity Pool:** Stop-loss cluster just below swing low at 1.0935.
4. **Entry:** Enter long on 1H chart when price retests OB and forms a bullish rejection candle at 1.0948.
5. **Stop-Loss:** Set at 1.0930 (below liquidity pool and OB).
6. **Take-Profit:** First target at FVG fill (1.0945), second target at previous swing high (1.0980).
7. **Outcome:** Trade reaches both targets with proper risk-reward; journal notes confirm alignment with SMC principles.

Key Takeaways

- Step-by-step breakdowns illustrate how multiple SMC factors—OBs, FVGs, liquidity pools, and market structure—combine to create high-probability trades.
- Real examples reinforce the importance of preparation, confluence, and disciplined execution.
- Post-trade analysis ensures learning from both successful and unsuccessful setups, strengthening probabilistic decision-making.
- Practicing structured trade breakdowns builds intuition and confidence for live market execution.

By systematically following these steps, traders convert abstract Smart Money Concepts into actionable strategies, improving accuracy, consistency, and overall trading performance across multiple markets.

15.3 Analysis of Successful and Failed Trades

Learning from past trades is essential to refine strategy, improve decision-making, and internalize Smart Money Concepts (SMC). Both successful and failed trades provide valuable lessons. Success confirms the validity of your approach, while failures expose weaknesses in execution, understanding, or discipline.

Analyzing Successful Trades

Successful trades reinforce patterns, risk management, and probabilistic thinking:

- **Entry Alignment:** Trades that succeed typically occur when all high-probability conditions align—order block retest, fair value gap fill, liquidity pool location, and trend bias.
- **Market Structure Confirmation:** Verification of break of structure (BoS), change of character (CHoCH), and swing highs/lows ensures institutional alignment.
- **Risk Management:** Proper stop-loss placement, position sizing, and R:R adherence prevent small errors from eroding profits.
- **Behavioral Consistency:** Successful trades often correlate with patience, waiting for confirmations, and avoiding emotional decisions such as chasing the market or entering impulsively.

Analyzing Failed Trades

Failures are equally instructive and often highlight recurring pitfalls:

- **Premature Entries:** Entering before full confirmation from OBs, FVG fills, or multi-timeframe alignment leads to stops being triggered unnecessarily.
- **Ignoring Liquidity Pools:** Overlooking stop-loss clusters or institutional liquidity zones often results in being caught in smart money traps (SMTs).
- **Emotional Decisions:** FOMO, revenge trading, or impatience to capture "quick profits" can override the SMC process, increasing loss probability.
- **Poor Risk Management:** Oversized positions, inadequate stop-losses, or ignoring R:R targets amplify losses even on high-probability setups.

Structured Post-Trade Review

A methodical review process ensures that lessons from each trade are internalized:

1. **Document Setup:** Record all aspects of the trade including entry rationale, stop-loss, take-profit, market context, and timeframes.
2. **Compare Outcome vs Plan:** Analyze deviations from your trade plan and whether they influenced the result positively or negatively.
3. **Identify Key Learnings:** Determine whether success was due to proper SMC alignment or if failure occurred due to emotional/behavioral factors.
4. **Actionable Adjustments:** Adjust future entries, stops, or analysis methods to mitigate repeated errors.

Case Example: A Failed Trade in Crypto

Scenario: BTC/USD showing an apparent bullish OB retest on 1H chart.

- Entry was made early before candle confirmation.
- Liquidity pool above swing high was ignored.
- Price triggered stop-loss within minutes due to a liquidity sweep.
- Post-trade review identified impatience and overconfidence as the main errors.

Case Example: A Successful Forex Trade

Scenario: EUR/USD bullish reversal aligning with daily OB and FVG.

- Entry waited for confirmation with bullish rejection candle.
- Stop-loss placed below liquidity pool, respecting institutional zones.
- Trade hit first and second take-profit targets with proper R:R adherence.
- Review confirmed strict adherence to SMC process as the key to success.

Key Takeaways

- Both successful and failed trades provide critical insights; success validates, failure educates.
- Emotional discipline, adherence to high-probability setups, and structured post-trade review are essential for long-term consistency.
- Understanding why a trade fails is as important as understanding why it succeeds; it strengthens probabilistic decision-making.
- Over time, systematically analyzing all trades fosters intuition for market behavior, enhances accuracy, and builds confidence for executing SMC strategies.

By consistently reviewing both successes and failures, traders develop a feedback loop that improves precision, reinforces institutional alignment, and creates a disciplined approach to navigating complex markets with confidence.

Chapter 16

Data-Driven Performance

Successful trading is not just about intuition or spotting high-probability setups; it is fundamentally a numbers game. Smart Money Concepts (SMC) and ICT strategies provide a framework to identify institutional behavior, but consistent profitability requires a disciplined, data-driven approach. Tracking performance, analyzing outcomes, and quantifying edge are essential to transform probabilistic strategies into measurable results.
This chapter focuses on the metrics, tools, and methodologies necessary to assess your trading objectively. By leveraging win/loss ratios, statistical analysis, and performance tracking templates, traders gain insights into the efficiency of their strategies, identify areas for improvement, and develop confidence rooted in evidence rather than emotion.

16.1 Win/Loss Ratios & Statistical Analysis

In trading, consistent profitability stems not only from identifying high-probability setups but also from objectively analyzing performance. Win/loss ratios and statistical metrics provide a quantitative framework to evaluate trading decisions, validate strategies, and identify areas for improvement.

Understanding Win/Loss Ratios

The win/loss ratio is the most fundamental metric in assessing performance. It represents the proportion of profitable trades compared to losing trades over a given period.

$$\text{Win/Loss Ratio} = \frac{\text{Number of Winning Trades}}{\text{Number of Losing Trades}} \tag{16.1}$$

For example, if a trader executes 100 trades in a month, winning 60 and losing 40, the win/loss ratio is:

$$\frac{60}{40} = 1.5$$

A ratio greater than 1 indicates more winning trades than losing ones. However, this metric alone is insufficient because profitability also depends on the risk-reward ratio of each trade.

Integrating Risk-Reward Analysis

The risk-reward (R:R) ratio measures potential reward relative to potential risk for each trade. Combining R:R with the win/loss ratio allows traders to assess the expected value of their strategy:

$$\text{(EV)} = (\text{Win Probability} \times \text{Average Win}) - (\text{Loss Probability} \times \text{Average Loss}) \tag{16.2}$$

For example, consider a trader with a 60% win rate, an average gain of 50 pips, and an average loss of 30 pips:

$$EV = (0.6 \times 50) - (0.4 \times 30) = 30 - 12 = 18 \text{ pips per trade}$$

A positive EV indicates a statistically profitable strategy over the long term, even if some trades are losses.

Additional Statistical Metrics

- **Profit Factor:** Ratio of total profits to total losses. A profit factor above 1 indicates overall profitability.
- **Average Gain vs. Average Loss:** Helps determine if gains sufficiently compensate for occasional losses.
- **Maximum Drawdown:** Largest peak-to-trough loss in the account. Crucial for risk management and psychological preparedness.
- **Consistency Metrics:** Track win/loss streaks, time-in-trade analysis, and trade frequency to identify behavioral or systemic inefficiencies.

Applying Statistical Analysis to SMC Trades

Smart Money Concepts (SMC) setups often involve complex multi-factor conditions, including order blocks, fair value gaps, liquidity pools, and market structure. By quantifying their performance:

- Identify which OB/FVG combinations yield the highest win probability.
- Determine session-specific tendencies (e.g., London vs. New York) for edge optimization.
- Evaluate multi-timeframe alignment effectiveness in improving trade success.

Practical Tracking Example

Suppose a trader records 50 trades over one month:

- **Winning Trades:** 30 trades with an average gain of \$150 each.
- **Losing Trades:** 20 trades with an average loss of \$90 each.

Win/Loss Ratio: $30/20 = 1.5$
Expected Value: $(0.6 \times 150) - (0.4 \times 90) = 90 - 36 = 54$
This demonstrates a profitable setup with consistent positive expectancy, despite 40% of trades being losses. Over time, this kind of statistical discipline compounds advantage.

Key Takeaways

- Win/loss ratios and statistical analysis provide objective measures of strategy effectiveness.
- Combining win rate with risk-reward evaluation creates a complete picture of expected performance.
- Tracking consistency, drawdowns, and session-specific tendencies allows traders to refine SMC strategies for maximum edge.
- Regular data analysis instills discipline, reinforces probabilistic thinking, and transforms intuition into measurable, repeatable results.

By systematically applying statistical analysis to trades, traders gain actionable insights, improve decision-making, and develop a data-driven edge that aligns with Smart Money Concepts and ICT methodologies.

16.2 Edge Quantification for Setups

In trading, having a probabilistic edge is what separates consistent winners from those who rely on luck. Smart Money Concepts (SMC) provide a framework to identify institutional activity, but not every setup offers the same level of statistical advantage. Edge quantification allows traders to measure which setups are truly high-probability and optimize their strategy for long-term profitability.

Defining Edge in Trading

Trading edge refers to the measurable advantage a trader has in the market. It can be expressed in terms of expected value (EV), win probability, risk-reward ratio, or the consistency of favorable outcomes over time. Mathematically:

$$\text{Edge} = (\text{Win Probability} \times \text{Average Gain}) - (\text{Loss Probability} \times \text{Average Loss}) \quad (16.3)$$

A positive edge indicates that, over many trades, the strategy is expected to generate profits, even if some trades result in losses.

Identifying High-Edge Setups in SMC

Not all SMC setups provide equal advantage. Edge quantification involves evaluating historical performance and setup-specific probabilities:

- **Order Blocks (OBs):** Assess which bullish or bearish OBs historically lead to higher win rates. For instance, daily OB retests may offer a stronger edge than lower timeframe OBs due to institutional influence.
- **Fair Value Gaps (FVGs):** Measure how often price fills these gaps and reverses as expected. Some FVGs in trending markets provide greater probability than others in sideways conditions.
- **Liquidity Pools:** Evaluate how frequently stops above swing highs or below swing lows are taken before a continuation, giving insight into stop-hunt reliability.
- **Confluence Factors:** Combine multiple SMC elements—OB + FVG + liquidity pools + market structure—to identify setups with the highest statistical probability.

Measuring Edge with Historical Data

A systematic approach to edge quantification involves:

1. **Collecting Data:** Record trades for each type of setup, including entry/exit, timeframe, and market context.
2. **Calculating Probabilities:** Determine win rate, average gain, and average loss for each setup.
3. **Expected Value (EV):** Calculate EV to quantify whether the setup is profitable over time.
4. **Comparing Setups:** Rank setups based on EV, risk-reward, and consistency to prioritize trades with the highest edge.

Example: Quantifying Edge in EUR/USD OB Retests

Suppose a trader reviews 100 OB retests on the 4-hour EUR/USD chart:

- 70 trades were winners with an average gain of 50 pips.

- 30 trades were losers with an average loss of 25 pips.

Win Probability: $70/100 = 0.7$
Loss Probability: $30/100 = 0.3$
Expected Value: $(0.7 \times 50) - (0.3 \times 25) = 35 - 7.5 = 27.5$ pips per trade
This setup demonstrates a significant positive edge, validating the inclusion of 4H OB retests in the trader's strategy.

Edge Optimization Tips

- Prioritize trades with higher EV and stronger confluence of SMC factors.
- Avoid setups with low win probability or inconsistent outcomes, even if they appear attractive visually.
- Continuously update statistical analysis as market conditions evolve; edge is not static.
- Use multi-timeframe alignment to further improve the probability of success.

Key Takeaways

- Quantifying edge transforms SMC setups from subjective observations into data-driven decisions.
- Positive expected value, high win probability, and risk-reward analysis are critical components of measurable edge.
- Historical trade analysis is essential to determine which setups consistently outperform.
- Edge quantification enables traders to focus on setups that offer the highest probability of success, optimizing performance and reducing guesswork.

By systematically quantifying edge for each SMC setup, traders gain a disciplined, probabilistic approach, ensuring that every trade contributes to long-term profitability and consistent execution aligned with institutional behavior.

16.3 Performance Tracking Templates

Consistent trading success is not achieved by intuition alone. Systematic record-keeping and structured performance tracking provide the foundation for improvement, discipline, and long-term profitability. Using performance tracking templates, traders can quantify results, identify strengths and weaknesses, and refine Smart Money Concepts (SMC) strategies over time.

Purpose of Performance Tracking

Performance tracking allows traders to:

- Maintain an accurate historical record of trades, setups, and outcomes.
- Measure win/loss ratios, risk-reward performance, and statistical edge.
- Identify patterns of success and recurring mistakes.
- Adjust position sizing, timing, and entry/exit strategies based on empirical evidence.
- Reinforce discipline and probabilistic thinking by separating emotions from decisions.

Essential Elements of a Tracking Template

A comprehensive performance tracking template should capture the following data for every trade:

1. **Trade Metadata:**
   - Date and time of entry and exit
   - Market and instrument (Forex, Crypto, Stocks, Commodities)
   - Timeframe used for analysis
2. **Setup Details:**
   - Order block (OB) type and location
   - Fair value gap (FVG) details
   - Liquidity pool or stop-loss cluster
   - Market structure context (trend, break of structure, change of character)
   - Multi-timeframe alignment
3. **Trade Execution:**
   - Entry price and rationale
   - Stop-loss placement and justification
   - Take-profit targets
   - Position size and risk percentage
4. **Outcome Metrics:**
   - Profit or loss in pips or currency
   - Risk-reward ratio achieved

- Win or loss indicator
- Duration of trade

5. **Post-Trade Notes:**
   - Emotional state during the trade
   - Deviations from trade plan
   - Observations of institutional behavior
   - Lessons learned

Template Formats

Performance tracking templates can be implemented in multiple formats:

- **Spreadsheets:** Excel or Google Sheets with structured columns for each data point; allows automatic calculation of metrics like win/loss ratio, expected value, and average risk-reward.
- **Trading Journals:** Digital or physical journals where trades are logged with notes, screenshots, and charts; useful for qualitative analysis.
- **Specialized Software:** Platforms such as TradingDiary Pro, Edgewonk, or custom-built databases can automate statistics, track performance, and provide visual analytics.

Using Templates for SMC Analysis

When tracking SMC-based trades, templates help evaluate:

- Which OB or FVG setups consistently produce positive expectancy.
- Session-specific performance (London, New York, Asia) to optimize timing.
- Multi-timeframe alignment effectiveness in different market conditions.
- Recurring mistakes or deviations from plan that reduce edge.

Practical Example: Spreadsheet Layout

A simplified performance tracking sheet may include the following columns:

Date	Pair	TF	Setup Type	Entry	SL	TP	Outcome
10 Oct	EUR/USD	1H	Bullish OB + FVG	1.0945	1.093	1.098	Win
11 Oct	BTC/USD	4H	Bearish OB	29500	29700	29000	Loss

Additional columns can track R:R, EV, session, trade duration, and notes for comprehensive analysis.

Key Takeaways

- Structured performance tracking transforms intuition into measurable, data-driven results.
- Templates allow identification of high-edge SMC setups, session biases, and multi-timeframe efficiencies.
- Post-trade notes reinforce learning from both wins and losses, improving discipline and emotional control.
- Regular review of tracked data enhances probabilistic thinking and long-term trading consistency.

By systematically maintaining performance tracking templates, traders create a feedback loop that strengthens strategy, validates setups, and aligns execution with institutional behavior, ensuring sustainable, evidence-based trading growth.

16.4 Equity Curve Analysis

Equity curve analysis is one of the most important components of evaluating a trader's performance. While win rate, risk-to-reward ratios, and profitability metrics provide partial insights, the **equity curve** reveals the true quality, stability, and sustainability of a trading system.

An equity curve reflects the growth (or decline) of account equity over time, capturing the cumulative effects of:

- winning streaks,
- drawdowns,
- volatility,
- risk management,
- consistency of execution,
- psychological discipline.

Professional funds, prop firms, and algorithmic desks treat the equity curve as the **primary diagnostic tool** for assessing a trader's long-term edge.

What Is an Equity Curve?

An equity curve is a graphical representation of the account's equity across a sequential series of trades.

If E_t represents the equity after trade t, then the equity curve is simply:

$$\{E_1, E_2, E_3, \ldots, E_n\}$$

The slope, curvature, and structure of this curve provide insights into:

- the robustness of a strategy,
- the smoothness of performance,
- the level of drawdown,
- the volatility of returns.

Why Equity Curve Analysis Matters

Equity curve analysis answers critical questions that raw profit numbers cannot:

1. Is the performance stable or unstable?
2. Is the strategy reliant on a few big wins?
3. Are drawdowns increasing over time?
4. Is variance too high for long-term survival?
5. Is the trader becoming more or less consistent?

A "good" equity curve is not just profitable—it is:

- smooth,
- controlled,
- volatility-adjusted,
- risk-governed,
- statistically reliable.

Key Components of Equity Curve Analysis

1. Smoothness (Equity Stability)

Smoothness reflects how evenly equity grows over time.

A smooth curve indicates:

- consistent execution,
- small and controlled drawdowns,
- stable risk.

A jagged curve often indicates:

- inconsistent risk-taking,
- emotional trading,
- high-variance strategies.

2. Drawdowns

Drawdowns measure the depth of the worst losses relative to the equity peak.

$$\text{Drawdown}(t) = \frac{E_{\text{peak}} - E_t}{E_{\text{peak}}} \times 100\%$$

A safe equity curve maintains:

- shallow drawdowns,
- rapid recovery,
- no consecutive deep drops.

3. Consecutive Losing Streaks

Losing streaks reveal:

- psychological resilience,
- strategy variance,
- risk exposure during poor market conditions.

A good system limits streak length (typically 3–5 losses).

4. Variance and Volatility of Returns

Variance measures how much returns fluctuate from trade to trade.

High variance suggests:

- unstable risk management,
- inconsistent position sizing,
- strategy weakness in certain conditions.

5. Equity Curve Regression Slope

The regression line of the curve defines the long-term trend of performance.

Let $y = mx + b$ be the linear regression of the equity curve. A higher slope m represents stronger average profitability.

6. Equity Curve Derivative (Momentum of Performance)

The rate of change reveals:

- when trader performance is accelerating,
- when performance is deteriorating.

$$\Delta E_t = E_t - E_{t-1}$$

Tracking ΔE_t highlights subtle behavioral or strategy shifts.

Equity Curve Patterns and Their Meaning

1. Smooth Upward Curve

Indicates:

- consistent execution,
- disciplined risk,
- stable edge.

2. Stair-Step Curve

Represents long flat periods followed by sharp jumps. Usually caused by:

- relying on a few big wins,
- low trade frequency strategies.

3. Jagged, Volatile Curve

Signals:

- inconsistent performance,
- improper risk scaling,
- possible overtrading or revenge trading.

4. Declining Equity Curve

Warns:

- edge deterioration,
- market condition mismatch,
- emotional instability,
- poor risk management.

How to Improve the Equity Curve

1. Smoothing the Curve

Achieved by:

- reducing position size,
- avoiding low-quality setups,
- filtering trades by time-of-day or market session,
- enhancing confluence requirements.

2. Controlling Drawdowns

Use:

- daily DD limits,
- weekly DD caps,
- losing streak rules,
- risk tiering (risk increases only after hitting equity milestones).

3. Maintaining Consistency

Consistency improves when:

- the strategy is applied mechanically,
- psychological errors decrease,
- journal-based feedback loops are used.

Advanced Metrics for Equity Curve Evaluation

1. Expectancy

$$E = (P_w \times A_w) - (P_l \times A_l)$$

Where:

- P_w = probability of winning,
- A_w = average win,
- P_l = probability of losing,
- A_l = average loss.

2. System Quality Number (SQN)

A Van Tharp metric evaluating strategy quality:

$$SQN = \frac{\text{Mean}(R)}{\text{StdDev}(R)} \times \sqrt{n}$$

3. Ulcer Index

Measures depth of sustained drawdowns:

$$UI = \sqrt{\frac{1}{n}\sum(DD_t^2)}$$

Using the Equity Curve as a Feedback Loop

The equity curve is not just an evaluation tool—it is a **self-correcting system**. Traders should adjust behavior based on curve feedback:

- Rising curve: maintain or gradually increase risk.
- Flat curve: refine filters, avoid marginal setups.
- Falling curve: stop trading and diagnose errors.

Summary

- The equity curve is the most important performance measurement tool.
- It reveals consistency, stability, risk exposure, and emotional control.
- Smooth upward curves reflect strong execution and risk governance.
- Jagged or declining curves indicate instability requiring intervention.
- Advanced metrics (expectancy, SQN, ulcer index) refine analysis.

- Proper equity curve evaluation transforms trading into an adaptive, feedback-driven process.

Analyzing the equity curve with discipline allows traders to foresee risks, improve strategy robustness, and evolve into consistent professional operators.

16.5 Expectancy Formula

A trading system's true profitability cannot be evaluated by win rate alone. Nor can it be measured solely by average return, risk-to-reward ratios, or drawdowns in isolation. The most accurate method for determining the long-term viability of any strategy is the **Expectancy Formula**.

Expectancy reveals the *average amount a trader can expect to win or lose per trade* over a large sample. It transforms performance into a quantifiable statistical edge.

Definition of Expectancy

Expectancy measures how much money, on average, a trader earns for every risked unit (1R) after many trades.

Formally:

$$E = (P_w \times A_w) - (P_l \times A_l)$$

Where:

- P_w = probability of a winning trade,
- A_w = average win (in R-multiple or percentage),
- P_l = probability of a losing trade,
- A_l = average loss (in R-multiple or percentage).

If $E > 0$, the trader has a **positive edge**. If $E < 0$, the system will lose long term regardless of win rate.

Why Expectancy Matters

Expectancy provides answers to essential questions:

- Does the system truly have an edge?
- Is the trader consistently profitable or lucky?
- Will the system survive 100+ or 1000+ trades?
- Is the reward-to-risk ratio strong enough to offset losses?
- Can the trader scale position sizes safely?

Professional traders and quantitative systems rely on expectancy—not win rate—to validate a strategy.

Components of Expectancy

Expectancy depends on two critical dimensions:

1. Win Probability (P_w)

Represents the proportion of trades that end in profit.

2. Win/Loss Size Ratio

Captures the relationship between:

- average winner (A_w),
- average loser (A_l).

A low win rate can still produce high expectancy if average winners are large:

$$A_w \gg A_l$$

A high win rate may still produce negative expectancy if losses are too large:

$$A_l > A_w$$

Examples of Expectancy Calculations

Example 1: High Win Rate, Low R:R

$$P_w = 0.70, \quad A_w = 1R, \quad P_l = 0.30, \quad A_l = 2R$$

$$E = (0.70 \times 1R) - (0.30 \times 2R) = 0.70 - 0.60 = 0.10R$$

This system is barely profitable.

Example 2: Low Win Rate, High R:R

$$P_w = 0.40, \quad A_w = 3R, \quad P_l = 0.60, \quad A_l = 1R$$

$$E = (0.40 \times 3R) - (0.60 \times 1R) = 1.20 - 0.60 = 0.60R$$

Despite a lower win rate, this system is far stronger.

Example 3: Negative Expectancy System

$$P_w = 0.55, \quad A_w = 1R, \quad P_l = 0.45, \quad A_l = 2R$$

$$E = (0.55 \times 1R) - (0.45 \times 2R) = 0.55 - 0.90 = -0.35R$$

Even with a 55% win rate, the strategy loses long term.

Expectancy and Sample Size

To be statistically meaningful, expectancy must be calculated over a sufficiently large number of trades. A minimum sample size:

- 100 trades = acceptable,
- 300 trades = reliable,
- 1000 trades = statistically robust.

Small sample sizes produce misleading expectancy due to variance.

Expectancy per Risk Unit

Expectancy is typically normalized per 1R risk. This ensures fairness regardless of position size, account size, or instrument.

Expected growth per trade:

$$E_{\%} = E \times \text{Risk per Trade (\%)}$$

For example:

$$E = 0.6R, \quad \text{Risk per Trade} = 1\%$$

$$E_{\%} = 0.6\%$$

Meaning: *On average, the trader grows the account by 0.6% per trade.*

Expectancy in Real-World Trading

Expectancy helps traders:

- understand the true value of their strategy,
- control emotions during losing streaks,
- increase risk in a controlled manner,
- build confidence in long-term performance,
- evaluate performance over weeks, months, or years.

Even when short-term results appear poor, positive expectancy ensures profitability over time.

Improving Expectancy

Expectancy can be improved by:

- increasing average win size (improving R:R),
- reducing average loss size (tightening risk),
- increasing win rate via better filtering,
- removing marginal trades,
- increasing confluence,
- avoiding emotional or impulsive actions.

Small improvements to expectancy produce exponential long-term effects due to compounding.

Summary

- Expectancy measures the average profit or loss per trade.
- Positive expectancy ($E > 0$) is essential for long-term success.
- Win rate alone is not enough—win/loss size matters equally.
- Expectancy must be calculated over a large sample of trades.
- Testing expectancy reveals whether a strategy is scalable and robust.
- Improving expectancy improves long-term equity curve stability.

The expectancy formula is the mathematical foundation of professional trading performance evaluation and a core component of edge quantification.

Part V

Trader Psychology & Discipline

Chapter 17

Mindset & Discipline

Trading is as much a psychological endeavor as it is a technical one. Even the most precise Smart Money Concepts (SMC) setups and ICT strategies can fail if the trader's mindset is misaligned with the probabilistic nature of markets. Emotional control, disciplined execution, and mental resilience are critical components that distinguish consistently profitable traders from those who succumb to impulse or stress.

This chapter explores the mental framework required to trade like an institution. It delves into the principles of patience, consistency, and emotional control, highlighting how cognitive biases such as overtrading, FOMO (Fear of Missing Out), and revenge trading undermine results. Traders will also learn techniques for achieving flow states, managing stress, and maintaining composure while waiting for high-probability setups.

17.1 Patience, Consistency, Emotional Control

Mastering Smart Money Concepts (SMC) and ICT strategies requires more than understanding market structure, order blocks, and liquidity pools. Without the right mental approach, even the most technically sound trades can fail. Patience, consistency, and emotional control are foundational traits that separate professional traders from retail participants who chase impulsive trades.

Patience: The Art of Waiting for Optimal Setups

Patience is the ability to wait for the market to present high-probability setups that align with institutional behavior. Many retail traders fall into the trap of "market FOMO," entering trades prematurely or on weak setups. Key aspects include:

- **Waiting for Confluence:** Only take trades where multiple factors align—OBs, FVGs, liquidity pools, and market structure confirm the setup.

- **Timeframe Discipline:** Avoid forcing trades on lower timeframes when higher timeframe analysis does not support a direction.
- **Mental Patience:** Accept that not every day offers trading opportunities; missing trades is preferable to entering suboptimal setups.

Example: A trader identifies a bullish order block on the daily chart but notices that price is currently in a downtrend on the 1-hour chart. Patience dictates waiting for a break of structure and retracement into the OB before executing, even if it takes several days.

Consistency: Following a Systematic Process

Consistency is the discipline to follow your trading plan and methodology across multiple trades, irrespective of short-term outcomes. This is achieved by:

- **Standardized Routine:** Implement pre-trade analysis, checklists, and journaling for every trade.
- **Reproducible Execution:** Enter trades using defined criteria, position sizing, and risk management rules without deviation.
- **Long-Term Perspective:** Focus on expected value and edge over hundreds of trades, rather than individual wins or losses.

Example: Even after a streak of losses, a disciplined trader follows the same SMC setup criteria without changing stop-losses or risk allocation impulsively, trusting the statistical edge of the methodology.

Emotional Control: Managing Psychological States

Emotional control prevents fear, greed, and frustration from dictating trading decisions. Key strategies include:

- **Recognizing Emotional Triggers:** Identify moments when FOMO, revenge trading, or overconfidence may influence entries.
- **Breathing and Pause Techniques:** Use micro-breaks, deep breathing, or brief meditation during high-volatility periods.
- **Objective Evaluation:** Focus on data-driven decisions; rely on your edge and statistical advantage rather than intuition alone.
- **Acceptance of Losses:** Treat losses as part of the probabilistic nature of trading rather than personal failures.

Example: After a sudden market spike triggers a stop-loss, a trader resists revenge trading, reviews the setup objectively, and waits for the next high-probability OB retest, maintaining composure.

Integrating Patience, Consistency, and Emotional Control

These three traits reinforce each other:

- Patience reduces impulsive trades, which in turn improves consistency.
- Consistency builds confidence, which helps regulate emotions during drawdowns.
- Emotional control allows a trader to adhere to both patience and consistency under stress.

Developing these traits is a continuous process, often requiring journaling, self-reflection, and repeated practice. Traders who internalize patience, consistency, and emotional control are better positioned to execute high-probability SMC setups with confidence and discipline, transforming probabilistic edge into tangible, long-term results.

Key Takeaways

- Patience ensures entry only at optimal setups, avoiding unnecessary losses.
- Consistency builds a reproducible process, emphasizing expected value over individual outcomes.
- Emotional control prevents impulsive decisions and maintains alignment with statistical edge.
- Mastery of these mental traits is as crucial as technical expertise in achieving sustainable trading success.

17.2 Cognitive Biases: Overtrading, FOMO, Revenge Trading

Even the most technically sound strategies can fail if cognitive biases influence decision-making. In trading, psychological tendencies often override logic, leading to suboptimal entries, exits, and risk management. Understanding, identifying, and mitigating these biases is crucial for consistently executing Smart Money Concepts (SMC) and ICT strategies.

Overtrading

Overtrading occurs when a trader takes too many trades in a short period, often ignoring the quality of setups. It is driven by the desire to generate profits quickly, impatience, or attempting to recover from losses.

Causes:

- Lack of patience for high-probability setups.
- Attempting to capitalize on every minor market movement.
- Emotional responses to previous losses or streaks of wins.

Consequences:

- Diminished edge: Entering low-probability trades reduces expected value.
- Increased transaction costs and slippage.
- Emotional fatigue and stress, leading to further mistakes.

Mitigation Strategies:

- Establish a daily or weekly limit on trades.
- Use strict entry criteria based on OB, FVG, liquidity pools, and market structure.
- Focus on quality over quantity; wait for setups with confluence and statistical edge.

Example: A trader notices minor retracements in a trending market and enters multiple trades without waiting for confluence. This leads to small but repeated losses, eroding both capital and confidence.

FOMO (Fear of Missing Out)

FOMO is the anxiety of missing a profitable move, causing impulsive entries before the market aligns with a high-probability setup. It is especially prevalent during volatile sessions or strong trending markets.

Causes:

- Observing strong price movement without a setup confirmation.
- Comparing oneself to other traders or perceived "opportunities."
- Overestimation of personal skill in predicting market turns.

Consequences:

- Entering trades with poor risk-reward ratios.
- Breaching predetermined stop-loss or entry rules.
- Increased stress and decreased trading discipline.

Mitigation Strategies:

- Rely strictly on pre-defined entry rules; ignore impulsive signals.

- Maintain a trade journal to review missed setups objectively.
- Practice probabilistic thinking: missing a trade is not a loss if your edge remains intact.

Example: Price breaks a bullish OB while the trader is away. Fear of missing out prompts an immediate market entry without waiting for a retracement or confirmation, resulting in a stop-loss hit.

Revenge Trading

Revenge trading is the attempt to recover previous losses by taking impulsive or riskier trades. It is driven by frustration and emotional reactivity, not by market logic or high-probability setups.

Causes:

- Reacting emotionally to a losing trade.
- Desire to quickly regain lost capital.
- Impaired judgment due to heightened stress or anger.

Consequences:

- Increasing losses exponentially.
- Breaking trading plan and risk management rules.
- Psychological fatigue and loss of confidence.

Mitigation Strategies:

- Step away from trading after a loss to reset emotional state.
- Review losses objectively using trade journals.
- Implement daily maximum loss limits to prevent emotional overreaction.

Example: A trader loses on a failed OB retest and immediately doubles position size in the next trade, violating risk management rules. This impulsive action leads to further capital loss.

Recognizing and Controlling Cognitive Biases

The key to mitigating cognitive biases lies in awareness, structured routines, and self-reflection:

- Maintain a trading journal to track emotional states, decisions, and deviations from plan.

- Predefine rules for entries, exits, and risk management to reduce impulsivity.
- Schedule breaks and review periods to reflect on past trades without immediate pressure.
- Practice mindfulness and emotional regulation techniques to stay calm under market stress.

Key Takeaways

- Overtrading, FOMO, and revenge trading are common cognitive biases that erode edge and consistency.
- Awareness and structured routines are essential for controlling these biases.
- Journaling, pre-defined rules, and probabilistic thinking help transform emotional reactions into disciplined, strategic decisions.
- Mastering cognitive control allows traders to fully leverage SMC setups and ICT strategies without letting emotions undermine their probabilistic advantage.

17.3 Flow & State Management

Achieving peak performance in trading is not solely a matter of technical knowledge or strategy. The trader's mental and emotional state plays a pivotal role in executing Smart Money Concepts (SMC) and ICT strategies effectively. Flow and state management involve cultivating the optimal psychological and physiological condition to make clear, disciplined, and probabilistic trading decisions.

Understanding Flow in Trading

The concept of flow, popularized by psychologist Mihaly Csikszentmihalyi, refers to a mental state of deep focus, immersion, and effortless engagement in an activity. In trading, flow enables a trader to:

- Analyze markets efficiently without distractions.
- Make split-second decisions with clarity and confidence.
- Maintain emotional equilibrium even during high-volatility periods.
- Execute trades with discipline and adherence to strategy.

Flow is often described as being "in the zone," where time seems to slow, distractions fade, and performance reaches its peak. For traders, this state allows SMC setups to be identified and executed with precision.

Techniques for Achieving Flow

Traders can adopt several strategies to consistently enter and maintain flow states:

1. **Pre-Session Rituals:** Develop a structured routine before trading, including reviewing charts, news, and session plans. Rituals prepare the mind and body for focused engagement.

2. **Goal Setting:** Define clear, achievable objectives for each trading session, such as analyzing a specific number of setups or practicing trade journaling. Focused goals facilitate flow.

3. **Environmental Control:** Minimize distractions by creating a quiet, organized workspace. Use dual monitors for charts and analysis, ensuring everything is within reach.

4. **Mindfulness and Breathing:** Engage in brief meditation or deep-breathing exercises to calm the nervous system, reducing stress and enhancing concentration.

5. **Physical State Optimization:** Maintain energy levels through proper sleep, hydration, and nutrition. Physical well-being directly affects mental clarity and reaction times.

Maintaining State During Volatile Markets

High volatility can disrupt focus and induce emotional responses. State management techniques include:

- **Anchoring Attention:** Focus on predefined setups (OBs, FVGs, liquidity pools) rather than reacting to every market movement.

- **Micro-Breaks:** Short breaks between trades or analysis periods help prevent cognitive fatigue.

- **Emotional Check-ins:** Periodically assess emotional state; if stress or excitement is high, pause and reset.

- **Limiting Screen Exposure:** Avoid over-monitoring markets; rely on alerts for key zones and setups to reduce sensory overload.

Flow and Probabilistic Trading

Probabilistic trading requires detachment from outcomes and reliance on edge, not certainty. Flow states support this mindset by:

- Reducing impulsive reactions to noise.

- Allowing clear recognition of high-probability SMC setups.

- Enhancing decision-making speed without sacrificing accuracy.
- Strengthening discipline in risk management and position sizing.

Key Takeaways

- Flow is a state of deep focus and effortless engagement critical for high-probability trading execution.
- Structured pre-session routines, goal setting, and environmental control help induce flow consistently.
- Managing physiological and psychological state reduces impulsivity and enhances decision-making under volatile conditions.
- Flow supports probabilistic thinking, allowing traders to trust their edge and execute SMC strategies with confidence and discipline.

17.4 Psychology of Waiting for Optimal Setups

One of the most challenging aspects of trading is learning to wait. Markets do not always present opportunities, and high-probability setups based on Smart Money Concepts (SMC) and ICT strategies may occur infrequently. The psychology of waiting is critical: it is the mental discipline to remain patient, observant, and prepared, resisting the urge to act prematurely.

Understanding the Need for Patience

Retail traders often struggle because they mistake activity for productivity. Entering trades without confluence or proper setup alignment leads to poor results, regardless of the strategy's theoretical edge. Waiting ensures:

- Entry into trades with optimal risk-reward ratios.
- Alignment with market structure, order blocks, and liquidity zones.
- Execution of trades that have a statistically favorable edge.

Example: A trader identifies a bullish order block on the daily chart. Instead of immediately buying, the price moves against them slightly, forming a retracement that perfectly aligns with the high-probability entry zone. Waiting allowed the trader to enter with minimal risk and maximum potential reward.

Probabilistic Mindset in Waiting

The psychology of waiting is deeply connected to probabilistic thinking:

- **Edge over Certainty:** Accept that no trade is guaranteed to win; focus on setups where statistical edge exists.
- **Long-Term Perspective:** A missed trade is not a loss if it preserves capital and avoids a low-probability scenario.
- **Confidence in Methodology:** Trust your SMC and ICT rules; the market will offer the right opportunity in time.

Patience combined with probabilistic thinking transforms trading from reactionary to strategic, where every entry is deliberate and every exit purposeful.

Techniques for Maintaining Discipline While Waiting

- **Pre-Defined Alerts:** Use chart alerts or notifications to signal when key zones or setups are approaching, reducing the temptation to constantly watch the market.
- **Journaling During Downtime:** Analyze past trades, review charts, or study upcoming setups while waiting to stay productive.
- **Mental Visualization:** Practice visualizing high-probability setups and how you would enter them. This reinforces discipline and readiness.
- **Micro-Goals:** Set small objectives for each session (e.g., identify three potential OBs) instead of chasing immediate execution.

Common Psychological Pitfalls

Even experienced traders can fall victim to impatience:

- **Chasing the Market:** Entering trades after price has already moved significantly, often resulting in poor risk-reward ratios.
- **Overanalyzing:** Spending too much time anticipating setups without executing when conditions are met.
- **Emotional Fatigue:** Restlessness from inactivity can trigger impulsive decisions; it is essential to remain mentally calm.

Key Takeaways

- Waiting for optimal setups is a strategic skill, not a passive behavior.
- Patience preserves capital, ensures high-probability entries, and aligns trades with institutional activity.

- A probabilistic mindset helps maintain confidence and reduces emotional pressure during periods without actionable trades.
- Structured routines, alerts, visualization, and journaling aid in maintaining discipline while waiting.

17.5 Self-Sabotage Patterns

One of the greatest challenges in trading is not technical skill, but the psychological and behavioral patterns that cause traders to sabotage their own success. Self-sabotage occurs when a trader's actions contradict their trading plan, risk rules, or long-term goals. These destructive behaviors often arise from emotional impulses, cognitive biases, unresolved fear, and an inability to tolerate uncertainty.

Understanding self-sabotage is essential for developing consistency, discipline, and long-term professional-level performance.

What Is Self-Sabotage in Trading?

Self-sabotage is any behavior that:

- undermines a trader's edge,
- violates predefined rules,
- increases risk beyond acceptable limits,
- results from emotional decision-making,
- disrupts long-term growth.

These patterns are not accidental. They emerge from deep psychological responses to risk, reward, fear, and unresolved emotional conditioning.

Why Self-Sabotage Occurs

Self-sabotage stems from:

- fear of missing out (FOMO),
- fear of losing,
- fear of being wrong,
- loss aversion,
- impulsive reactions to market noise,
- perfectionism and over-control,

- stress and emotional overload.

Traders often know what they *should* do, yet fail to execute because emotions override logic.

Common Self-Sabotage Patterns

1. Overtrading

Overtrading occurs when traders enter excessive trades without valid signals. Triggers include:

- boredom,
- revenge trading,
- chasing the market,
- trying to "make back" losses.

Overtrading increases variance and undermines expectancy.

2. Moving Stop-Losses

Changing stops after entry reflects:

- unwillingness to accept a loss,
- emotional attachment to a position,
- fear of being wrong.

This often turns a small controlled loss into a catastrophic drawdown.

3. Premature Entry (FOMO)

Entering trades before confirmation causes:

- entering during inducement,
- getting trapped before liquidity sweeps,
- inconsistent execution.

FOMO erodes discipline and leads to unnecessary drawdowns.

4. Premature Exit (Fear of Reversal)

Traders who exit too early often:

- do not trust their strategy,
- fear profits turning into losses,
- anchor on recent losing streaks.

This reduces average win size and destroys expectancy.

5. Increasing Position Size After Losses

This revenge mechanism reflects:

- emotional frustration,
- the desire to recover quickly,
- an escalation of risk without justification.

Such behavior can break max drawdown rules and accelerate account ruin.

6. System-Hopping

Traders abandon strategies after a few losses, seeking:

- "perfect" systems,
- guaranteed wins,
- elimination of uncertainty.

Frequent system switching prevents statistical edge from playing out.

7. Ignoring the Trading Plan

Deviation from the trading plan includes:

- taking setups outside session rules,
- ignoring HTF bias,
- trading impulsively based on emotion.

This reduces consistency and increases randomness in results.

8. Emotional Trading

Emotional trading emerges from:

- fear,
- greed,
- frustration,
- impatience.

Emotionally driven decisions lack structure, objectivity, and edge.

Underlying Psychological Drivers

Self-sabotage patterns originate from deeper psychological forces:

1. Loss Aversion

Losses are psychologically felt twice as strongly as equivalent gains, leading to:

- closing trades early,
- avoiding valid trades,
- holding losers too long.

2. Ego Protection

Traders often equate being wrong with personal failure, leading to:

- refusing to close losing trades,
- doubling down on bad positions,
- avoiding stop-losses.

3. Impulse-Based Decision Making

Neural reward circuits punish uncertainty, causing:

- impatience before confirmation,
- reacting to noise,
- chasing immediate reward.

4. Fear Conditioning

Past trauma (financial or emotional) creates:

- hesitation to take trades,
- closing trades too early,
- inconsistent risk management.

How to Break Self-Sabotage Patterns

1. Build Structured Rules

Self-sabotage thrives on ambiguity. Rules create safeguards:

- fixed risk per trade,
- predefined entry models,
- session limitations,
- max drawdown protocols.

2. Use a Trading Journal

Journaling reveals:

- emotional triggers,
- decision flaws,
- recurring patterns.

Reflection reduces repetition of harmful behaviors.

3. Automate Where Possible

Automation reduces emotional interference:

- alerts for entry zones,
- algorithmic partials,
- predefined stop-loss and take-profit.

4. Enforce Cooling-Off Periods

When emotional, a trader should:

- pause for the day,
- take a walk,
- analyze journal notes.

Self-regulation prevents catastrophic decisions.

5. Strengthen Process Orientation

Focusing on process rather than outcome reduces emotional swings. A good trade is defined by:

- following rules,
- acting on valid signals,
- managing risk correctly.

Outcome is secondary; execution quality is primary.

Summary

- Self-sabotage patterns arise from emotional, cognitive, and behavioral biases.
- Common patterns include overtrading, premature entries/exits, stop manipulation, system-hopping, and revenge trading.
- These behaviors undermine edge, consistency, and long-term profitability.
- Awareness and structured risk/process rules are essential for preventing self-destructive tendencies.
- Mastery of self-sabotage prevention is a prerequisite for achieving professional level trading discipline.

Self-awareness, structure, and psychological discipline form the backbone of long-term trading success.

Chapter 18

Stress & Performance Management

Trading is inherently stressful. Even the most methodical Smart Money Concepts (SMC) and ICT strategies expose traders to drawdowns, volatile markets, and unpredictable price action. How a trader manages stress, maintains focus, and sustains performance directly impacts long-term profitability.
This chapter explores the psychological and practical aspects of handling stress, controlling emotional swings, and maintaining peak performance over extended periods. It provides tools and techniques for daily mental preparation, decision-making under pressure, and strategies to achieve consistency, even in challenging market conditions.

18.1 Managing Drawdowns & Emotional Swings

Drawdowns—periods when trading capital declines due to a series of losses are an inevitable part of the trading journey. Emotional swings, such as fear, frustration, and overconfidence, often accompany drawdowns, leading traders to make impulsive decisions. Successfully managing these challenges is critical for preserving capital, maintaining discipline, and achieving long-term success.

Understanding Drawdowns

A drawdown is a temporary decline in account equity from a previous peak. They vary in depth and duration, depending on strategy, market conditions, and risk management. Understanding drawdowns helps traders:

- **Set Realistic Expectations:** Accept that losses are part of probabilistic trading.

- **Avoid Panic Responses:** Recognize that drawdowns do not indicate strategy failure if managed correctly.
- **Maintain Long-Term Perspective:** Focus on statistical edge over many trades rather than short-term results.

Example: A trader following SMC setups experiences a 10% drawdown over three trades due to unusual volatility. Recognizing this as part of the normal distribution of outcomes allows the trader to stick to the plan and avoid rash decisions.

Common Emotional Swings During Drawdowns

- **Fear:** Leads to hesitation, early exits, or skipping high-probability trades.
- **Frustration:** Can cause revenge trading, overtrading, or ignoring risk limits.
- **Overconfidence:** Following a streak of wins, traders may increase position sizes or deviate from their strategy, exposing themselves to larger losses.

Practical Strategies for Managing Drawdowns

- **Risk Management Rules:** Define maximum loss per trade and per day to limit drawdown exposure.
- **Position Sizing Discipline:** Use techniques like the Kelly Criterion or fixed fractional sizing to maintain consistent risk across trades.
- **Trade Journaling:** Document all trades, including emotional state and reasoning, to identify patterns and prevent repetition of mistakes.
- **Pause and Reset:** Take short breaks after consecutive losses to recalibrate mentally before executing new trades.
- **Probabilistic Mindset:** Focus on the edge and expected value of setups, not individual outcomes, to reduce emotional impact.

Techniques for Emotional Regulation

- **Mindfulness and Meditation:** Regular practice improves focus, reduces stress, and enhances emotional control during volatile periods.
- **Breathing Exercises:** Deep, controlled breathing helps calm the nervous system and prevent impulsive decisions.
- **Visualization:** Mentally rehearsing trades and handling losses reduces anxiety when facing real market scenarios.

- **Positive Self-Talk:** Replace negative thoughts like "I am losing" with constructive statements such as "I am following my edge and strategy."

Key Takeaways

- Drawdowns are a normal and expected part of trading; they do not define your skill or strategy.
- Emotional swings—fear, frustration, and overconfidence—can amplify losses if unmanaged.
- Implement structured risk management, position sizing, and journaling to maintain discipline during drawdowns.
- Mindfulness, breathing exercises, and visualization techniques help regulate emotions and improve decision-making.
- Adopting a probabilistic mindset allows traders to focus on statistical edge rather than individual trade outcomes, ensuring long-term consistency.

18.2 Daily Practices for Focus & Mental Clarity

Successful trading requires not just technical knowledge but also a sharp, focused mind. Mental clarity allows traders to interpret charts accurately, follow SMC and ICT setups, and execute trades without emotional interference. Establishing daily practices for focus and cognitive optimization is essential for consistent performance.

Morning Preparation Rituals

Starting the day with a structured routine sets the tone for disciplined trading:

- **Market Review:** Analyze pre-market news, economic calendars, and key levels from the previous session to anticipate potential market behavior.
- **Visualization of Trades:** Mentally rehearse high-probability setups you expect to encounter, reinforcing preparedness.
- **Mindfulness or Meditation:** Even 5–10 minutes of focused breathing or meditation reduces stress and primes the brain for clear decision-making.
- **Physical Activity:** Light exercise or stretching increases blood flow to the brain, improving alertness and cognitive function.

Structured Trading Routine

During market hours, following a structured routine enhances focus and reduces impulsive actions:

- **Checklists:** Use pre-trade and post-trade checklists to ensure setup validity, risk management, and confluence alignment.
- **Micro-Breaks:** Short, scheduled breaks prevent fatigue and mental drift, especially during long sessions.
- **Single-Tasking:** Focus on one analysis or trade at a time to avoid cognitive overload and reduce errors.
- **Alert Systems:** Utilize chart alerts for OBs, FVGs, and liquidity zones to avoid continuous screen monitoring, which can induce stress.

Cognitive Enhancements

Maintaining mental clarity is supported by cognitive optimization techniques:

- **Mindful Breathing:** Periodic deep-breathing exercises calm the nervous system and enhance decision-making under pressure.
- **Hydration and Nutrition:** Proper hydration and balanced meals stabilize energy and focus throughout trading sessions.
- **Focus Music or White Noise:** Some traders benefit from low-level background sounds that reduce distractions without breaking concentration.
- **Visualization and Mental Rehearsal:** Before key trades, visualize potential market scenarios and your planned responses to reinforce calm, decisive action.

Evening Reflection and Reset

Post-market practices consolidate learning and prepare the mind for the next session:

- **Trade Journaling:** Record trades, setups, emotional state, and adherence to strategy for objective review.
- **Reflection on Emotions:** Identify moments of impatience, FOMO, or frustration and plan strategies to mitigate them.
- **Wind-Down Routine:** Engage in activities that relax the mind, such as reading, stretching, or light exercise, to improve sleep quality and recovery.

Key Takeaways

- Mental clarity and focus are as critical as technical skill in trading success.
- Structured daily routines—morning preparation, in-session practices, and evening reflection—enhance cognitive performance and discipline.
- Mindfulness, physical wellness, and environmental control support optimal decision-making under market stress.
- Journaling and reflection transform experience into learning, improving both emotional resilience and trading performance over time.

18.3 Long-Term Consistency Strategies

In trading, consistency over months and years is far more important than short-term wins. Long-term success is achieved by combining a robust strategy, disciplined execution, and psychological resilience. This section outlines practical strategies to maintain high performance and avoid burnout, emotional decision-making, or deviation from probabilistic trading principles.

Establishing Core Trading Habits

Consistency begins with daily habits that reinforce discipline:

- **Pre-Trade Preparation:** Always perform top-down analysis, check confluence of SMC setups, and verify market context before entering trades.
- **Adherence to Rules:** Stick strictly to risk management, position sizing, and trade entry criteria.
- **Regular Review:** Schedule weekly and monthly reviews of performance metrics, including win/loss ratios, drawdowns, and edge quantification.
- **Continuous Learning:** Keep studying markets, refining strategies, and learning from both successes and failures.

Probabilistic Mindset for Long-Term Success

Consistency is deeply rooted in probabilistic thinking:

- **Edge Over Certainty:** Focus on high-probability setups rather than trying to predict every market move.
- **Acceptance of Drawdowns:** Understand that losing streaks are natural; maintaining strategy adherence ensures long-term profitability.

- **Detachment from Outcomes:** Evaluate performance over many trades, not single outcomes, to avoid emotional overreaction.

Managing Emotional and Physical Resilience

Long-term consistency requires managing both mind and body:

- **Stress Management:** Utilize mindfulness, meditation, and relaxation techniques to reduce anxiety and impulsive decisions.
- **Sleep and Recovery:** Prioritize adequate rest to maintain cognitive sharpness and emotional stability.
- **Balanced Lifestyle:** Incorporate exercise, nutrition, and personal activities to prevent burnout and sustain motivation.

Tracking Performance Objectively

Data-driven review reinforces consistency:

- Maintain a detailed trade journal including setups, risk-reward ratios, and emotional states.
- Calculate key performance metrics such as expectancy, edge, and win rate to evaluate strategy effectiveness.
- Use statistical analysis to identify patterns, refine setups, and adjust position sizing without compromising discipline.

Adapting Without Compromising Principles

Markets evolve, and traders must adapt while preserving core methodology:

- Adjust strategies based on market regime shifts (trending vs. ranging).
- Incorporate new tools or technical integrations only after proper testing and validation.
- Avoid impulsive changes during drawdowns or winning streaks; changes should be methodical and data-driven.

Key Takeaways

- Long-term consistency is the result of disciplined habits, probabilistic thinking, and emotional resilience.
- Objective tracking and review of trades and performance metrics help maintain alignment with high-probability strategies.

- Physical and mental well-being are foundational to sustained trading performance.
- Adaptation is necessary, but must be controlled, data-driven, and aligned with core SMC and ICT principles.

18.4 How to Avoid Burnout for Traders

Burnout is one of the most pervasive and underestimated threats to long-term trading performance. Trading demands continuous decision-making under uncertainty, emotional regulation, and constant exposure to financial risk. Over time, these pressures accumulate and lead to psychological and cognitive exhaustion. Burnout not only affects emotional well-being but also destroys consistency, damages discipline, and directly increases drawdowns.

Understanding how burnout forms—and how to prevent or recover from it—is essential for sustainable, professional-level trading.

What Causes Burnout in Traders

Burnout occurs when the mental load placed on the trader exceeds their psychological capacity for an extended period. Common causes include:

- **Excessive screen time** and over-monitoring the market,
- **Overtrading** or chasing setups,
- **Unrealistic expectations** and pressure for constant growth,
- **Emotional exhaustion** from drawdowns or losing streaks,
- **Decision fatigue** from making too many micro-decisions,
- **Lack of work–life boundaries**,
- **Never fully disconnecting** from charts, even during downtime.

From the perspective of cognitive load theory, the human brain has limited capacity for processing information. Continuous exposure to charts, price movement, and uncertainty depletes this capacity, leading to impaired judgment and emotional sensitivity.

Early Warning Signs of Burnout

Burnout rarely occurs suddenly; instead, it progresses gradually. Recognizing early signs allows traders to intervene before performance collapses.

Early Warning Indicators

If three or more indicators appear regularly, the trader is entering the burnout zone.

Indicator	Meaning	Recommended Action
Loss of focus	Cognitive overload	Take a session break
Irritability or frustration	Emotional fatigue	Deep breathing or reset
Premature entries/exits	Impulsivity	Review checklist before trading
Charts "stop making sense"	Mental exhaustion	Stop trading for the day
Overtrading	Compulsive response	Enforce session limits
Fear of taking valid trades	Stress response	Reduce size and recenter
Violating trading rules	Discipline collapse	Mandatory cooldown period

Table 18.1: Early Signs of Trader Burnout

Core Principles to Prevent Burnout

1. Structured Trading Routine

A stable routine reduces cognitive load and emotional wear. A professional routine includes:

- fixed trading hours,
- predefined sessions (e.g., London + New York Open),
- a limited number of monitored instruments,
- pre-market analysis and end-of-day journaling,
- strict session cutoff times to prevent over-engagement.

2. Reduce Screen Time

The goal is to observe key areas—not the entire market. Use:

- alerts for HTF levels,
- automated notifications for OB/FVG zones,
- structured killzone-only active trading.

Less screen time results in fewer emotional decisions and greater mental clarity.

3. Avoid Decision Fatigue

Decision fatigue occurs when too many choices deplete cognitive energy. Prevent this by:

- using one primary entry model (e.g., CHoCH → FVG → OB),
- limiting setups to A+ trades only,
- establishing a maximum of 1–3 trades per session,
- eliminating unnecessary chart hopping.

The fewer decisions required, the more precise the execution.

4. Mandatory Rest and Recovery

Rest is not optional; it is part of the trading process.

- Take short breaks every 60 minutes during sessions.
- Step away after a losing streak or emotional spike.
- Have at least one non-trading day per week.
- Include regular monthly reset days for psychological recovery.

5. Psychological and Physical Health

Trading performance is directly tied to mental and physical health. Effective tools include:

- mindfulness or meditation (5–10 minutes daily),
- breathwork for emotional regulation,
- daily physical exercise,
- consistent sleep routines,
- journaling emotional states before/after trades.

A regulated body supports a regulated mind.

6. Disconnect After Trading Hours

Set strong boundaries to prevent constant mental engagement:

- no chart-checking after cutoff time,
- no overnight monitoring,
- no revisiting trades after closing the platform,
- schedule "off-market" periods each week.

This mental separation accelerates recovery.

Burnout Recovery Protocol

When burnout has already begun, traders should follow a structured recovery system.

Step 1: Immediate Stop (24–72 Hours)

- cease all trading activity,
- avoid chart analysis entirely,
- review emotional and performance journals only.

This resets emotional intensity and restores objectivity.

Step 2: Diagnose the Cause

Identify the primary trigger:

- overtrading,
- sleep deprivation,
- drawdown stress,
- deviation from rules,
- external life pressure.

Awareness prevents repeating the pattern.

Step 3: Controlled Return with Half Risk

Once emotional stability returns:

- reduce risk per trade by 50%,
- limit trading to one session only,
- take only the highest-quality setups,
- stop immediately after one loss.

This allows confidence recovery without exposing large capital.

Step 4: Gradual Performance Rebuild

Increase size only when:

- rules are consistently followed,
- emotions remain stable,
- journal shows clean execution,
- no impulse trades occur.

Discipline must recover before risk increases.

Daily Reset Checklist

A daily mental reset helps prevent burnout accumulation. Before trading begins, confirm:

- My mind is calm and not stressed.
- I slept adequately and feel physically regulated.
- I reviewed HTF bias and know today's narrative.
- I accept uncertainty and risk.
- I am not trying to recover previous losses.
- I am committed to following the trading plan.
- I will stop immediately if emotional instability appears.

If any checklist item fails, the trader should reduce size or skip the session.

Summary

- Burnout emerges from prolonged psychological and cognitive overload.
- Early recognition prevents deeper emotional and financial damage.
- Prevention requires structure: routines, limited screen time, decision reduction, and mental boundaries.
- Recovery requires halting trading, diagnosing triggers, reducing risk, and rebuilding gradually.
- Long-term sustainability depends on regulating mental capital just as rigorously as financial capital.

Mastering burnout prevention is essential for consistent, long-term professional trading performance.

Part VI

Technology & Automation

Chapter 19

Tools & Indicators

In modern trading, having the right tools and indicators is essential for efficiently analyzing markets, identifying high-probability setups, and executing trades in alignment with Smart Money Concepts (SMC) and ICT strategies. While understanding market structure, order blocks, and liquidity zones is critical, leveraging advanced charting platforms and custom indicators allows traders to apply these concepts consistently and effectively.
This chapter explores the essential technological tools and indicators that professional traders use to gain an edge. It provides guidance on selecting charting platforms, implementing custom indicators for order blocks, fair value gaps, and liquidity pools, and setting up alerts and notifications to ensure you never miss critical market opportunities.

19.1 Charting Platforms: TradingView, MT5, NinjaTrader

A reliable and feature-rich charting platform is a foundational tool for traders implementing Smart Money Concepts (SMC) and ICT strategies. The platform you choose can significantly impact your ability to analyze market structure, identify order blocks, track liquidity zones, and execute trades efficiently. This section explores three widely used charting platforms TradingView, MetaTrader 5 (MT5), and NinjaTrader—and their relevance for professional trading.

TradingView

TradingView is a web-based platform renowned for its user-friendly interface, extensive charting tools, and active community. Key advantages include:

- **Advanced Charting:** Supports multiple chart types, timeframes, and drawing tools essential for identifying SMC setups.

- **Custom Indicators:** Access to both built-in and community-created indicators for order blocks, fair value gaps, and liquidity pools.
- **Alerts and Notifications:** Flexible alert system for price levels, indicators, and custom scripts, enabling timely responses to setups.
- **Accessibility:** Cloud-based, accessible from multiple devices without installation.

Considerations: While TradingView excels in analysis and visualization, it offers limited native execution capabilities for certain brokers. Traders may need to use it in conjunction with brokerage platforms for live orders.

MetaTrader 5 (MT5)

MT5 is a popular multi-asset platform, widely used for Forex and CFD trading. Its key features include:

- **Execution Capabilities:** Direct integration with brokers for instant order execution and trade management.
- **Custom Indicators and Expert Advisors (EAs):** Automate detection of order blocks, fair value gaps, and liquidity zones, enabling semi-automated or fully automated trading.
- **Multi-Timeframe Analysis:** Supports a wide range of timeframes to facilitate top-down analysis for SMC strategies.
- **Backtesting:** Robust historical testing for strategies and indicators.

Considerations: MT5's interface may be less intuitive than TradingView, and its charting visuals are sometimes limited. However, its execution and automation capabilities make it essential for serious traders.

NinjaTrader

NinjaTrader is a professional-grade platform tailored for futures, Forex, and equities trading. Its standout features include:

- **Advanced Order Execution:** Highly customizable order types, OCO (one-cancels-other), and automated execution strategies.
- **Custom Indicators:** Build or import indicators for SMC-specific analysis such as order blocks, liquidity pools, and fair value gaps.
- **Market Replay and Backtesting:** Simulate historical market conditions to refine trade execution and decision-making.
- **Performance Analytics:** Track trade statistics and strategy performance for continuous improvement.

Considerations: NinjaTrader requires installation and may have a steeper learning curve compared to web-based platforms. However, for traders seeking professional execution and advanced analytics, it is highly valuable.

Key Takeaways

- Selecting the right charting platform depends on your trading style, need for custom indicators, execution requirements, and preference for interface.
- TradingView excels in visualization, community scripts, and accessibility.
- MT5 is ideal for automated strategies, broker integration, and multi-asset execution.
- NinjaTrader provides professional execution, analytics, and backtesting for serious traders.
- Combining platforms—such as using TradingView for analysis and MT5 / NinjaTrader for execution—can optimize workflow and enhance trading precision.

19.2 Custom Indicators: OB, FVG, Liquidity Pools

While charting platforms provide standard indicators like moving averages and RSI, SMC and ICT traders benefit significantly from custom indicators tailored to market structure, liquidity, and institutional activity. Custom indicators allow traders to visualize order blocks (OB), fair value gaps (FVG), and liquidity pools—core elements of Smart Money Concepts.

Order Block (OB) Indicators

Order blocks are price zones where institutions place large orders, often leading to future support or resistance levels. Custom OB indicators:

- Automatically detect bullish and bearish order blocks based on previous market structure.
- Highlight potential retracement zones where high-probability entries may occur.
- Provide visual cues for confluence with other market structure elements, such as swing highs/lows and liquidity zones.

Usage Tips: Combine OB indicators with trend analysis, top-down timeframes, and multi-session context to identify optimal trade setups.

Fair Value Gap (FVG) Indicators

Fair Value Gaps represent areas where price moves too quickly, leaving inefficiently traded zones that often get revisited. Custom FVG indicators:

- Automatically mark gaps in price action where institutional imbalance may exist.
- Highlight mitigation zones that can act as reversal or continuation points.
- Assist in combining OB and liquidity zones for layered, high-probability setups.

Usage Tips: Observe FVGs in alignment with order blocks and liquidity pools for confluence; not every FVG will trigger a trade, so context is critical.

Liquidity Pool Indicators

Liquidity pools are areas where stop-loss orders and resting limit orders cluster, often targeted by institutional activity. Custom liquidity indicators:

- Identify clusters of pending orders above or below swing highs/lows.
- Highlight potential stop-hunt areas where price may spike to capture liquidity.
- Provide advanced warning of potential reversals or manipulative moves.

Usage Tips: Integrate liquidity pool visualization with OBs and FVGs to anticipate institutional maneuvers and align entries with high-probability zones.

Integration and Best Practices

- **Layer Indicators:** Use OB, FVG, and liquidity indicators together to find confluence points, improving trade probability.
- **Customize Alerts:** Set alerts for price entering these critical zones to reduce screen time and avoid missed opportunities.
- **Test and Refine:** Backtest indicator settings across multiple timeframes and instruments to fine-tune sensitivity and reduce false signals.
- **Adapt to Market Context:** Indicators are tools, not absolute rules. Always validate with broader market structure and session bias.

Key Takeaways

- Custom indicators provide visual clarity for core SMC concepts: OBs, FVGs, and liquidity pools.
- Proper integration of these indicators with market structure and time-frames enhances high-probability trade setups.
- Alerts, backtesting, and confluence layering are essential for effective use.
- Indicators are aids, not replacements, for trader judgment—context and analysis remain paramount.

19.3 Alerts & Notifications for Key Zones

In modern trading, alerts and notifications are essential tools to maintain focus, reduce screen fatigue, and ensure timely reactions to high-probability setups. When combined with Smart Money Concepts (SMC) and ICT strategies, automated alerts help traders monitor critical levels such as order blocks (OBs), fair value gaps (FVGs), and liquidity pools without constantly staring at charts.

Setting Up Alerts for Order Blocks

Order blocks represent institutional buying or selling zones. Alerts can be configured to notify when price approaches these critical levels:

- **Price Entry Alerts:** Trigger when price enters a bullish or bearish OB, indicating a potential setup for entry or confirmation.
- **Retest Alerts:** Notify when price revisits a previously broken OB for potential retest trades.
- **Confluence Alerts:** Combine OB alerts with other factors such as FVG or liquidity pool proximity for higher probability signals.

Monitoring Fair Value Gaps

FVG alerts help traders identify imbalanced zones likely to be revisited by price:

- **Gap Entry Alerts:** Trigger when price enters an identified FVG.
- **Mitigation Zone Alerts:** Notify when price reaches the area that may fill the gap or reset liquidity.
- **Multi-Timeframe Alerts:** Set alerts across higher and lower time-frames to catch both major and minor FVG interactions.

Tracking Liquidity Pools

Liquidity pools are areas where stop-loss clusters and resting orders accumulate. Alerts for these zones help anticipate institutional manipulation:

- **Stop-Hunt Alerts:** Trigger when price approaches a cluster of likely stop-losses above or below swing highs/lows.
- **Volume Spike Notifications:** Detect sudden changes in volume near liquidity zones, indicating potential sweep or trap activity.
- **Time-of-Day Filters:** Activate alerts during key sessions (London/New York) when liquidity sweeps are more probable.

Best Practices for Alerts

- **Prioritize High-Probability Zones:** Avoid alert overload by focusing only on critical OBs, FVGs, and liquidity pools aligned with market structure.
- **Use Multiple Notification Channels:** Enable desktop, mobile, and email notifications to ensure you never miss a key level.
- **Regularly Review Alerts:** Adjust alert levels as market structure evolves to maintain relevance and accuracy.
- **Avoid Over-Reliance:** Alerts are tools to enhance awareness, not substitutes for active analysis and judgment.

Key Takeaways

- Alerts and notifications increase efficiency, focus, and timely responses to high-probability SMC setups.
- Properly configured alerts for OBs, FVGs, and liquidity pools reduce missed opportunities and help manage risk.
- Use multi-timeframe and session-based filters to improve alert quality and relevance.
- Alerts complement analysis—they are most effective when integrated with sound market structure, confluence, and probabilistic thinking.

Chapter 20

Algorithmic & Semi-Automated Trading

As markets become faster and more complex, algorithmic and semi-automated trading has emerged as a powerful tool for professional traders. By combining Smart Money Concepts (SMC) and ICT strategies with automation, traders can systematically detect high-probability setups, reduce emotional interference, and enhance execution speed. Automation does not replace the need for understanding market structure, order blocks, or liquidity zones, but it complements manual trading by increasing efficiency and consistency.

20.1 Scripts for Trade Setup Detection

Scripts for trade setup detection are specialized algorithms or custom indicators designed to automatically identify potential high-probability trading opportunities based on Smart Money Concepts (SMC) and ICT principles. These scripts serve as a technological extension of the trader's analysis, enabling faster recognition of key zones such as order blocks (OBs), fair value gaps (FVGs), and liquidity pools.

Purpose and Benefits

- **Efficiency:** Quickly scan multiple instruments and timeframes for potential setups without manually analyzing every chart.
- **Accuracy:** Reduce human error in identifying critical levels and market structure elements.
- **Consistency:** Ensure systematic application of SMC rules, avoiding emotional or impulsive decisions.

- **Time Management:** Free up time for higher-level analysis, trade planning, and risk management while scripts handle repetitive detection tasks.

Key Features of Effective Scripts

An effective trade setup detection script should include the following elements:

- **Order Block Detection:** Identify bullish and bearish order blocks based on predefined criteria such as last institutional swing and market structure.
- **Fair Value Gap Identification:** Highlight inefficiently traded price zones where institutions may target liquidity or retracements.
- **Liquidity Pool Visualization:** Detect clusters of stop-loss orders or pending limit orders that may act as magnet zones for price manipulation.
- **Multi-Timeframe Analysis:** Allow simultaneous detection across higher and lower timeframes to align entries with the broader market context.
- **Alerts Integration:** Trigger notifications when price interacts with these zones for timely decision-making.

Practical Implementation

When implementing scripts, consider the following:

- **Customization:** Adjust sensitivity and parameters to match your trading style, timeframes, and risk tolerance.
- **Backtesting:** Test scripts on historical data to validate accuracy, reduce false signals, and understand typical behaviors.
- **Confluence:** Use scripts as a guide, not as a standalone decision-maker. Always verify setups with market structure, session bias, and other SMC principles.
- **Broker Compatibility:** Ensure scripts are compatible with your charting platform and broker's API if trade execution is integrated.

Best Practices

- Combine script detection with manual analysis for confluence and context.

- Avoid over-reliance on automation; maintain an understanding of the underlying principles.
- Regularly update and refine scripts as markets evolve or new patterns emerge.
- Incorporate alerts and notifications to act promptly on detected setups.

Key Takeaways

- Scripts enhance efficiency, accuracy, and consistency in detecting OBs, FVGs, and liquidity pools.
- They are a complement to, not a replacement for, manual SMC analysis.
- Proper customization, backtesting, and integration with alerts are essential for maximizing their effectiveness.
- Traders who combine scripts with disciplined strategy adherence can significantly improve their probability of success while reducing cognitive load.

20.2 Optional Advanced Automation for SMC/ICT Strategies

Advanced automation allows traders to take Smart Money Concepts (SMC) and ICT strategies beyond manual execution, combining algorithmic detection with semi-automated or fully automated trade management. While manual discretion remains critical for interpreting market context, automation can streamline repetitive tasks, improve execution speed, and help maintain discipline.

Scope of Advanced Automation

- **Semi-Automated Trading:** Automation handles trade setup alerts, partial order execution, and stop/limit placement, while the trader retains final decision-making authority.
- **Fully Automated Execution:** Algorithms manage order entries, exits, risk management, and position sizing based on pre-defined rules derived from SMC and ICT principles.
- **Integration with Scripts:** Combines trade setup detection scripts with automation to execute trades automatically when conditions are met.

Key Components of Automation

- **Rule-Based Entries and Exits:** Define precise criteria for order blocks, fair value gaps, liquidity zones, and confluence for automated trade execution.
- **Risk Management Rules:** Implement position sizing, stop-loss, and take-profit strategies using automated calculations like the Kelly Criterion or fixed fraction methods.
- **Dynamic Adjustments:** Adapt orders in real-time based on changes in market structure, session bias, or volatility.
- **Multi-Instrument Management:** Handle simultaneous trades across Forex, commodities, crypto, or indices efficiently without missing setups.

Practical Implementation Tips

- **Start Small:** Test automation on a single instrument or small position size before scaling.
- **Backtesting and Forward Testing:** Validate automated strategies on historical data and in a simulated environment to ensure reliability.
- **Monitoring:** Even fully automated systems require monitoring for anomalies, slippage, or unexpected market behavior.
- **Customization:** Tailor automation rules to your trading style, risk tolerance, and preferred timeframes. Avoid generic "one-size-fits-all" solutions.

Benefits of Advanced Automation

- Increases efficiency and execution speed, reducing missed opportunities.
- Reduces emotional interference in high-stakes decision-making.
- Enables systematic application of SMC and ICT strategies across multiple instruments and timeframes.
- Provides consistent adherence to predefined risk management rules.

Limitations and Considerations

- Automation cannot replace understanding of market structure and context.
- Requires regular monitoring and adjustment to adapt to changing market conditions.

- System reliability depends on platform, broker, and internet stability.
- Over-optimization for historical data may lead to poor performance in live conditions.

Key Takeaways

- Advanced automation enhances SMC/ICT trading by streamlining execution, risk management, and multi-instrument monitoring.
- Semi-automated approaches provide a balance between human discretion and algorithmic efficiency.
- Proper implementation, testing, and ongoing monitoring are critical for effective automated trading.
- Automation should complement, not replace, trader judgment, confluence analysis, and probabilistic thinking.

Part VII

Appendices & Resources

Cheat Sheets & Glossary

This chapter is designed as a quick reference guide for traders using Smart Money Concepts (SMC) and ICT strategies. It provides concise definitions, visual cues, and actionable guidelines to help you recall key concepts, avoid common mistakes, and improve trade efficiency. Think of it as your pocket-sized manual for market structure, order blocks, liquidity, and probabilistic trading.

.1 Quick Reference for Setups, Zones, OBs, FVG, SMT, BoS, CHoCH

Setups and Entry Guidelines

- **Optimal Trade Entry (OTE):** Enter trades near the 61.8%–79% Fibonacci retracement of the last swing, preferably aligning with OBs and liquidity zones.
- **Breaker Blocks:** Enter when a previously broken order block is retested and validated as a support/resistance flip.
- **Liquidity Sweeps:** Wait for stop-loss hunting or liquidity sweeps to complete before confirming entry.

Zones and Key Levels

- **Order Blocks (OBs):** Areas where institutions accumulate positions; bullish OBs below price, bearish OBs above price.
- **Fair Value Gaps (FVGs):** Price gaps created by rapid institutional moves; often act as future retracement targets.
- **Liquidity Pools:** Clusters of stop-loss orders; anticipate potential stop-hunts or reversals around these zones.

Market Structure Terms

- **Break of Structure (BoS):** Price breaking a previous swing high-/low, signaling a shift in trend or institutional bias.
- **Change of Character (CHoCH):** Confirmation of trend reversal or transition, typically after liquidity is absorbed.
- **Swing Highs/Lows:** Key levels where price reverses; often coincide with liquidity and OB zones.

Smart Money Traps (SMT)

- **Bullish Traps:** False breakouts above resistance designed to trigger stop-losses of shorts.
- **Bearish Traps:** False breakdowns below support designed to trigger stop-losses of longs.
- Always validate SMTs with volume, market structure, and session bias before trading.

.2 Common Mistakes and Solutions

Overtrading and FOMO

- **Mistake:** Entering trades without proper setup due to fear of missing out.
- **Solution:** Wait for high-probability confluence zones with clear OB, FVG, and liquidity alignment.

Ignoring Higher Timeframes

- **Mistake:** Trading only on lower timeframes without considering the overall market context.
- **Solution:** Always perform top-down analysis: H4/D1 → H1 → M15 to align trades with the institutional bias.

Misinterpreting Order Blocks or FVGs

- **Mistake:** Treating every OB or FVG as tradable without checking confluence.
- **Solution:** Verify market structure, liquidity alignment, and session context before executing trades.

Poor Risk Management

- **Mistake:** Ignoring proper position sizing, stop-loss placement, or risk-to-reward ratios.
- **Solution:** Apply Kelly Criterion, fixed-fraction sizing, or other validated position-sizing methods; ensure R:R $\geq 1:2$ for most trades.

Neglecting Journaling and Review

- **Mistake:** Not tracking trades, setups, or outcomes; repeating the same errors.
- **Solution:** Maintain a structured trade journal with setup type, entry/exit, mistakes, lessons, and edge quantification.

Ignoring Session and Time-of-Day Bias

- **Mistake:** Trading during low liquidity periods or ignoring session overlap effects.
- **Solution:** Focus trades during London, New York, and overlapping sessions; note session-specific behaviors in your journal.

Key Takeaways

- Cheat sheets and glossary serve as quick reminders, improving decision speed and accuracy.
- Consistent application of OB, FVG, liquidity, BoS, and CHoCH concepts reduces trading errors.
- Awareness of common mistakes and corrective measures accelerates learning and builds probabilistic thinking.
- This chapter acts as a mental model framework to reference during live trading, ensuring discipline and high-probability setups.

Recommended Resources

Trading Smart Money Concepts (SMC) and ICT strategies requires both theoretical knowledge and practical guidance. While this book provides a strong foundation, continuous learning from trusted resources can accelerate mastery. This chapter compiles high-quality references including books, courses, mentorships, forums, and communities to help traders deepen their understanding and stay connected with evolving market strategies.

.3 Books

- **Market Wizards by Jack D. Schwager:** Interviews with top traders, offering insights into psychology, risk management, and strategy.
- **The Art of Currency Trading by Brent Donnelly:** Practical guide to Forex trading, including market structure and institutional perspective.
- **Technical Analysis of the Financial Markets by John Murphy:** Comprehensive reference for chart patterns, indicators, and multi time-frame analysis.
- **ICT Mentorship Notes:** Original ICT notes and concepts that pioneered Smart Money and order block-based trading methodology.

.4 Courses

- **ICT Mentorship Program:** Offers structured lessons on market structure, liquidity concepts, order blocks, and high-probability setups.
- **Advanced Price Action and SMC Courses:** Focused on institutional trading behavior, liquidity sweeps, and confluence strategies.
- **Algorithmic and Automation Courses:** Teach scripting, alerts, and semi-automated trading aligned with SMC principles.

.5 Mentorships

- **Personal Mentorship:** Working one-on-one with experienced traders accelerates understanding of market psychology, execution timing, and risk management.
- **Group Mentorship Programs:** Collaborative learning environment with feedback, shared case studies, and Q&A sessions on trade setups.
- **Trade Review Mentorship:** Mentors analyze past trades to identify mistakes, highlight strengths, and improve decision-making under real conditions.

.6 Forums and Communities

- **TradingView Community:** A platform to share charts, ideas, and strategies with traders worldwide.
- **Reddit Trading Communities (e.g., r/Forex, r/Daytrading):** Discussion forums to exchange knowledge and market insights.
- **Discord Groups:** Active SMC and ICT-focused communities that offer real-time alerts, trade breakdowns, and mentorship support.
- **Specialized SMC Forums:** Private or invitation-based communities for advanced discussions on institutional trading concepts.

.7 Best Practices for Using Resources

- Cross-reference multiple resources to validate concepts and avoid misinformation.
- Apply learned techniques in a demo environment before live trading.
- Participate actively in communities and forums to reinforce knowledge through discussion and observation.
- Seek mentors to accelerate the learning curve, particularly for understanding subtle institutional behaviors.
- Keep a reading and learning journal to track progress and integrate new insights into your trading workflow.

.8 Key Takeaways

- Continuous education is crucial in mastering SMC and ICT strategies.

- Books provide foundational knowledge, while courses and mentorship offer structured and practical guidance.
- Communities and forums help traders stay updated with market behaviors and share experiences.
- Combining multiple learning resources ensures both theoretical understanding and practical application.

FAQ Section

This chapter addresses frequently asked questions from beginner to advanced traders, as well as common misconceptions about Smart Money Concepts (SMC) and ICT strategies. The goal is to clarify doubts, provide actionable insights, and help traders avoid pitfalls while reinforcing correct trading principles.

.9 Common Questions (Beginner → Advanced)

Beginner Questions

- **Q: What is Smart Money?**
  A: Smart Money refers to the capital controlled by institutional traders, banks, and professional market participants who move markets due to their large positions and deep understanding of market structure.
- **Q: How do order blocks work?**
  A: Order blocks are areas where institutions accumulate or distribute positions. Bullish OBs occur below price and act as support; bearish OBs occur above price and act as resistance. They are validated by retests, liquidity interaction, and confluence with market structure.
- **Q: Do I need advanced indicators to trade SMC?**
  A: No. While scripts and indicators can help detect OBs, FVGs, and liquidity pools, the core skill is understanding market structure, institutional behavior, and confluence analysis.

Intermediate Questions

- **Q: How do I combine multiple timeframes?**
  A: Perform top-down analysis from higher timeframes (H4, D1) to lower (H1, M15). Align trade direction with institutional bias and key liquidity zones across these timeframes to increase probability of success.
- **Q: What is the role of fair value gaps?**
  A: FVGs represent inefficiently traded zones where price skipped levels,

often due to institutional aggression. They act as potential retracement targets and areas for trade confluence.

- **Q: How should I manage risk?**
A: Use proper position sizing (Kelly Criterion or fixed fraction), maintain favorable risk-to-reward ratios, and diversify across setups or correlated instruments to reduce exposure.

Advanced Questions

- **Q: How can I anticipate institutional moves?**
A: By understanding liquidity pools, stop-loss clusters, and order block structure, combined with session bias and market flow, traders can probabilistically anticipate where institutions are likely to push price.

- **Q: Can I fully automate SMC trading?**
A: Full automation is possible but requires robust scripting, rule-based entries, and continuous monitoring. Human oversight is recommended to adapt to unexpected market conditions.

- **Q: How do I differentiate false breakouts from genuine moves?**
A: Evaluate market structure, liquidity sweeps, and confluence with OBs, FVGs, and higher timeframe trends. False breakouts often occur in low-liquidity periods or around stop-hunts.

.10 Misconceptions and Clarifications

- **Misconception: SMC guarantees profits.**
Clarification: SMC improves the probability of high-quality setups but does not eliminate risk. Losses are still possible; disciplined risk management is critical.

- **Misconception: You must trade every setup.**
Clarification: Patience is key. Only trade setups with high confluence, proper structure, and session alignment. Overtrading reduces edge.

- **Misconception: Indicators alone are sufficient.**
Clarification: Indicators can assist but are secondary to understanding market structure, liquidity, and institutional behavior. Blind reliance on indicators often leads to poor decisions.

- **Misconception: SMC works only in Forex.**
Clarification: SMC principles apply across all liquid markets including Forex, commodities, indices, and crypto. The core idea is institutional behavior, not the asset class.

- **Misconception: Automation removes the need for analysis.** Clarification: Automated systems execute trades based on rules but do not replace the need for market understanding, context evaluation, or risk management.

.11 Key Takeaways

- FAQs help bridge gaps in understanding, clarify practical application, and reduce common mistakes.
- Misconceptions are prevalent but avoidable with disciplined study and real-world application.
- Consistent review of these questions and answers reinforces probabilistic thinking and high-probability decision-making.

Conclusion: Key Takeaways & Encouragement

As we reach the end of this book, it's important to consolidate the principles, strategies, and mindset lessons that define successful Smart Money Concepts (SMC) and ICT trading. The journey through market structure, liquidity, order blocks, fair value gaps, confluence, risk management, and psychology has provided both the tools and the perspective necessary to think like an institution and trade with probabilistic confidence.

.12 Key Takeaways

- **Think Like Institutions:** Understand that the market is primarily driven by institutional participants. Recognizing where liquidity resides and how large players manipulate price is central to trading with an edge.
- **Master Market Structure:** Breaks of structure (BoS), changes of character (CHoCH), swing highs/lows, and trend identification form the foundation of high-probability setups. Use them in conjunction with order blocks and liquidity zones.
- **Use Confluence for Precision:** Layer multiple factors—OBs, FVGs, liquidity pools, session bias, and multi-timeframe alignment—to improve the probability of successful trades.
- **Risk Management is Non-Negotiable:** Proper position sizing, risk-to-reward evaluation, and hedging strategies protect your capital and enable consistent growth over time.
- **Mindset Matters:** Patience, discipline, emotional control, and probabilistic thinking are as important as technical skills. Avoid overtrading, FOMO, and impulsive decisions.

- **Technology and Automation are Tools:** Utilize charts, indicators, and semi-automated scripts to enhance execution and efficiency—but never let them replace your understanding of market behavior.
- **Continuous Learning is Essential:** Markets evolve, so ongoing education, mentorship, community engagement, and journaling are crucial for long-term success.
- **Probabilistic Thinking is the Edge:** Every trade is a probability, not a certainty. Embrace uncertainty, plan for multiple outcomes, and focus on expected value rather than individual wins or losses.

.13 Encouragement for Traders

Trading is both an art and a science. Even with the best strategies, there will be losing trades and challenging periods. What separates successful traders is the ability to learn, adapt, and remain disciplined. By internalizing the concepts in this book, consistently applying high-probability strategies, and maintaining a strong psychological framework, you set yourself apart from retail traders who follow the market blindly.

Remember, mastery takes time. Start with a single concept, practice it rigorously, journal your results, and gradually integrate advanced strategies. Patience compounded over months and years is the true advantage in trading. Treat each trade as a learning opportunity and each loss as a lesson, not a failure.

Above all, trade with respect for the market and your capital. Let curiosity, discipline, and probabilistic thinking guide your decisions. The journey toward understanding Smart Money Concepts and ICT strategies is ongoing, but with persistence, you can consistently align yourself with the forces that drive market success.

.14 Final Thoughts

- Apply knowledge, not just theory.
- Observe institutional behavior and let it guide your trades.
- Prioritize risk management above all else.
- Cultivate patience, discipline, and emotional control.
- Continue learning, reviewing, and refining your strategies.

With these principles, you are well-equipped to navigate the markets with confidence, discipline, and an edge. The journey has only just begun—embrace it fully, stay curious, and trade with integrity.

Bonus Sections: AI in SMC, Retail vs Institutional Perspective, Psychology of Liquidity Hunting

This bonus chapter explores advanced concepts that bridge modern technology with Smart Money Concepts (SMC) and ICT strategies, providing a deeper understanding of how AI can enhance trading, how retail behavior differs from institutional behavior, and the psychology behind liquidity hunting.

.15 AI in Smart Money Concepts

Artificial Intelligence (AI) is increasingly becoming a powerful tool for traders. Within the context of SMC, AI can assist in:

- **Pattern Recognition:** AI algorithms can detect order blocks, liquidity pools, fair value gaps, and market structure patterns faster than manual observation.
- **Backtesting and Simulation:** AI can simulate thousands of historical scenarios, helping traders evaluate the statistical edge of specific setups and refine strategies.
- **Trade Filtering and Confluence Detection:** By automatically scanning multiple timeframes and identifying zones of confluence, AI can help focus on high-probability trades.
- **Adaptive Learning:** Machine learning models can adjust to changing market conditions, learning from new price behaviors and institutional patterns.

While AI can augment a trader's decision-making, it is essential to remember that understanding market structure, liquidity, and institutional behavior remains irreplaceable. AI is a tool, not a replacement for probabilistic thinking and discipline.

.16 Retail vs Institutional Perspective

Understanding the differences between retail traders and institutions is crucial for anticipating market behavior:

- **Capital and Influence:** Institutions control large volumes of capital that can move markets, while retail traders operate with relatively small positions.
- **Access to Information:** Institutions often have faster access to market data, order flow, and macroeconomic insights, giving them an informational edge.
- **Psychology and Patience:** Retail traders are prone to emotional decisions like FOMO and revenge trading. Institutions execute strategies based on liquidity, probability, and risk management.
- **Trade Goals:** Retail traders often focus on short-term profits, whereas institutions aim for predictable returns, managing drawdowns and exploiting liquidity imbalances.

By aligning your trading approach with institutional principles—identifying liquidity, waiting for confluence, and thinking probabilistically—you can bridge the gap between retail limitations and institutional-level decision-making.

.17 Psychology of Liquidity Hunting

Liquidity hunting is the process by which institutions target clusters of stop-loss orders, retail positions, or key price levels to execute their trades efficiently. Understanding the psychology behind this process can improve trade timing and reduce losses:

- **Stop-Loss Clusters:** Retail traders often place stops at obvious swing highs/lows. Institutions anticipate these clusters and push price to trigger them, capturing liquidity.
- **FOMO and Overextension:** Retail traders frequently enter late, chasing breakouts. Institutions use these reactions to reinforce moves in their favor.
- **Liquidity Sweeps:** Price temporarily breaches key levels to absorb liquidity before resuming the intended trend, creating optimal entry zones for institutional positions.

- **Behavioral Patterns:** Recognizing repetitive retail reactions—panic selling, impulsive buying, or premature entries—allows traders to anticipate where liquidity is likely to be hunted.

By internalizing these psychological patterns and combining them with market structure, OBs, FVGs, and session bias, traders can align with institutional intent rather than against it, improving the probability of successful trades.

.18 Key Takeaways

- AI enhances speed, pattern recognition, and statistical evaluation but cannot replace core market understanding.
- The institutional perspective emphasizes patience, probability, liquidity, and risk management, which retail traders must adopt for consistent edge.
- Liquidity hunting is a central component of market behavior; understanding the psychology behind it provides insights into price manipulation and optimal entry points.
- Integrating these advanced insights with SMC frameworks elevates trading from reactive to strategically proactive, increasing both confidence and probability of success.

Bibliography / References

This chapter lists the key references, books, articles, courses, and online resources that have informed the concepts, strategies, and principles presented in this book. Traders and readers are encouraged to explore these resources to deepen their understanding of Smart Money Concepts (SMC), ICT strategies, market structure, liquidity, and trading psychology.

.19 Books

- Schwager, Jack. *Market Wizards: Interviews with Top Traders.* Wiley, 1989.
- Murphy, John J. *Technical Analysis of the Financial Markets.* New York Institute of Finance, 1999.
- Donnelly, Brent. *The Art of Currency Trading.* McGraw-Hill Education, 2010.
- ICT Mentorship Notes. Original Smart Money Concepts and Institutional Trading Methodology, 2017–2023.
- Elder, Alexander. *Trading for a Living.* Wiley, 1993.

.20 Articles and Papers

- Lo, Andrew W., and Hasanhodzic, Jasmina. *The Evolution of Technical Analysis.* Journal of Investment Management, 2007.
- Murphy, John J. *Behavioral Finance and Market Structure.* Technical Analysis of Stocks & Commodities, 2005.
- Chan, Ernest P. *Algorithmic Trading: Winning Strategies and Their Rationale.* Wiley, 2013.

.21 Online Resources

- TradingView: `https://www.tradingview.com` – Charts, scripts, and trading community insights.
- Reddit Forex and Daytrading Communities: `https://www.reddit.com/r/Forex/`, `https://www.reddit.com/r/Daytrading/` – Discussion forums for trading ideas.
- Discord SMC/ICT Communities: Invitation-based discussion groups for real-time trade analysis and mentorship.
- Investopedia: `https://www.investopedia.com` – Definitions, tutorials, and explanations of financial concepts.

.22 Courses and Mentorship Programs

- ICT Mentorship Program – Institutional Trading, Order Blocks, Liquidity Concepts.
- Advanced SMC/Price Action Courses – Available through various online platforms, focused on high-probability setups and market manipulation understanding.
- Algorithmic and Semi-Automated Trading Programs – Covering scripting, alerts, and trading automation aligned with SMC.

.23 Key Notes

- The references above include foundational materials, practical guides, and advanced methodologies to support continued learning.
- Readers are encouraged to cross-reference multiple resources to validate concepts and strengthen their understanding of probabilistic, institutional-based trading.
- Many of the principles in this book are synthesized from direct observation of market structure, ICT mentorships, and verified trading strategies over multiple asset classes including Forex, crypto, commodities, and indices.

www.ingramcontent.com/pod-product-compliance
Lightning Source LLC
Chambersburg PA
CBHW050522240926
51846CB00003B/661
* 9 7 8 9 3 3 4 4 4 4 7 5 9 *